The New Politics of Briti

The New
Politics of
British Local
Governance

Edited by

Gerry Stoker

Foreword by R. A. W. Rhodes

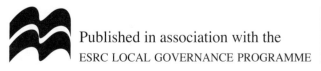

Published in association with the
ESRC LOCAL GOVERNANCE PROGRAMME

E·S·R·C
ECONOMIC
& SOCIAL
RESEARCH
COUNCIL

First published in Great Britain 2000 by
MACMILLAN PRESS LTD
Houndmills, Basingstoke, Hampshire RG21 6XS and London
Companies and representatives throughout the world

A catalogue record for this book is available from the British Library.

ISBN 0–333–72817–3 hardcover
ISBN 0–333–72818–1 paperback

First published in the United States of America 2000 by
ST. MARTIN'S PRESS, INC.,
Scholarly and Reference Division,
175 Fifth Avenue, New York, N.Y. 10010

ISBN 0–312–22803–1

Library of Congress Cataloging-in-Publication Data
The new politics of British local governance / edited by Gerry Stoker ;
foreword by R.A.W. Rhodes.
p.   cm. — (Government beyond the centre)
Published in association with the ESRC Local Governance Programme.
Includes bibliographical references and index.
ISBN 0–312–22803–1 (cloth)
1. Local government—Great Britain.   I. Series.

JS3111 .N48   1999
320.8'0941—dc21
                                                    99–047267

This book is printed on paper suitable for recycling and made from fully managed and
sustained forest sources.

10   9   8   7   6   5   4   3   2   1
09   08   07   06   05   04   03   02   01   00

Printed in Hong Kong

This book is dedicated to the memory of

Kieron Walsh

who died in May 1995. He was a member of the
ESRC's Local Governance Programme and a good
friend and valued colleague.

Contents

List of Tables and Figures   ix

Foreword by R.A.W. Rhodes   xi

Notes on the Contributors   xvi

Introduction
Gerry Stoker   1

1   Governance Failure
    Bob Jessop   11

2   Local Government After Fordism: A Regulationist
    Perspective
    Joe Painter and Mark Goodwin   33

3   Regime Formation in Manchester and Edinburgh
    Alan Harding   54

4   Policy Networks and Local Political Leadership
    in Britain and France
    Peter John and Alistair Cole   72

5   Understanding Urban Governance:
    The Contribution of Rational Choice
    Keith Dowding, Patrick Dunleavy, Desmond King,
    Helen Margetts and Yvonne Rydin   91

6   Local Governance in the Shadow of Juridification
    Davina Cooper   117

7   Local Governance: The Assessments of Councillors,
    Quango Members and the Public
    Bill Miller and Malcolm Dickson   130

8   The Changing Nature of Local Labour Politics
    Declan Hall and Steve Leach   150

9   The Conservative Party in Local Government,
    1979–1997
    Ian Holliday   166

10 Participation Strategies and Local Environmental
    Politics: Local Agenda 21
    Stephen C. Young   181

11 Technical Expertise and Public Participation in
    Planning for Housing: 'Playing the Numbers Game'
    Jonathan Murdoch, Simone Abram and Terry Marsden   198

12 User Participation in Community Housing: 'Is Small
    Really Beautiful?
    David Clapham, Keith Kintrea and Helen Kay   215

13 Patterns of Inclusion and Exclusion: Ethnic Minorities
    and Urban Development Corporations
    *Sue Brownill, Konnie Razzaque, Tamsin Stirling and
    Huw Thomas*   234

14 Feminist Intervention and Local Domestic Violence
    Policy
    Stefania Abrar   249

Bibliography   268

Index   288

List of Tables and Figures

Tables

2.1 The role of local governance in the post-Fordism
    mode of regulation   40
2.2 Sectoral distribution of employment   47
5.1 Different policy network models   100
5.2 Main actors in London policy networks   101
5.3 Known serviced tourist accommodation in
    Greater London   104
7.1 Party and ideology   133
7.2 Identification – a sense of belonging   133
7.3 A mission to mobilise   135
7.4 Representation and responsiveness   136
7.5 Too much or too little influence?   137
7.6 Self interest   139
7.7 Efficiency   140
7.8 Local versus central control?   141
7.9 Populism   142
7.10 Best form of control?   143
7.11 Monitoring quango boards   145

Figures

5.1 Goods and services in the modern state   108
5.2 A three-stage budget flow diagram   110
11.1 The planning-for-housing network   201

Foreword

Introduction

I first became involved with the Economic and Social Research Council's 'Local Governance' Research Programme in April 1990. As I write this Foreword, it is February 1999, a mere nine years later. Time flies when you are having fun and as chair of the Steering Committee I had my fair share of fun, and frustrations and tears (with the death of a still missed colleague, Kieron Walsh). It also produced some fascinating research and this Foreword is probably the last time I will reflect on what we set out to do and what we achieved.

What we set out to do

The Local Governance Programme had four aims:

- To document the transformation of the structure of government beyond Westminster and Whitehall from a system of local government into a system of local governance involving complex sets of organisations drawn from the public and private sectors.
- To develop a cumulative multi-theoretic approach to the study of local governance by comparing and contrasting the strengths and weaknesses of current theoretical approaches rather than espousing any one approach.
- To identify, encourage and co-ordinate the participation of a new generation of researchers from the social science disciplines.
- To place the changing British system of local governance in an international context.

The Programme was formally launched in 1992. There were 27 research projects. The first-phase projects started in March 1993. The second-phase projects started in January 1994. The Programme finished in April 1997.

The ESRC is the United Kingdom's leading social science funding agency. It is an independent organisation, financed solely by government. Its activities fall into three groups: research grants, research centres and programmes, and postgraduate training. Research Programmes seek to harness and strengthen the United Kingdom's social science research capacity to address scientific and policy relevant topics of strategic and national importance. Typically, there will be 10–15 projects drawn from several social science disciplines and spread among UK universities. Researchers work independently on individual projects with the support of a Programme Director and his or her advisory Steering Committee. The shared focus, the opportunities for co-operation between research teams, the encouragement of inter-disciplinary working and a communication plan to increase the impact on practitioners provide the rationale for Programmes.

One of the main reasons for the 'Local Governance' Programme was a recognition by both practitioners and academics that the local government system of the United Kingdom had been subject to considerable legislative change and institutional restructuring. Governance refers to institutional diversity; to the complex of local authorities with other local organisations drawn from the public, private and voluntary sectors. It also covers the processes for governing these interwoven and interweaving sets of organisations. The boundaries are blurred and there can be no presumption that governing mechanisms reside in the commanding heights of the state. All the projects explored the ways in which local government became transformed into local governance and how decision making in and about local areas changed in consequence. The role of local authorities now extends beyond direct provision to encompass contracting, regulating, enabling and providing leadership for a local arena characterised by a complex array of interactive relationships. The Programme describes and analyses the new governance and assesses its significance for government and citizen, service provision and local democracy.

Phase 1 had six themes. Theme one provided a historical perspective, examining the history of the institutions of local governance from 1801 onwards. Theme two looked at the changing context of local governance, focusing on: Europeanising local governance; local economic and social restructuring; and the structure and practices of post-Fordist local governance. Theme three focused on the changing map of local power, examining the community power structures of London; and coalition building between public and private interest in urban development in a comparative study of cities in Denmark, Germany, the Netherlands and the United Kingdom. Theme four looked at changes in local politics, and specifically: the changing nature of political leadership, parties and decision making; the recent history of the Conservative party on local government; and the impact of legal change on local government. Theme five was concerned with new forms of service delivery and examined the performance of opted out schools, hospitals and housing action trusts; and the empowerment of users in health and social care services. Theme six explored the changing role of management in local authorities, looking at emerging patterns of management in local governance; inter-organisational co-operation in housing management; and new forms of school and college management.

Phase 2 had four themes. Theme one looked at public opinion and local citizenship. Theme two examined targeting and control in financing local governance; and accounting for infrastructure assets. Theme three explored the changing role of the voluntary sector, covering community based housing organisations and the voluntary sector and local sustainable development. Theme four focused on intergovernmental management and local networks, looking at networks of participation in local planning; and local policy networks in Britain and France. Finally, there were six applied strategic projects which were low cost, short and targeted on issues of direct concern to practitioners. They covered: economic culture; gender; labour market fragmentation; race equality; local strategies for crime prevention; and local economic governance.

What did we achieve?

Gerry Stoker (1999) identifies several, negative unintended consequences of the new public management (NPM), including fragmentation, loss of accountability and a decline in the public service ethic. He also identifies important unintended benefits. First, NPM disrupted the system. Second, local authorities were increasingly forced to account for their actions in public. Third, these twin pressures produced a sense of crisis which helped to create new policy ideas. The delicious irony is that the new ideas were not those of NPM but of local governance; of service delivery through organisational networks spanning the public, private and voluntary sectors (Rhodes, 1997, Chapter 3). NPM aimed at 'a more efficient and customer-oriented service delivery' but got 'a broader vision of a new community governance' (Stoker, 1999). So, the key terms for analysing the new local governance are interdependence, exchange, trust, diplomacy and reciprocity (Rhodes, 1999).

In the Introduction to this volume Gerry Stoker explores the implications of this shift to governance for local politics and policy making. The new politics of local government stresses the emergence of governing coalitions based on many public, private and voluntary sector actors; and the changing organisation and style of party politics. Public managers and private actors now inhabit a strange new world in which the role of government is redefined and a network style of working is paramount. Although party leaders are an integral part of this world, their backbench colleagues are cast adrift in a sea of changes they do not comprehend which offers them no clear role. Moreover, these changes are a reaction to the changing informational and financial dynamics of local governance. Shifts in the structure of the private sector economy, the effects of globalisation, and the complex mechanisms of financial rationing and control interweave to produce an ever-shifting backcloth, the long-term and permanent effects of which remain difficult to judge.

So, as government fragments and networks vie with markets and bureaucracy as key service delivery mechanisms, there are many consequences for local politics and policy, including: complexity and confusion, opaque accountability and a diminished capacity to steer. As networks obscure formal accountability so they create opportunities for diverse interests to influence policy and the micro-politics of the city challenges representative democracy. The core ideas of managerialism and marketisation have restricted the tool kit available to local government for steering networks. Networks are pervasive. As local government develops the skills of political steering and indirect management, NPM, whether in the guise of managerialism or institutional economics, is no longer the challenge confronting government. The challenge is diplomacy in governance; that is, sitting where the other person is sitting and negotiating an agreement about means and objectives (and for a more detailed analysis, see Rhodes, 1997).

The 'Local Governance' Programme told a story of 'the shift from local government to local governance'. But the social sciences offer only provisional knowledge and prediction is mainly an aspiration; we have 'the capacity to offer some hindsight, a little insight and almost no foresight' (Hayward, 1986, p. 17). But an awareness of our limitations does not render the social sciences useless. If we cannot offer solutions, we can define and redefine problems in novel ways. We can tell the policy makers and administrators distinctive stories about their world and how it is governed. The new public management told a story of economy, efficiency and effectiveness which contrasted sharply with the story of the local government officer as professional with clients and the permanent secretary as policy adviser and fire-fighter for the minister. Governance tells a story of differentiation, networks, trust, diplomacy and coalition-building which contrasts sharply with the prescriptions of managerialism and the world of markets and contracts. In other words, 'governance' provides a language for re-describing the world and the 'Local Governance' Programme has played no small part in challenging the dominant managerial ideology of the 1980s and arguing for a view of the world in which networks vie with markets and bureaucracy as the appropriate means for delivering services. So, if we achieved anything it is the simple message that for every problem there is a simple solution, and it is always wrong. The language of governance makes no apology for describing a complex world in all its complexity and arguing it is the mix of steering strategies that matters; there is no simple solution based on either markets or hierarchies or networks.

R. A. W. Rhodes
Professor of Politics
University of Newcastle-upon-Tyne
and Chair, ESRC Local Governance Steering Committee

This book is the companion volume to G. Stoker (ed.), *The New Management of British Local Governance* (London, Macmillan, 1999). A list of the projects of the ESRC Local Governance Programme and their key publications can be obtained from Gerry Stoker. Contact G. Stoker @ strath. ac. uk.

Notes on the Contributors

Simone Abram Department of Geography, University College of Swansea

Stefania Abrar was a researcher for the 'Gender and New Urban Governance' project.

Sue Brownill School of Planning, Oxford Brookes University, Headington, Oxford

David Clapham Professor, Department of City and Regional Planning, University of Wales, Cardiff

Alistair Cole Department of European Studies, Bradford University

Davina Cooper Professor, Faculty of Law, University of Keele, Staffordshire

Malcolm Dickson Lecturer, Department of Government, University of Strathclyde

Keith Dowding Reader, London School of Economics and Political Science

Patrick Dunleavy Professor, London School of Economics and Political Science

Mark Goodwin, Institute of Earth Studies, University of Wales, Aberystwyth

Declan Hall Lecturer, Institute of Local Government Studies, University of Birmingham

Alan Harding Professor, European Institute for Urban Affairs, John Moores University, Liverpool

Ian Holliday Senior Lecturer, Department of Government, University of Manchester

Bob Jessop Professor, Department of Sociology, University of Lancaster

Peter John Reader, Department of Politics, University of Southampton

Helen Kay was a researcher for the 'Sustainability and Maturity of Community Based Housing Organisations project.

Desmond King Professor of Politics, St John's College, University of Oxford

Keith Kintrea Professor, Centre for Housing and Urban Studies, University of Glasgow

Steve Leach Professor, Department of Public Policy and Managerial Studies, De Montfort University, Leicester

Helen Margetts Lecturer in Politics, Birkbeck College, London

Terry Marsden Professor, Department of City and Regional Planning, University of Wales, Cardiff

Bill Miller Professor of Politics, University of Glasgow

Jonathan Murdoch Department of City and Regional Planning, University of Wales, Cardiff

Joe Painter Department of Geography, University of Durham

Konnie Razzaque Faculty of the Built Environment, University of the West of England

R A W Rhodes Professor of Politics, University of Newcastle

Yvonne Rydin Reader, Department of Geography, London School of Economics and Political Science

Tamsin Stirling Chartered Institute of Housing, Wales

Gerry Stoker Professor of Politics, University of Strathclyde

Huw Thomas Department of the City and Regional Planning, University of Wales, Cardiff

Stephen C Young Senior Lecturer, Department of Government, University of Manchester

Introduction

Gerry Stoker

The study of local politics has been prone to some of the same cycles and trends as the wider field of political science (Stoker, 1998a). Fifty years ago – as in political science in general – the focus was on institutions. Local politics was the study of local government: its legal competences and structure and its core actors – mayors, councillors, bureaucrats. The literature was often descriptive and generally concerned with examining semi-constitutional questions and administrative doctrines about the appropriateness of local autonomy or how best politicians could hold bureaucrats. This relatively quiet backwater was given a radical shake-up by the arrival of behavioural political science with its focus on 'how things are rather than how they should be' and its new commitment to empirical analysis. The dry study of institutions was under pressure to look at what happened in practice rather than formal rules and expectations. The most prominent expression of the revolution was the emergence of a community power debate and associated competing elitist and pluralist interpretations. These studies, and more broadly the behavioural style of analysis, became the cutting-edge of the sub-discipline of local politics in the 1960s (for a more detailed review see Judge *et al.*, 1995).

In the 1970s, however, something happened to the study of local politics. It got Marxism – or, rather, Marxism got it. As a result research moved even further away from institutional analysis and was steered towards a concern with external social and economic influences and the distributional impact of policy (Pickvance, 1995). The study of local politics became situated in the context of capital accumulation and the social conflicts endemic to market societies. This shift in focus in many respects 'made sense' in the light of the considerable observable social conflicts in cities and the substantial processes of dislocation and change associated with the late urbanisation of some capitalist economies and the processes of deindustrialisation in others (Brindley *et al.*, 1996).

The study of local politics may have left behind some of the specific Marxist-inspired studies but the broader political economy perspective associated with these studies has helped to frame key research and theoretical themes in the 1980s and 1990s. Local politics is seen as shaped by two fundamental and connected external factors. The first can be termed the 'market' effect. Land-use, employment, leisure and welfare in urban areas are profoundly shaped by the forces of the private market. Urban politics is the study of how the state at various levels meets the challenge posed by key decision-making capacity and resources being held in private hands (Lindblom, 1977). The second external factor is captured by the phrase 'globalisation'. The politics of localities, it is argued, is subject to a wide range of pressures for homogenisation as a result of technological, political and economic developments that are global in scope (Leo, 1997). The information revolution, the processes of global economic competition and the increasing tendency for political systems to look beyond their boundaries for lessons and ideas from elsewhere all contribute to a homogenising stimulus. At the same time much urban governance is seen as about asserting particularity – about identifying a niche for a particular locality.

Beyond these broad forces local politics is shaped by its attempt to grapple with some intractable and difficult policy issues (Stoker and Young, 1993). The list for many local governments would include: economic development and property development, finance (balancing spending with revenues), training and employment, crime prevention and public safety, transport congestion and pollution and environmental problems.

The challenge posed by each policy issue is considerable but made more problematic still by features integral to these core and critical policy arenas. The first is a high degree of institutional fragmentation. The core actors associated with each policy issue are spread not only among a wide variety of institutions but also across public, private and voluntary sectors. Second, each policy arena is one of high bounded rationality. It is difficult to know what to do and gaining understanding is time-consuming and demanding. Defining the problem, let alone designing appropriate solutions, is a difficult and daunting task. Third, each of the core policy issues relies on action in situations characterised by power dependence. Power to impose solutions is limited and the crucial challenge is to create a power to act. In a complex, fragmented world the paradigmatic form of power is that which enables certain interests to blend their capacities to achieve common purposes (Stone, 1993).

To put the issue another way, a key concern in the study of local politics has become 'governance', which can be broadly defined as a concern with governing, achieving collective action in the realm of public affairs, in conditions where it is not possible to rest on recourse to the authority of the state (see Stoker, 1998c). Governance involves working across boundaries within the public sector or between the public sector and private or voluntary sectors. It focuses attention on a set of actors that are drawn from but also beyond the formal institutions of government. A key concern is processes of networking and partnership. Governance recognises the capacity to get things done which does not rest on the power of government to command or use its authority. Governing becomes an interactive process because no single actor has the knowledge and resource capacity to tackle problems unilaterally (Stoker, 1998b).

The interest in governance has in turn encouraged a reformulated concern with institutions but this time framed within the wider context of what has been termed the 'new institutionalism' (Lowndes, 1996). The new institutionalism harks back to the early concern with institutions but attempts to move beyond its descriptive style and its focus on constitutional and administrative doctrines. New institutionalism argues for the importance of institutionalised social conventions to explain human action and inaction. Intellectual currents and developments in the world of local politics have combined to encourage a focus on how individuals act collectively and the institutional structure – both informal and formal – that shapes collective action. Approaches to the study of the new institutionalism range from the historical to rational choice. There is, however, a shared concern with the framing of collective action.

This book, which draws together findings from the ESRC Local Governance Programme 1992–97, explores the implications of the emergence of governance for the operation of local politics. It begins with two chapters that remind the reader of the complexity and scale of the tasks taken on by governance and as a consequence the inevitable limitations and weaknesses of the institutional devices and processes that have emerged. The next three chapters in different ways explore the attempt to build leadership capacity in the context of governance. The intersection between public and private and voluntary sectors is at the heart of the new local governance and a range of theoretical and empirical issues are explored by the authors of Chapters 3–5. Chapter 6 reminds us of the still substantial effect of central government of the local political system. The theme of Chapter 7 is the varied and uncertain response of the public and local political elites to the challenges posted by governance. There follow two chapters on the changing nature of local party politics. The concluding five chapters explore in different settings the implications of the new governance for citizen participation and mobilisation. What emerges in all the chapters is a picture of a system that is experiencing institutional flux as new ways of working, in the light of new challenges are developed, tried and tested.

As a guide for the reader the themes of individual chapters are examined further below.

Chapter 1, by Bob Jessop, reflects on how all mechanisms for governing are prone to failure. This applies as much to the new emerging forms of local governance as to any other institutional devices. Drawing on his research into local economic development, Jessop identifies three main factors which limit success. First, there are limitations to effective intervention in the market. Second, partnerships may operate at a scale or over a time period which makes the full achievement of economic development objectives problematic. Third, the difficulties of developing effective interpersonal, interorganisational and, finally, intersystemic coordination are considerable. Jessop's conclusion is, paradoxically, not pessimistic but rather realistic. His argument is that failure is normal to a degree and, if it is expected, can be allowed for by flexible and adaptable strategies. The new governance can therefore help solve economic and social problems by constantly reviewing and extending the diversity of its co-ordination mechanisms. What it needs, in addition, is greater legitimacy which can be delivered only by a more participatory politics involving a wider range of stakeholders.

Painter and Goodwin, in Chapter 2, consider how economic and social forces have reshaped the world of local governance. They conclude that local authorities while reacting to dramatic forces of change, in particular de-industrialisation on a massive scale in the case study area of Sunderland, are not equipped to establish a fully successful new mode of social and economic regulation. Action has been undertaken and economic, training and other initiatives have been developed in partnership between local authorities and other agencies in the world of governance but a successful and stable 'post-Fordist' regime to structure state–society–economy relations has not emerged. British local authorities lack the power and institutional capacity to develop a sufficiently broad-ranging response to the challenges they face. Moreover, their spatial scale and boundaries may make them unsuitable for the task. One possible implication of this analysis is to suggest that a regional level of organisation may be appropriate. The introduction of Regional Development Agencies (RDAs) and the possibility of further constitutional development in the regions of England to match the assemblies in Wales and Northern Ireland and the parliament in Scotland suggest that the issue of the appropriate level of social and economic intervention by the state will remain a matter of policy debate.

In Chapter 3, Harding's analysis of circles of powerful public and private sector actors in Manchester and Edinburgh captures the politics of elite partnership-building that has been a developing feature of local politics from the late 1970s onwards. After a period of tension in the early 1980s, Manchester emerged as an exemplar of the new style of partnership of local officialdom and business partnership. A reasonably strong regime, exhibiting relatively high levels of energy, trust and co-operation, was built. Edinburgh also saw sustained efforts at partnership-building, although of less intensity and lower quality compared with Manchester. Business–local government partnership in both cities focused largely on particular development and economic issues and did not extend, to any substantial degree, to the mainstream activities of the authorities in providing education, housing and welfare services. The new rules and relationships of the politics of 'production', as Harding puts it, were not transferred to the more traditional 'consumption' concerns of local politics. The introduction of 'Best Value' procedures to the provision of local services may herald an attempt under the Labour government to extend partnership-type relations from economic development concerns to the mainstream service delivery of local authorities.

John and Cole, in Chapter 4, explore the development of networks by local political leaders. Like Harding, they are interested in identifying the centre of gravity of urban governance and, more particularly, local economic development policy making. Their empirical evidence relates to four cities: Leeds and Southampton in Britain, and Lille and Rennes in France. In both Britain and France, John and Cole find that political leaders have forged new coalitions as development politics has become more fragmented and complex. Yet, the visibility of French mayors and the public's capacity to hold them to account gives a stronger local democratic element in the French cities in what are fragmented frameworks of governing in both countries. There are risks of the abuse of personal power by the mayor, but these are countered by enhanced local accountability and a stronger capacity to deliver integrated strategies. John and Cole lend support to the call for stronger political leadership – for example, elected mayors – in British local governance.

Dowding and his colleagues, in Chapter 5, again explore the power structures in local communities, but use a framework drawing on the rational choice perspective rather than regimes or networks. The empirical focus of their analysis is London. They provide a judgement on the state of London governance following the abolition of the Greater London Council (GLC). They argue that the strategic concerns of the city were left in the hands of disparate and competing organisations. Some issues were tackled but others were neglected. It will be interesting to see if the elected Mayor and the Assembly that will be established in Greater London in 2000 will provide a stronger and more wide-ranging political capacity. This chapter makes some strong claims for rational choice as a method of study and argues that it can illuminate the central features of modern urban governance: community power and leadership, coordination through networks, new managerial service delivery and the shifting boundaries of the appropriate scale and arenas for intervention.

Chapter 6, by Cooper, explores how local politicians and officials have reacted to the process of 'juridification'. The legal framing of local actions, and the willingness of the centre to use legal instruments to impose its policies, were features of the world of local politics from the 1980s onwards. The impact on the consciousness – and, indeed, behaviour – of councillors and local government officers has been complex. In terms of Labour's post-1997 reform programme it is not clear what the impact of the experience of juridification will be. Law and legality remain open to local interpretations and responses. The long period of Conservative domination and intervention may have conditioned in some local actors a rather negative image of their own capacity to take and shape an agenda of change. Cooper's analysis suggests however, that the impact of juridification has been complex, so that there remains scope for creativity and a positive response to a reform agenda.

In Chapter 7, Miller and Dickson present findings from an extensive attitude survey which tested not only public opinion, but also the opinions of local councillors and the board members of quangos in the health and training fields. The chapter presents an overview of key findings and, in particular, considers the differences and similarities in the views of councillors and quango members on the nature of modern local governance. The public emerge as generally supportive of the principle of local democracy, yet willing to tolerate appointed boards or even private company involvement in service delivery provided that it works to improve service quality. The public have a fairly jaundiced view of the way local democracy works at the moment and give strong support to measures such as elected mayors and local referendums to increase the direct say of people in decision making.

The concern of Hall and Leach, in Chapter 8 is with the organisation of Labour Party politics at the local level and the relationship with the national party. They argue that the scope for effective national party intervention is much greater in relation to procedural than to policy matters. Overall, their research suggests that, despite noteworthy examples of strong intervention, the influence of the national party is largely contingent upon local party group acquiescence. The authors recognise that both party groups on local authorities (because of the weakness of local election turnout) and the broader local party organisations (because of the limited number of activists) have serious problems of legitimacy. The national Labour agenda of democratic renewal launched after the general election in May 1997 addresses these concerns. However, according to Hall and Leach, the need for radical change in the way politics is conducted is more strongly recognised at the national than at the local level.

Holliday presents, in Chapter 9, an analysis of the fortunes of the Conservative Party in local politics between 1979 and 1997. The backcloth to the chapter is the loss of power at the local level for the Conservatives that matched their period of long domination of national politics. Holiday identifies three types of local Conservatism: apolitical, mainstream and radical. He suggests that the Conservatives paid a high price for their success both in national politics and in imposing national discipline on local government. The issue for them is not only winning back voters, but also attracting back into local government service Conservative activists turned off by loss of local authority power and the decline in the tradition of disinterested public service.

Chapter 10 begins a series of chapters that shift attention towards public participation and the active involvement of community and voluntary organisations in decision making. Young provides an account of the rise of public participation around Local Agenda 21 environmental issues. He identifies four different types of participation strategy developed by local authorities, ranging from the top-down to the bottom-up. Evaluating the participation experience leads Young to ask how far it has led to changes in policy, better processes or more effective partnership. He attempts to work out the balance between optimistic and pessimistic interpretations of participation, and concludes that there is a need for a more long-term strategic approach to participation by local councils and a greater commitment to producing a substantial civic infrastructure. Such a view chimes in with guidance produced by the DETR (1998) which aims to encourage and facilitate the best practice on local participation that has emerged in the last decade or so.

Murdoch and his colleagues, in Chapter 11, examine a top-down participation process over the allocation of land for new building housing. They offer a case study of Buckinghamshire. They argue that the way the debate is framed gives priority to the views of experts, policy makers, developers and, to a lesser extent, campaigning groups seeking to protect the rural environment. However, other actors, including many local residents, are not effectively included in the process.

In Chapter 12, Clapham and his colleagues provide a more upbeat assessment of a participation initiative in Glasgow. They evaluate the community-ownership housing schemes that were launched there in the mid-1980s. Compared to standard council provision they find greater resident satisfaction with the quality of the service and a stronger sense of accountability and legitimacy in relation to the running of community-based organisations. The schemes launched over a decade ago have a record of success that suggests they are not short-term 'fixes', but have a sustainable role in the future. 'Ordinary' people have become involved, but the organisations do rely heavily on their staff. The quango funding their operations, Scottish Homes, and the local authority that influences surrounding development have a constraining and limiting effect.

Brownill and her colleagues, in Chapter 13, show that quangos are interested in public involvement and community participation. They provide a study of the extent to which Urban Development Corporations (UDCs) have included or excluded ethnic minorities from their decision making and related activities. They note a variety of practices and experience reflecting local circumstances. They argue that the need for UDCs and other quangos to achieve legitimation and to promote a positive public image ensures a continued role for consultation and some limited opportunities for influence. The constraints remain considerable, however, and in many respects the involvement of black and ethnic minorities is not seen as a priority.

In Chapter 14, Abrar examines how feminists have operated to influence the uptake of policy on domestic violence by local authorities. Case studies of three authorities reveal a range of experiences, but in each locality crucial avenues to influence policy were found by campaigning groups. A complex pattern of working both inside the local authority and the voluntary sector is a characteristic feature of political organisation against domestic violence.

1 Governance Failure

Bob Jessop

The 1970s saw growing assertions that state intervention was failing and that the state itself was in crisis. In the UK in the 1980s, the dominant neo-liberal response to this alleged crisis largely involved turning to the market and, to a lesser extent, to community or family self-help. The Thatcher and Major governments promoted privatisation, liberalisation, de-regulation, the use of market proxies in the residual state sector, cuts in direct taxes to enhance consumer choice, and internationalisation to promote capital mobility and the transfer of technology and 'know-how'. They also advocated an enterprise culture and popular capitalism to make civil society more market-friendly. This project was intended to re-equip the UK with a liberal, nightwatchman state with progressively smaller and more balanced budgets thereby boosting this slimmed-down state's capacity to perform its remaining core functions. However, while this neo-liberal programme was still being pursued and, indeed, intensified, it also became apparent that the turn to the market had not delivered all that had been promised. Market failures and inadequacies had not been eliminated, yet an explicit return to the state was ideologically and politically unacceptable. Thus, as early as the 1980s, one could discern increasing government interest at all levels in how public–private partnerships and similar forms of governance might contribute to public policy and purposes. This alternative to marketisation was steadily reinforced during the Conservative years and is likely to become yet stronger under 'New Labour' with its declared commitment to a 'stakeholding society'. The expansion of governance is not meant to return Britain to a discredited corporatism (let alone a tripartite corporatism with the active involvement of organised labour) but, rather, to address the real limitations of the market, state and mixed economy as means of dealing with various complex economic, political and social issues. One area where a turn to governance has been popular is local economic and social development, and it is this area that provides the empirical focus of the following theoretical reflections on the various ways in which coordination mechanisms can fail and how tendencies to failure may themselves be governed.

Market failure

Many economists tend to assume that the 'procedural rationality' of perfect markets guarantees market success. Failure occurs when economic exchanges do not produce what a perfect (hence imaginary) market would deliver. Since market rationality depends on free and equal exchange rather than on the purposes of economic transactions, success or failure cannot, on most accounts, be judged through substantive criteria such as the uneven impact of market forces on wealth, income, life-chances, or regional imbalance. Provided that inequalities derive from (or are consistent with) the operation of perfect markets, then they must be judged as rational and fair. At best, one could see such problems as market 'inadequacies' rather than genuine market failures. There is no shortage of claims about such inadequacies, however, nor about the need to remedy them, as well as market failures, through social and political action of various kinds.

In a market-rational framework, state and market are strictly demarcated. The state should stay at arm's length from market forces, merely establishing and defending the framework for market institutions. The latter can then allocate goods and services in the most efficient way. The market also functions as a learning mechanism. Thus, Hayek argues that market failure is an essentially 'trial-and-error' discovery mechanism whereby markets prompt economic agents to learn and innovate. In the long run, according to this view, the market provides the most flexible and least disastrous mechanism for coordinating and adapting in the face of complex interdependences and turbulent environments. Moreover, for neoclassical and Austrian theorists alike, the initial response to market failure is 'more market, not less' – even if this often requires further state intervention in the short term. But it is debatable, to say the least, whether even perfect markets could eliminate all forms of market failure. Even neoclassical economists recognise the extent to which markets may not 'suitably capture the full social benefits or levy the full social costs of market activity' (Wolf, 1978, p. 138).

The critique of markets has been taken furthest by Marxists and political ecologists. Marxists argue that capitalism is distinctive not for markets as such, but for their extension to labour-power. It is market-mediated exploitation of wage-labour that drives 'economic growth' – not the inherent efficiency of markets. Markets may mediate the search for added value, but cannot produce it. The commodification of labour-power also generates basic contradictions which cannot be resolved through the market mechanism. Among other examples, the commodity is both an exchange-value and use-value, the wage is both a cost of production and source of demand, money is both national money and international currency, and productive capital is both abstract value in motion and a concrete stock of time-and-place-specific assets in the process of valorisation. Thus, for Marxists, phenomena attributed to market failures or inadequacies often express the underlying contradictions of capitalism. It follows that state intervention may, at best, only modify the forms or sites of these contradictions – introducing class struggles into the state and/or generating tendencies towards fiscal crisis, legitimacy crisis, rationality crisis, etc. Political ecologists add the market-mediated despoliation of the environment and the commitment to unsustainable development to such criticisms.

State failure

Whereas neoclassical economists' solution for market failure or inadequacy is to extend the market, welfare economists call for more state intervention. This is intended to avoid or correct market failures and to subordinate market forces to specific public purposes. More generally, the rationale for state activity is not procedural (as with the market) but substantive. It is found in the definition and enforcement of collectively binding decisions in the name of the public interest or general will. This rationale is expressed through imperative coordination (or hierarchy) rather than the anarchy of market forces. State failure is judged in turn according to this substantive rationality: it refers to the failure to realise the state's own political project(s) within the terms of its own operating rules and procedures. In democratic regimes these rules and procedures include respect for legality and the regular renewal of popular mandates for action. In this context, the primary criterion for identifying state failures is not allocative efficiency (as this is defined in terms of the procedural rationality of the market). Instead, it is the effectiveness (as often symbolic as material) with which specific state projects are realised. It is certainly possible, however, for efficiency to count among criteria for the success of specific projects. Thus 'value for money' was one objective of the recent neoliberal state project.

Moreover, just as market failure can be related to substantive factors that block the realisation of its procedural rationality, so state failure can be linked to specific procedural factors that block effective policy-making and implementation. Thus, various commentators suggest that planning, bureaucracy, participation, reliance on professional expertise, etc., may each fail in different ways to generate adequate policies and/or to secure their effective realisation. Resulting tendencies towards implementation and fiscal crises can lead, in turn, to problems of political legitimacy where the state's public purposes are not seen to be achieved. One response to this within the state is a constant cycling through these different modes of policy-making and implementation in the attempt to compensate for their respective tendencies to failure.

Just as neoclassical economists make unrealistic assumptions about markets, welfare economists make implausible claims about states. They assume that states not only have all the information necessary to maximise social welfare, but also have both the internal organisational capacities and the powers of external intervention needed to achieve their public objectives. Yet it is widely recognised that:

- state managers (especially elected politicians) have short-term time horizons and are vulnerable to lobbying;
- states are subject to bounded rationality (limited information, uncertainty and time pressures) when acting;
- states often pursue multiple and even contradictory goals – many of which are also inherently infeasible;
- state capacities are limited both by 'internalities' (calculations of private costs and benefits which differ from public goals) and external resistance;
- nonmarket outputs are usually hard to define in principle, ill-defined in practice, and difficult to measure;

- state intervention may prompt rent-seeking behaviour among policy-takers which merely redistributes rather than creates resources (Offe, 1975; Wolf, 1978).

There are different responses to state failure. Liberal critics see the market as a self-correcting learning mechanism and the state as inherently incorrigible and ineducable. They do not ask whether state failure could be corrected in ways similar to market failure, but instead seek to replace it with the market. Other critics, however, allow for self-correcting policy cycles and/or institutional redesign within the state. Measures to improve policy coordination and implementation can include redefining the division of labour in the state and wider political system, increasing state autonomy so that it is less vulnerable to particularistic lobbying, boosting reflexivity (including through auditing and the contract culture), and reorienting time horizons in favour of longer-term policy-making and policy-taking.

Governance as a response to market and state failure

Discussions of market and state failure often appear to rest on diametrically opposed theoretical and politico-ideological positions. Yet they share some core assumptions. Both presume a dichotomistic 'public–private' distinction and a zero-sum conception of the respective spheres of the market and state. Thus, on the one hand, critics of state failure see the economy as the site of mutually advantageous, voluntary exchange among formally free, equal, and autonomous economic agents; and, on the other hand, they regard the state as premised on organised coercion, which intrudes on the private liberties of citizens (especially in their capacity as economic agents). Conversely, critics of market failure see the state as a sovereign authority, empowered to pursue the public interest against the particularistic, egoistic, short-term interests of citizens (especially those of property owners). In both cases, the more there is of the state, the less there is of the market; what varies is the positive or negative evaluation of this ratio.

Literature on governance rejects this rigid polarisation between the anarchy of the market and the hierarchy of imperative coordination, in favour of the concept of 'heterarchy', i.e. horizontal self-organisation among mutually interdependent actors. It recognises the equivalence of the twin tendencies to market and state failure and proposes to reconcile and transcend them by relying on procedures which cut across the market and state divides. These include interpersonal networking, interorganisational negotiation, and 'decentred, intersystemic context steering' (dezentrierte Kontextsteuerung). The first two of these forms of governance should be familiar; the last requires some initial comment. It comprises efforts to steer (guide) the development of different systems by taking account both of their own operating codes and rationalities and of their various substantive, social, and spatio-temporal interdependencies. This is aided by communication intended to reduce intersystemic 'noise' (and to aid mutual understanding), as well as by negotiation, negative coordination, and cooperation in shared projects. It is reflected in the use of symbolic media of communication such as money, law, or knowledge to modify the structural and strategic contexts in which different systems function so that compliance with shared projects follows from their own operating codes rather than from imperative coordination (see Glagow and Willke, 1987).

The rationality of governance is neither procedural nor substantive; it is best described as 'reflexive'. The procedural rationality of the capitalist market is essentially formal in nature, prioritising an endless 'economising' pursuit of profit maximisation; the substantive rationality of government is goal-oriented, prioritising 'effective' pursuit of successive policy goals. Both approaches are particularly prone to problems of bounded rationality, opportunism, and asset specificity (Coulson, 1997). Advocates of governance suggest that these problems can be avoided by instituting negotiation around a long-term, consensual project as the basis for both negative and positive coordination among interdependent actors. The key to success is continued commitment to dialogue in order to generate and exchange more information (thereby reducing, without ever eliminating, the problem of bounded rationality), to weaken opportunism by locking partners into a range of interdependent decisions over short-, medium-, and long-term time horizons, and to build on the interdependences and risks associated with 'asset specificity' by encouraging solidarity among those involved. The rationality of governance is dialogic rather than monologic, pluralistic rather than monolithic, heterarchic rather than either hierarchic or anarchic. In turn, this suggests that there is no one best governance mechanism.

The conditions for such reflexive rationality are as complex as those for well-functioning markets or state planning. Interpersonal networking, interorganisational negotiation, and intersystemic steering are different modes of coordination and pose different problems in this regard. Specific objects of governance also affect the likelihood of success. For example, governing the global economy, human rights regimes, and transnational social movements clearly involve very different problems. Turbulent environments pose different governance problems from those that are relatively stable – especially as time is required for self-organisation to operate consensually. Governance mechanisms must provide a framework in which relevant actors can reach agreement over (albeit possibly differential) spatial and temporal horizons of action *vis-à-vis* their environment. They must also stabilise the cognitive and normative expectations of these actors by shaping and promoting a common 'world view' as well as developing adequate solutions to sequencing problems, i.e. predictably ordering various actions, policies or processes over time, especially where they have different temporal logics. At stake here is establishing secure bases of coordination with their own structurally inscribed strategic selectivity.

Governance failure?

The growing interest in governance mechanisms as a solution to market failure or state failure should not lead to neglect of governance failure. Governance mechanisms need not prove more efficient procedurally than market and states as means of economic or political coordination, nor are they guaranteed to produce more adequate outcomes. A commitment to continuing deliberation and negotiation does not exclude eventual governance failure. The criterion for such failure is not, however, immediately obvious. There is no pre-given formal maximand or reference point to judge governance success, as there is with monetised profits in the economy and/or the (imaginary) perfect market outcome. Nor is there a contingent substantive criterion – the realisation of specific political objectives connected to the (imagined) public interest – as there is with imperative coordination by the state. The primary point of governance is that goals will be modified in and through ongoing negotiation and reflection. This suggests that governance failure may comprise failure to redefine objectives in the face of continuing disagreement about whether they are still valid for the various partners.

One can also apply procedural and substantive criteria to heterarchy, however, and assess whether it produces more efficient long-term outcomes than the market and more effective long-term outcomes than imperative coordination by states. This involves adopting an evolutionary perspective and requires comparative evaluation of all three modes of coordination in terms of all of their respective rationalities. This can be seen in the increasing interest in heterarchy as a mechanism for reducing transaction costs in the economy in cases of bounded rationality, complex interdependence, and asset specificity. It is also reflected in the state's increasing interest in heterarchy's potential for enhancing the state's capacity to secure political objectives by sharing power with forces beyond it and/or delegating responsibilities for specific objectives to partnerships (or other heterarchic arrangements). Likewise, of course, partnerships (or other heterarchic arrangements) may simplify the pursuit of their own goals by relying on the market and/or state to fulfil certain aspects of their jointly-agreed projects.

Potential sources of governance failure

Rather than pursue the relatively abstract arguments about markets, states, and governance and their forms of failure outlined above, I will now try to relate them to local economic and social development. This analysis moves in three steps: an initial review of possible sources of governance failure, identification of some basic dilemmas of governance at the level of public–private partnerships (as derived from case studies in the North West and Thames Gateway regions); and some brief references to specific examples of governance arrangements and their tendencies to failure.

There are three main sets of factors which limit the success of governance in local economic and social development. The first set affects all forms of economic and social coordination and is inscribed in capitalism itself. Capitalism has always depended on a contradictory balance between marketised and non-marketised organisational forms. Although this was previously understood mainly in terms of the balance between market and state, governance does not introduce a neutral third term but adds another site upon which the balance can be contested, for new forms of governance provide a new meeting ground for the conflicting logics of accumulation and political mobilisation.

The second set concerns the contingent insertion of partnerships into the more general state system, especially in terms of the relative primacy of different modes of coordination and of access to institutional support and material resources to pursue governance objectives arrived at through reflection. Among crucial issues here are the supporting measures which are taken by the state, the provision of material and symbolic support, and the extent of any duplication or counteraction by other coordination mechanisms.

We can distinguish three aspects of this second set of constraints. First, as both governance and government mechanisms exist on different scales (indeed one of their functions is to bridge differences in scales), success at one scale may well depend on what occurs on other scales. Second, coordination mechanisms may also have different time horizons. One function of governance (as of quangos and corporatist arrangements beforehand) is to enable decisions with long-term implications to be divorced from short-term political (especially electoral) calculations. Disjunctions may still arise, however, between the time scales of different governance and government mechanisms. Third, although various governance mechanisms may acquire specific techno-economic, political, and/or ideological functions, the state typically monitors their effects on its own capacity to secure social cohesion in divided societies. It reserves to itself the right to open, close, juggle, and re-articulate governance arrangements not only in terms of particular functions but also from the viewpoint of partisan and overall political advantage.

The third set of constraints is rooted in the nature of governance as self-organisation. First, attempts at governance may fail because of over-simplification of the conditions of action and/or deficient knowledge about causal connections affecting the object of governance. This is especially problematic when this object is an inherently unstructured but complex system, such as the insertion of the local into the global economy. Indeed, this leads to the more general 'governability' problem, i.e. the question of whether the object of governance could ever be manageable, even with adequate knowledge (Mayntz, 1993; Malpas and Wickham, 1995). Second, there may be coordination problems on one or more of the interpersonal, interorganisational, and intersystemic levels. These three levels are often related in complex ways. Thus interorganisational negotiation often depends on interpersonal trust; and de-centred intersystemic steering involves the representation of system logics through interorganisational and/or interpersonal communication. Third, linked to this is the problematic relationship between those engaged in communication (networking, negotiation, etc.) and those whose interests and identities are being represented. Gaps can open between these groups leading to representational and legitimacy crises and/or to problems in securing compliance. Fourth, where there are various partnerships and other governance arrangements concerned with interdependent issues, there is a problem of coordination among them. I address this problem below in terms of metagovernance (see pp. 23–5).

Partnership dilemmas

The potential sources of governance failure discussed above assume different forms in different contexts. From interviews with those involved in partnerships in the North West and the Thames Gateway regions, we can specify four sets of strategic dilemmas that affect economic development partnerships as they seek to develop a consensual approach to the joint pursuit of a medium- to long-term strategy which advances both the individual and collective interests of their various members. These dilemmas oppose cooperation with competition, openness with closure, governability with flexibility, and accountability with efficiency.

Cooperation vs competition

Capitalist economies operate through an unstable mix of cooperation and competition. One horn of the resulting dilemma is how to maintain interpersonal trust, secure generalised compliance with negotiated understandings, reduce 'noise' through open communication, and engage in negative coordination in the face of the many and varied opportunities that exist for short-term, self-interested competitive behaviour – behaviour which could soon destroy the basis for continuing partnership. The other horn is that an excessive commitment to cooperation and consensus could block the emergence of creative tensions, conflicts, or efforts at crisis-resolution which could promote learning and/or learning capacities and thereby enhance adaptability. This horn is especially acute when the environment is turbulent, speedy action is required, incrementalism is inappropriate, and it would take time to build consensus. Such dilemmas have been widely discussed in recent analyses of flexible industrial districts, learning regions, innovative milieux, etc. These dilemmas also occur politically in the trade-off between partnership and partisanship, for partnerships are typically linked to differential advantages for political parties, tiers of government, and departmental interests as well as to differential economic interests of various kinds. This poses dilemmas both in relation to any given partnership and, even more acutely, in relation to the opportunities that may exist for juggling multiple partnerships to secure partisan advantage.

Openness vs closure

Heterarchic governance arrangements operate in complex, often turbulent, environments. They face problems in remaining open to the environment at the same time as securing the closure needed for effective coordination among a limited number of partners. One horn of the resulting dilemma is that closure may lock in members whose exit would be beneficial (e.g. inefficient firms, underemployed workers, 'sunset' sectors) or block recruitment of new social partners (e.g. new firms, marginalised workers, 'sunrise' sectors). The other horn is that openness may discourage partners from entering into long-term commitments and sharing long-term time horizons. This may prompt opportunism in the (potentially self-fulfilling) cases where partnerships dissolve or involve high turnover. It is reflected in the choice of maximising the range of possible actions by expanding relevant bases of membership or of favouring the 'small is beautiful' principle for the purpose of focused and timely action, and in the choice of variable geometries of action *versus* fixed spatial boundaries for membership of a governance arrangement. An interesting variant of this latter version of the dilemma (especially given the increasing importance of interregional cooperation in Europe) is whether to permit transnational partnerships or to insist on the defence of national sovereignty.

Governability vs flexibility

Heterarchic arrangements are said to permit longer-term strategic guidance (lacking in markets) whilst still retaining flexibility (lacking in hierarchies with their rule-governed procedures). This is also the site of a dilemma, however: that between governability (the capacity for effective guidance) and flexibility (the capacity to adapt to changed circumstances). This assumes several forms. Reducing complexity through operational rules as a precondition for governing a complex world needs to be balanced against the recognition of complexity to mobilise the 'requisite variety' of actors and resources. Avoiding duplication to limit resource costs needs to be balanced against maintaining an adequate repertoire of actions and strategic capacities. A third variant is posed in the choice between exploiting past organisational and interorganisational learning to standardise 'best practice', and maintaining adaptability in the face of a turbulent environment by avoiding 'locking-in' to outmoded routines. This last problem is particularly associated with efforts to impose 'best practice' from above rather than encourage diversity and allow for horizontal communication and learning among partnerships.

Accountability vs efficiency

Most public–private partnerships are expected to serve the public interest as well as to deliver private benefits. This blurs the public–private distinction, however, and poses a familiar dilemma in terms of accountability *versus* efficiency. On the one hand, there are problems about attributing responsibility for decisions and non-decisions (i.e. acts of commission or omission) in interdependent networks. These problems are more acute when partnerships are interorganisational, rather than interpersonal. On the other hand, attempts to establish clear lines of accountability can interfere with the efficient, cooperative pursuit of joint goals. A related dilemma is that public–private arrangements run the risk of allowing the exploitative capture of public resources for private purposes and/or extending the state's reach into the market economy and civil society to serve the interests of the state or governing party. A third version of this dilemma concerns the relative primacy of economic performance and social inclusion – how far the maximand in public–private partnerships is marketised economic performance as opposed to the addressing of problems of social cohesion.

Metagovernance

If markets, states, and governance are each prone to failure, how is economic and political coordination for economic and social development ever possible and why is it often judged to have succeeded? In part, this can be explained through the multiplicity of satisficing criteria and the range of potential vested interests, so that at least some aims are realised to a socially acceptable degree for at least some of those affected. A further explanation can be derived from the observation that 'governing and governance itself should be dynamic, complex and varied' (Kooiman, 1993: 36). This highlights the role of the 'metastructures' of interorganisational coordination (Alexander, 1995: 52) or, more generally, of 'metagovernance', i.e. the governance of government and governance.

Metagovernance should not be confused with some superordinate level of government in control of all governance arrangements, nor with the imposition of a single, all-purpose mode of governance. Rather, it involves managing the complexity, plurality, and tangled hierarchies characteristic of prevailing modes of coordination. It involves defining new boundary-spanning roles and functions, creating linkage devices, sponsoring new organisations, identifying appropriate lead organisations to coordinate other partners, designing institutions, and generating visions to facilitate self-organisation in different fields. It also involves providing mechanisms for collective feedback and learning about the functional linkages and the material interdependences among different sites and spheres of action, and encouraging a relative coherence among diverse objectives, spatial and temporal horizons, actions, and outcomes of governance arrangements. It involves the shaping of the context within which these arrangements can be forged rather than the development of specific strategies and initiatives for them.

Governments play a major and increasing role in metagovernance. They:

- provide the ground rules for governance and the regulatory order in and through which governance partners can pursue their aims;

- ensure the compatibility or coherence of different governance mechanisms and regimes;
- act as the primary organiser of the dialogue among policy communities;
- deploy a relative monopoly of organisational intelligence and information with which to shape cognitive expectations;
- serve as a 'court of appeal' for disputes arising within and over governance;
- seek to re-balance power differentials by strengthening weaker forces or systems in the interests of system integration and/or social cohesion;
- try to modify the self-understanding of identities, strategic capacities, and interests of individual and collective actors in different strategic contexts and hence alter their implications for preferred strategies and tactics;
- assume political responsibility in the event of governance failure.

This emerging role means that networking, negotiation, 'noise' reduction, and negative as well as positive coordination occur 'in the shadow of hierarchy' (Scharpf, 1994: 40). It also suggests the need for almost permanent institutional and organisational innovation to maintain the very possibility (however remote) of sustained economic growth.

Thus, metagovernance does not eliminate other modes of coordination. Markets, hierarchies, and heterarchies still exist, but they operate in a context of 'negotiated decision-making'. Thus, on the one hand, market competition will be balanced by cooperation, the invisible hand will be combined with a visible handshake. On the other hand, the state is no longer the sovereign authority; it becomes but one participant among others in the pluralistic guidance system and contributes its own distinctive resources to the negotiation process. As the range of networks, partnerships, and other models of economic and political governance expand, official apparatuses remain at best *primi inter pares*, for, although public money and law would still be important in underpinning their operation, other resources (such as private money, knowledge, or expertise) would also be critical to their success. The state's involvement would become less hierarchical, less centralised, and less dirigiste in character. The exchange of information and moral suasion become key sources of legitimation and the state's influence depends as much on its role as a prime source and mediator of collective intelligence, as on its command over economic resources or legitimate coercion (Willke, 1992).

Metagovernance failure

Recognising possible contributions of reflexive metagovernance to economic and social coordination is no guarantee of success. It is certainly not a purely technical matter which can be resolved by experts in organisational design or public administration, for all the technical activities of the state in whatever domain are conducted under the primacy of the political, i.e. the state's concern with managing the tension between economic and political advantages and its ultimate responsibility for social cohesion. This fact plagues the liberal prescription of an arms' length relationship between the market and the nightwatchman state, since states are rarely strong enough to resist pressures to intervene when anticipated political advantage is at stake or there is a need to respond to social unrest. This can be seen in the telling title of Michael Heseltine's 1985 report to Cabinet on the change of direction on policies for the inner city: *It took a riot.*

To minimise the risks of metagovernance failure, a repertoire of responses is needed to retain the ability flexibly to alter strategies and to select those that are more successful. This may well seem inefficient from an economising viewpoint because it introduces slack or waste, but it also provides major sources of flexibility in the face of failure (cf. Grabher, 1994), for, if every mode of economic and political coordination is failure-laden, then relative success in coordination over time depends on the capacity to switch modes of coordination as the limits of any one mode become evident. This provides the basis for displacing or postponing failures and crises. It also suggests that the ideologically-motivated destruction of alternative modes of co-ordination could prove counter-productive, for they may well need to be re-invented in one or another form. There are further dilemmas here from an evolutionary viewpoint: (a) learning *versus* forgetting; and (b) removing particulars *versus* retaining the general. If one affirms the maxim that 'it is necessary to change society to preserve it', then there should be mechanisms for social forgetting as well as social learning. One should also recognise that, even if specific institutions and organisations are abolished, it may be necessary to safeguard the underlying modes of coordination which they embody.

These dilemmas are evident from the experience of the Thatcher and Major governments. The neoliberal hostility to the interventionist state, trade unionism and corporatism, municipal socialism, and other features of the postwar settlement, was reflected in continuing efforts to destroy, weaken, or marginalise them. Whilst this was perhaps necessary to change attitudes in the attempted modernisation of the British economy, state, and society, it also dissipated experience and knowledge that could still prove useful, and whilst it removed specific institutional and organisational obstacles to the neoliberal project, in the short-term it also deprived the central state of an adequate range of modes of coordination to deal with complex issues in an environment made more turbulent by the intended and unintended effects of its own radical policies. So the Thatcher and Major governments eventually found it necessary to relearn lessons about the limits of the market mechanism and to reinvent alternative modes of coordination to supplement, complement, or compensate for the operation of market forces. This rediscovery was usually disguised behind changed names, innovative discourses, and institutional turnover. Nonetheless the usual policy cycle of market, governance, and state was repeated in central government policies for urban regeneration.

Two case studies

This section briefly illustrates some of the themes developed above by considering two cases from our two regional research sites (the Thames Gateway and the North West). The first concerns an inter-organisational partnership centred in Dartford in north west Kent and concerned with a particular property-led development project. The second concerns networks mobilised around the Manchester Olympic bids as a larger place-marketing exercise for Manchester and the North West. Both cases can be interpreted as instances of governance failure as well as governance success.

Kent Thames-side Agency and London Science Park at Dartford

When we conducted interviews in Dartford at the beginning of our research on the Thames Gateway region some years ago, we were confidently informed by various politicans, local government officers, and spokesmen for Dartford Chamber of Commerce that one of the town's big successes was to have secured the London Science Park at Dartford (hereafter LSP). At the conclusion of our research, the Science Park project had been scaled down and was still far from being fully established. Exploring the reasons for this illustrates many of the constraints on local governance identified above (pp. 18–22).

The first set of constraints concerns the dynamic of capitalism which was far beyond the control of the local authority and its partners. Three major obstacles (among many) to the LSP's timely establishment can be noted: the uneven development of the South East economy; the problems of property-led development under a neoliberal regime; and the conflicting temporal and spatial horizons of action of different public and private sector partners. The Thames Gateway initiative (initially flagged as the East Thames Corridor) was intended to redress the overheating of the South East economy (especially to the west of London) and to exploit the opening towards Europe by promoting growth in the east; this would have the additional advantage of exploiting brownfield and derelict land along the Thames thus relieving pressure on the green belt. The problems of industrial and urban decay affecting the East Thames region were not removed simply through declaration of the Thames Gateway initiative, however (especially given the emphasis on private enterprise more than public funding), and continued to disfavour investment in 'high tech' projects in the region. Moreover, as the property-led development approach needs continued economic expansion to justify investment, the collapse of Lawson's boom in the late 1980s and the resulting overhang of property investments in the City and South East proved a further disincentive. This, in turn, produced conflicting expectations about the various time horizons and priorities for profitable development of the proposed LSP site between private and public sector partners. These were compounded by the greater spatial scope of action of two of the partners whose activities extended well beyond the local to the regional, national, and international scales. This was reflected in conflicts around three issues: the most appropriate uses, the ideal sequencing, and the proper distribution of profits from bringing parcels of land in different ownership into development. A merger between the Glaxo and Wellcome corporations also altered the interests of a key partner.

The second set of constraints concerns the insertion of the LSP project into the wider set of local government and governance arrangements. Of particular significance here was the turbulent political environment for the partners in the Kent Thames-side Agency concerned with the LSP. The rationale for the partnership was the pooled interdependence of Dartford Borough Council (a major local landowner and planning authority wishing to upgrade the town's image and economic prospects), Wellcome (a leading international pharmaceutical company and major local employer), the local health authority (with a redundant hospital site and plans for expansion), Blue Circle Industries (a major landowner and property developer by virtue of its disused chalk pits in North West Kent), and the University of Greenwich (interested in developing a new campus, including student accommodation, and boosting research links with industry by locating at the LSP site). Three sources of uncertainty and turbulence (among others) which affected the project were: (a) central government-induced changes in the status, powers, and ownership rights of the health authority (in turn a regional health authority, a district authority, and a NHS trust) and, hence, in its interests in the project; (b) politically-motivated delays in government commitments to infrastructural projects and spending essential to the overall growth dynamic of the sub-region, notably around the Channel Tunnel Rail Link, the international rail terminal, and road links; and (c) changes in central government policy on higher education and training which affected the interests of the University of Greenwich regarding campus accommodation and research strategy.

Paradoxically, the partnership itself appears to have worked well. A clear recognition of pooled interdependence provided a continuing framework for negotiation around the need to balance conflicting property interests and the overall economic, political, and social benefits of cooperation. A flexible framework which avoided a once-and-for-all decision on the appropriate legal form and membership of the partnership encouraged a balance between openness and closure and between governability and flexibility. The insertion of the LSP into a broader and largely consensual local and regional accumulation strategy developed by the borough council permitted balance between economic efficiency and political accountability. As delays in complementary economic projects (a major regional shopping centre, an international rail terminal, the high-speed Channel Tunnel Rail Link) are overcome and the Thames Gateway role as the bridge between London and Europe becomes a reality, the prospects for a scaled-down version of the LSP feeding into a more general pattern of synergetic growth look better than they did at the end of our research.

The Manchester Olympic bids

The Manchester Olympic bids illustrate the paradox of a successful failure – a project which could be successfully marketed despite failing in key respects (Bovaird, 1994). If one regards them as place-marketing exercises linked to property-led development, then they helped to market Manchester, mobilised important grants for urban regeneration, and secured widespread recognition and support at home and abroad. Indeed, if one accepts that the actual staging of the Games could prove costly, then the eventual failure to secure them could even be considered a success (contrast the Olympic experiences of Montréal and Barcelona, or Sheffield and the World Student Games). The presentational politics of the bidding process required a united front among local partners and this, combined with the broadly positive-sum nature of the Olympics-legitimated but state-aided and property-led development project, provided the context in which the various dilemmas of partnership were managed in the short term.

From a governance viewpoint, three points need to be made. First, Manchester's Olympic strategy illustrates the complementarity and interdependence among different scales of economic and political action. Local governance is not confined to the local level. The bid strategy and outcome involved a complex interplay between: (a) local economic and political capacities and priorities; (b) national and international systems of rule-setting (especially those of the Department of the Environment and the International Olympic Committee); and (c) European and central government political and economic strategies. Second, the broad-based grant-coalition which fronted the Olympic bids was firmly rooted not only in material interdependences, but also in established informal inter-personal networking among business leaders, political figures, and other local elites. This was the basis of trust for interorganisational negotiations and the formation of a broad-based hegemonic project for the region. Although Sir Bob Scott (whose role was famously described as 'a man and his secretary sitting in an office and mas-querading as an institution') achieved a high profile in the bid process as the public (and acceptable) face of private capital, a key metagovernance role was also performed by the local authori-ties under the leadership of Manchester City Council. This is clear not only in promotional activities, but also in various project man-agement activities. Third, the Olympic bids provided a positive-sum game for developing a broadly consensual local accumulation strat-egy and hegemonic project. They provided the basis for levering European and central government funding, secured property-led regeneration, enhanced the image of Manchester (with some skil-fully contrived confusion between Manchester City Council and Greater Manchester), promised benefits to the North West more generally, and attracted considerable local popular support. With the second failure to win the Olympics nomination, much of this unity and support has been dissipated. A pattern of fragmentation and duplication of partnerships has reasserted itself. This illustrates the role of strategy and vision, as well as structures, in maintaining local governance (for further details on this case study, see Cochrane *et al.*, 1996; and Jessop *et al.*, 1999).

Concluding remarks

In short, markets, states, and governance all fail. This is not surpris-ing, for failure is a central feature of all social relations: 'governance is necessarily incomplete and as a necessary consequence must always fail' (Malpas and Wickham, 1995, p. 40). Indeed, given the growing structural complexity and opacity of the social world, failure is the most likely outcome of most attempts to govern it, in terms of multiple objectives over extended spatial and temporal horizons, whatever coordination mechanism is adopted. This emphasis on the improbability of success serves to counter the rhetoric of partnership which leads commentators to highlight achievements rather than failures and, where they recognise failure, to see it as exceptional and corrigible in regard to their preferred mode of coordination even as they see coordination failure elsewhere as inevitable. This polarisation is reflected both in the succession of governments and in policy cycles within governments in which different modes of policy-making succeed each other as the difficulties of each become more evident. Postwar British politics offers plenty of evidence of this through the increasingly hectic oscillation among liberal, dirigiste, and corporatist modes of economic intervention (witness, in particular, the successive 'U-turns' in the Heath government of 1970–74 and the Wilson–Callaghan governments of 1974–79).

Once the incompleteness of attempts at coordination (whether through the market, the state, or heterarchy) is accepted as inevitable, it is necessary to adopt a satisficing approach which has at least three key dimensions:

- a reflexive orientation to what will prove satisfactory in the case of failure, to compare the effects of failure/inadequacies in the market, government, and governance, and to regularly re-assess the extent to which current actions are producing desired outcomes;
- deliberate cultivation of a flexible repertoire (requisite variety) of responses so that strategies and tactics can be combined to reduce the likelihood of failure and to alter their balance in the face of failure and turbulence in the policy environment. Moreover, as different periods and conjunctures require different kinds of policy mix, the balance in the repertoire will need to be varied;
- a self-reflexive 'irony', in the sense that participants must recognise the likelihood of failure but proceed as if success were possible. The supreme irony in this context is that the need for irony holds not only for individual governance mechanisms but also for metagovernance itself.

For reasons I have explored in more detail elsewhere (Jessop, 1997b, 1998a), I suggest that public–private partnership in its various forms is especially appropriate for securing economic, social, and community development in the current period despite its inevitable tendencies towards governance failure. This suggests the need to put such governance arrangements at the core of the coordination repertoire, with diverse flanking and supportive measures from other modes of coordination. There must also be greater commitment to a participatory politics based on stakeholding, and to sustainable economic and community development.

About this study

This study is based on research in Greater Manchester and the Thames Gateway into the nature and formation of economic development partnerships during the early and mid-1990s. The research involved extensive interviewing and documentary analysis. Other publications arising from the research include Jessop, 1995, 1997a, 1997c and 1998b.

2 Local Governance After Fordism: A Regulationist Perspective

Joe Painter and Mark Goodwin

Local governance is affected by, and in turn affects, wider processes of social and economic restructuring. Our recently completed research project on 'British local governance in the transition from Fordism' was designed to analyse the relationships between changes in local governance and broader socio-economic trans- formation. To do this, we adopted a conceptual framework and methodological approach drawn from regulation theory (partly because we had found regulation theory helpful in our earlier work, and partly because we wanted to test its usefulness in analys- ing change in local governance). This chapter presents a summary of the findings of our research.

Local governance and regulation theory

A number of political scientists, sociologists and geographers have begun to use the concepts and terminology of regulation theory to interpret contemporary changes in the structures and practices of local governance. Their work has shown that two broad approaches can be taken: the first examines the notion of post-Fordist local governance, and the second considers the role of local governance in a (potential) post-Fordist society. In most of the literature these two aspects have rarely been distinguished – indeed research has focused almost automatically on the former. Thus, several of these writers have claimed that local governance in the UK is changing from a Fordist to a post-Fordist form. In some cases this claim may amount to no more than the cataloguing of a series of changes which seem compatible with existing accounts of the characteristics of post-Fordist industrial organisation. This clearly does not amount to a demonstration of the linkage between social and economic restructuring and changes in local governance, nor does it involve a regulationist conceptualisation of local governance change. For us, the power of regulation theory lies in its ability to analyse both the consequences of a particular Mode of Regulation (MoR) for the nature of local governance and the role that the structure and practices of local governance play in the emergence and stabilisation of the MoR. This is much more akin to the second approach outlined above, which we regard as more theoretically coherent. We will amplify this by reference to the role of local governance in Fordism, before we turn to our analysis of local governance in the transition therefrom.

Jessop (1992) identifies four different meanings of the term 'Fordism': as labour process, regime of accumulation, mode of regulation and mode of societalisation. UK local governance could be related to each of these, however Jessop concludes that the concept of Fordism is most appropriately defined as a mode of regulation and we will treat it as such in our analysis. According to Jessop (1992, pp. 48–9), Fordism as an MoR involved a labour relations system based on collective bargaining which indexed wages to productivity increases, the separation of ownership from control in large monopolistic enterprises, 'national' money and consumer credit, mass marketing, and a Keynesian welfare state. The state operated demand management policies in the fiscal sphere and underwrote a minimum level of working class consumption to help complete the 'virtuous circle' between production and consumption.

These core features of Fordism as an MoR are expressed, in concrete form, differently in different countries, as actual regulatory influences and practices develop in specific historic and geographic contexts. In Britain, local governance played a central role. It both contributed to, and was influenced by, the MoR. The dynamics of the relationship between local governance and the Fordist MoR can be summarised briefly as follows:

1. Elected local government under Fordism in the UK was a key element of the Keynesian welfare state – both organisationally and discursively;

2. As such it provided and managed important elements of the social wage, such as housing, which helped to underwrite the mass consumption norm required to sustain Fordist growth;
3. It was also a key site where consensual social-democratic politics could be constructed and experienced. It provided services for which there were political demands, but which could not be mechanised and mass produced easily, and which were thus unprofitable for the capitalist sector to provide on a unive'sal basis. Hence, the paradox that the Fordist local state engaged in production using largely non-Fordist techniques.
4. Local government also contributed to regulation through infrastructural provision and the planning of local economic development.

   Although important parts of UK local government contributed to the dynamic of the Fordist MoR, the relationship was not a purely functional one. First, although it displaced certain crisis tendencies, for example through its contribution to the social wage, it exacerbated others. Outside local government, a key element of Fordist regulation was the organisation of labour in terms of collective bargaining. This was regulatory in the parts of the manufacturing sector where wage increases could be financed through productivity gains as a result of technical change. In contrast, however, when collective bargaining became widespread in the public services sector, there was relatively little scope for such productivity growth and the organisation of labour relations along these lines became dysfunctional. Second, the real heyday of Fordist local governance in Britain came at the end of the Fordist phase, when crisis tendencies were already apparent. The expansion of local government during the early 1970s, in fact, fed into a crisis of regulation, and local government, especially, moved from playing (among other things) a regulatory role, to being bound up in what Offe (1984) has termed the 'crisis of crisis management' within the welfare state. During the 1980s, we suggest, a particular political response to these crisis tendencies, coupled to the desire of the right to defeat socialism and labourism, led to local government itself becoming increasingly an object of regulation, as well as a part of the regulation process.

   To talk in these terms is to begin to chart the contribution made by local governance to the dynamics of the Fordist MoR. We are not simply identifying structures and practices of local governance that appear to be Fordist – centralised service delivery, hierarchical management, bureaucracy – and labelling them as such. We are, instead, tracing the connections and dynamics that operate (in both directions) between social and economic restructuring and changes in local governance. The same analytical method must be used to analyse the role of local governance in the transition away from Fordism – hence our main concern is with local governance in a post-Fordist society, rather than with post-Fordist organisational forms in local governance. This is difficult, for while it is relatively easy to chart a series of changes in the institutions and mechanisms of local government, and label them post-Fordist (or not, as the case may be), elucidating what part these changed structures and practices might play in helping to stabilise the functioning of any new MoR is an altogether more complex process, requiring careful theoretical reflection as well as empirical investigation.

Local state and governance in a post-Fordist mode of regulation

We have argued elsewhere that coherent 'modes of regulation' are likely to arise only very rarely (Goodwin and Painter, 1996). The effectiveness of regulation fluctuates over time and across space, and our research started from the premise that the 30 years following the Second World War represented a phase of particularly successful regulation in most of the advanced capitalist economies, which has been labelled 'Fordism'. The relationship between local governance and Fordism was outlined above, and the contradictions and failure of the Fordist mode of regulation have been documented elsewhere (Aglietta, 1979; Lipietz, 1987). While there are, as yet, few signs that a new phase of successful regulation is replacing Fordism, the theoretical possibility of such a new phase raises a counterfactual question: what kinds of possible regulatory arrangements could both resolve the contradictions of Fordism and promote the stabilisation of economic activity over the medium term and over a given geographical space? (To put it another way, what would a successful post-Fordist mode of regulation consist of?)

Taken together, these concepts allow us to frame the following questions as the core of our analysis, questions that arise logically from the adoption of a regulationist framework for research into the restructuring of local government and governance:

What would the roles of the local state, local government and local governance be in a successful post-Fordist mode of regulation, and how far are these being fulfilled currently?

Answering these questions involves using regulation theory to develop a theoretical account of the necessary features of a successful post-Fordist mode of regulation, and then comparing these with the contemporary restructuring of local governance.

Defining a 'post-Fordist mode of regulation'

Since no stable mode of regulation has yet arisen in the wake of the failure of Fordism, it is quite impossible to specify the character of post-Fordism in full. Nevertheless, it is possible to identify some minimum necessary features. There is no necessity for post-Fordism to emerge, but should it do so it would, by definition: (a) resolve the contradictions and crisis tendencies of the Fordist mode of regulation; and (b) enable and promote sustained capital accumulation. Jessop (1994) has outlined a possible mode of regulation which, he argues, could be termed 'post-Fordist' inasmuch as it would resolve the key contradictions and crisis tendencies of Fordism. The four key areas he identifies are the wage relation, the enterprise system, the money form and the state.

The wage relation

Under Fordism, the wage relation saw an indexing of wages to productivity. The benefits of this included the mitigation of class conflict and an expansion of mass markets. However, as wage increases became generalised through a system of national collective bargaining to sectors where productivity increases through technological change were not available, the costs of the Fordist form of the wage relation began to outweigh these benefits. To resolve these problems, therefore, Jessop proposes that the wage relation under post-Fordism would have the following characteristics: (a) polarisation between skilled and unskilled workers; (b) flexibility in internal and external labour markets; (c) firm- or plant-level bargaining; and (d) new forms of social wage.

The enterprise system

Under Fordism, the enterprise system involved large, bureaucratic, vertically integrated and hierarchically organised firms controlled from the centre. This allowed the coordination of mass workforces of semi-skilled workers, whose activities were linked through production systems organised by a cadre of technical and managerial staff. Production was for mass markets where competition took place principally on price, and in which large organisations permitted the exploitation of economies of scale. Increasingly, however, such organisational forms were unable to respond flexibly to the saturation of those mass markets and to consumer demand for more customised products. Within enterprises, the separation of control from execution led to dissatisfaction with the incremental degradation of work which it implied. In the perpetual search for productivity increases, large tiers of managerial staff not directly involved in production came to be more of a cost than a benefit. According to Jessop, the post-Fordist resolution of these problems would have the following features: (a) flatter, less bureaucratic organisations; (b) forms of intra- and inter-firm coordination between hierarchy and market; (c) profitability dependent on flexible production systems, product and process innovation and economies of scope; and (d) competition governed by non-price factors.

Money form

Under Fordism, money was national, and international transactions were governed by relatively stable exchange rates underpinned initially by gold and then by the US dollar. National monetary controls and currency issues were linked to Keynesian policy objectives of controlling aggregate demand. In due course, these arrangements came to be viewed as constraints on the ability of private capital to respond to heightened competition, and as potentially inflationary. The post-Fordist resolution outlined by Jessop would involve: (a) private, internationalised bank credit; (b) state credit subject to the limits set by global money markets; and (c) segmented markets served by new forms of commercial capital.

State

Under Fordism, the state played a key role as a Keynesian welfare state. It regulated demand and underwrote a minimum level of mass consumption through the social wage. It was also involved, in a variety of ways, in sponsoring and regulating the wage relation, the enterprise system and the money form. For a time, this was functional to sustained accumulation. In due course, however, the Fordist state became implicated in the contradictions and eventual failure of the Fordist mode of regulation. Much attention has been focused within regulation theory on the fiscal problems of the Fordist state, and its inability to finance a social wage in the face of the pincer movement generated by economic crisis (the simultaneous deterioration in the fiscal base and increase in the demands upon it as a result of economic downturn). In addition, however, it is important to consider the rationality crisis of the state (its inability to pursue its own strategies for technical, organisational and informational reasons) and the legitimation crisis of the state (the resulting decline in popular support). We will consider these additional problems in more detail below. For Jessop, the contradictions which stem from the role of the state in Fordism can potentially be resolved by the restructuring of the state from the Keynesian welfare state of Fordism to the post-Fordist 'Schumpeterian workfare state'. The Schumpeterian workfare state would: (a) promote product and process innovation ('Schumpeterianism'); and (b) subordinate social policy to the needs of labour market flexibility ('workfare'). (Note that Jessop intends the term 'workfare' to be understood metaphorically, not in the literal sense of traditional US workfare programmes.)

In addition, the post-Fordist state would be 'hollowed-out'. Hollowing out reflects the international character of post-Fordism and involves the weakening of the national state relative to international and local sources of power through: (a) the internationalisation of production; (b) the renaissance of local and regional government; and (c) the development of international networks of localities.

The roles of local governance in post-Fordism

Having presented an outline of the features which Jessop suggests would be likely to characterise post-Fordism were it to emerge, we are now in a position to consider the role of the local state (including local government) and local governance therein. These roles are of two sorts. First, there are functions within the post-Fordist mode of regulation which would have to be fulfilled by the local state and or local governance (necessary roles). Second, there are roles which might be played by the local state or local governance, but which could be fulfilled in other ways (contingent roles). (In addition there are roles which the local state or local governance might play which would actively prevent the emergence of post-Fordism.)

The necessary and contingent roles of the local state and local governance in relation to each of the elements of the post-Fordist mode of regulation are outlined in Table 2.1. Local government here is included within local state. At this stage, no attempt has been made to distinguish the roles of local governance from the roles of the local state, except where that distinction is obviously of material difference to the operation of the mode of regulation.

TABLE 2.1   **The roles of local governance in the post-Fordism mode of regulation**

Aspects of post-Fordist mode of regulation	Functions of institutions of local governance
Wage relation	
Skilled/unskilled polarisation	Training; management of social and spatial inequality; safety net welfare provision
Flexibility in internal and external labour markets	Training; management of growth of 'peripheral' labour force; promotion of new labour-market practices via own workforce; subcontracting of service delivery
Firm or plant level bargaining	Promotion of new practice via own workforce
New forms of social wage	Funding and/or delivery
Enterprise system	
Flatter, less bureaucratic organisations	Promotion of new practice through organisational change
Forms of intra- and inter-firm co-ordination between hierarchy and market	Move from state coordination to coordination through governance; facilitating networking, partnerships, and relations of trust; developing new forms of co-ordination

TABLE 2.1 Contd.

Profitability dependent on flexible production systems, product and process innovation and economies of scope.	Infrastructural provision; support for innovation; training
Competition governed by non-price factors	Environmental improvement; place marketing and place management to improve competitive advantage of local service sector
Money form	
Private, internationalised bank credit	Not directly relevant to local governance
State credit subject to limits set by global money markets	Observance of fiscal austerity; cost reductions promoted through organisational change, service reductions, flexibilisation of public sector labour market, and competitive tendering
Segmented markets served by new forms of commercial capital	Not directly relevant to local governance
Hollowed-out Schumpeterian workfare state	
Promote product and process innovation	Provision of infrastructure (especially new information and communication technologies); support for innovation; training
Subordinate social policy to needs of labour market flexibility	Policing and control of social unrest at local level; limitations on social welfare provision; training oriented towards needs of private sector
Weakening of national state: (a) internationalised production	Place marketing for inward investment
(b) local/regional government renaissance	Development of 'local regulatory capacity'; management of uneven development
(c) networks between localities across nations	Formation of international networks

Not surprisingly, there are many features of post-Fordism to which local governance and the local state are of no relevance. The money form, for example, is primarily determined at the national and international scale, with the only role for the local state being the observance of fiscal discipline to bear down on overall public sector debt. In other areas, however, it is not only clear that there *are* roles for the local state and governance, but also that the playing of these roles is a necessary, though not sufficient, condition for the emergence of post-Fordism. Training, for example, has rightly attracted a lot of attention from regulationist authors. In a competitive environment, there is a classic prisoner's dilemma for individual companies with regard to training. It is in the interests of industry as a whole that a trained labour force be available, but it is not in the interests of any one employer to provide training, which will be a short-term cost, and whose benefits may be siphoned off by competitors through labour poaching. Training, if it is to be provided at all, must be provided (at least to some extent) collectively. The coordination mechanism for such provision has traditionally been the state, but increasingly a process of governance is supplementing, or replacing this. However it is provided, though, it must be provided locally, both in order to bring the delivery of training to local populations, and in order to tailor training requirements to local labour markets. If we add to this the central role that workforce reskilling and technological innovation play in the definition of post-Fordism, it is clear that provision of training is a necessary feature of local state and/or governance in post- Fordism. A similar argument could be developed in relation to the other components in Table 2.1.

The contents of Table 2.1 might be summarised as follows. Under Fordism, for a period, the provision of social welfare was functional for economic growth and development, and also brought a degree of social cohesion and stability. Under post-Fordism, international economic competitiveness would be paramount, and social policy would be subordinated to supply-side requirements, particularly the need to provide a flexible labour force with training matched to the requirements of private investors. In consequence, new forms of coordination between the public and private sectors ('governance') would be required both to maintain the subordination of social need to economic competitiveness politically, and to ensure that supply-side provision was indeed tailored to the needs of the private sector. Welfare policy becomes decoupled from economic development and increasingly a mechanism for mitigating the social consequences of the restless search for competitive advantage. As it is no longer central to the mode of growth, welfare need no longer be provided or underwritten by the state, and new forms of coordination ('governance' again) can be introduced here too. This may also allow the costs of provision to be limited, especially where family members, voluntary agencies or 'the community' are the main providers.

Local governance is potentially one of the most significant mechanisms for the management of uneven development, but can only be effective if it forms part of a multi-scale system of regulation. Uneven development is expressed in local-level variation, but its causes lie, at least in part, elsewhere. Local governance, therefore, may have some scope for mitigating the social consequences of uneven development, for example by tailoring a welfare system to local conditions, but, at best, it can influence only the local half of the (unequal) relationship between global flows and local conditions.

In principle, therefore, local governance can only ever make a limited contribution to the stabilisation of a new, successful mode of regulation. On the other hand, that contribution is vital, if the tensions arising from uneven development are not to undermine the emergence of the new MoR.

Local regulatory capacity

We propose the concept of 'local regulatory capacity' to refer to the extent to which the local state, local governance (and other potential local-level regulatory mechanisms) contribute the necessarily local elements of the overall management of the tensions and contradictions of a mode of regulation.

We prefer this term to the alternative notion of 'local mode of regulation', since the latter seems to us to imply that a complete mode of regulation could arise at the local level. The idea of 'regulatory capacity' recognises that local mechanisms are only ever part of the picture. It also implies an *ability* to fulfil certain roles which may or may not be realised, depending on conditions at other spatial scales.

Case study of Sunderland

Our three case studies (see 'About This Study', p. 53) suggest that while many of the features of Jessop's outline of post-Fordism are developing, there is little evidence that the local state and local governance are capable of providing the necessary local regulatory mechanisms for the stabilisation or sustainability of a new mode of regulation. Moreover, some developments are clearly counter-regulatory, and seem likely to undermine any such emergent sustainability. Here there is space to report on only one of these studies – that of Sunderland.

The case study area

The case study covered the local governance of the area that falls within the boundaries of the Metropolitan Borough of Sunderland, one of five metropolitan districts that constituted the former Metropolitan County of Tyne and Wear. Tyne and Wear and its constituent districts (Newcastle, Gateshead, North Tyneside, South Tyneside and Sunderland) were established by the Local Government Act of 1972 and came into being in April 1974. The metropolitan county was abolished as a unit of local government from 1 April 1986 under the provisions of the Local Government Act of 1985. Its functions were divided among the five districts and a number of joint boards. At the 1991 Census, the population of Sunderland was 289 000, representing a decline of 2% since 1981. In 1992, the Borough was formally awarded the status of 'City'.

The territory of the Metropolitan Borough of Sunderland includes:

- the settlement of Sunderland itself, located in the north-east of the borough on both sides of the River Wear at its mouth;
- the new town of Washington, which was designated in July 1964 and which occupies 2270 hectares in the north-west of the borough;
- the former mining settlements of Houghton-le-Spring and Hetton-le-Hole in the south of the borough;
- rural land occupying 5700 hectares (about 40% of the area) of which approximately 4300 hectares is existing or proposed green belt, occupying an irregular area in the centre of the borough and a strip along its northern boundary (City of Sunderland, 1995).

Economic change in Sunderland

During the nineteenth century, the town was a major centre of industrialisation. The population grew rapidly from 20 000 in 1801, to 151 000 in 1911. Much of the expansion was a product of the development of the shipbuilding and coalmining industries. Despite major economic problems during the depression of the 1930s, these industries continued as major sources of employment until the second half of the twentieth century. In 1951, one-fifth of the male population of working age was employed in shipbuilding. In 1960, over 18 000 people in Sunderland worked in coalmining. As recently as 1981, the two industries together employed 10 000 workers, about 10% of the total workforce. Today, there are no shipyards left on the River Wear. In 1993, Wearmouth colliery, the last deep mine in the Durham coalfield, closed. The loss of these two industries has removed the traditional economic base of the city, with dramatic implications.

First, unemployment in Sunderland is high. The count of those claiming unemployment-related benefits peaked in 1986 at just under 30 000. It has now fallen significantly but the rate of unemployment remains high by national standards. This is shown by the estimates of the unemployment rate provided by the quarterly Labour Force Survey (LFS). (The LFS uses the internationally accepted definition of unemployment provided by the International Labour Organisation (ILO), one that is not affected by changes to the rules governing benefit entitlement.) According to the LFS estimates, between May 1992 and November 1996, the unemployment rate in Sunderland averaged 13.7%, compared with 9.5% for Great Britain as a whole.

Second, rates of employment are low relative to the national average. The level of employment is not the straightforward inverse of the level of unemployment, and is in many ways a significantly better indicator of the health and prosperity of the economy, particularly where comparisons between different areas are concerned. This is because many people who are not employed would take up a job if one were available locally, but may not be included in the unemployment figures because they fall outside the formal definition of 'unemployed'. The level of employment, measured as a proportion of the local population of working age, provides a good guide to the vibrancy of the local economy. A relatively low level of employment indicates that there is a high level of dependency in the local area on unearned income, whether from state benefits, savings or other household members. This, in turn, indicates that the formal local economy is unable to provide as high a standard of living for local people as is the case in other areas.

Data derived from the 1991 Census of Population relating to employment show that, while the British economy as a whole provides gainful employment or self employment for 69% of the population of working age, the figure for Sunderland is significantly lower, at just 59%. In other words, over two-fifths of the population of Sunderland that is of working age has no direct income from a job. The contrast is greater still among men, with the Sunderland economy able to provide employment for 63% of those of working age, compared with a national figure of 76%. The relatively low prosperity of the local economy at the time of the 1991 Census is also indicated by the low levels of car ownership (48.8% of households in Sunderland had no car compared with a figure for Great Britain of 33.4%) and of owner occupation (53.2% in Sunderland compared with 66.3% for Great Britain)

While more than half of women employees are in full-time jobs, part-time work is much more common among women than among men, so much so that part-time work may be said to be overwhelmingly undertaken by women. Levels of self employment are significantly lower among women than among men. Overall, though, female participation in the formal economy in Sunderland has expanded dramatically from 29% of all employees in 1951, to 47% in 1991.

The decline of the traditional industrial sectors in Sunderland has been accompanied by the rise of the service sector and significant employment growth in new manufacturing operations. These changes have had some paradoxical effects on the industrial structure of the city. In 1981 (in the depths of the deindustrialising recession of the early 1980s) the ratio of manufacturing to service employment was similar in Sunderland to that in Great Britain as a whole (see Table 2.2). By 1995, while the British economy had become overwhelming dominated by service sector jobs, the level of manufacturing employment in Sunderland had returned to its 1981 level (having fallen to a low of 23.6% in 1987).

TABLE 2.2   Sectoral distribution of employment

Sector	Great Britain		Sunderland	
	1981	1995	1981	1995
Service jobs (% of all jobs)	61.5	75.5	62.5	67.5
Manufacturing jobs (% of all jobs)	28.4	18.4	26.5	26.8

Source: NOMIS/Census of Employment

Of course this broad picture disguises major shifts in the character of the manufacturing sector in Sunderland. The disaggregated Census of Employment cannot be published in detail for Sunderland for reasons of confidentiality. However, while 1989 saw the end of shipbuilding on the Wear, there was significant employment growth in the clothing and footwear sector, and especially in motor vehicle manufacture, following the opening of the Nissan car assembly plant in Washington, where the workforce grew to nearly 5000 by 1994 (*Financial Times*, 7/11/94, p. 20).

Sunderland in Fordism and post-Fordism

According to Hudson (1989), the concepts of Fordism and post-Fordism cannot easily be applied to the changing urban and regional economy of old industrial areas like the north east of England. Hudson argues that the region was never truly Fordist because its economy was never dominated by the mass production industries supposedly typical of Fordism. This argument is valid if Fordism is defined (as it commonly is) as a form of labour process or production organisation. However, our definition of Fordism is different. Following Jessop (1992), we define Fordism as a mode of regulation, that is, as a particular institutional and political configuration. From this perspective, the prevalence or otherwise of mass production techniques in the key industrial sectors is not the issue. Of more importance is the social organisation associated with those key sectors and the institutional matrices through which they were regulated.

If Fordism is defined as a mode of regulation (in Jessop's sense of that term), then Sunderland was certainly Fordist. The dominance of heavy industry was closely associated with a labour market dominated by male full-time employment, organised in highly unionised mass workforces. Consumption practices were far more homogeneous than is the case today. The provision of consumption goods was socialised to a considerable extent, and the consumption norm was underwritten by a well developed social wage administered through the welfare state bureaucracy. Public sector services in Sunderland grew rapidly in the years after the Second World War and with them a large public sector labour force. As in any locality, these social and institutional patterns were given particular inflections reflecting local circumstances in Sunderland. In our view, however, this local variation did not amount to a distinctive *local* mode of regulation. Rather, Sunderland was fully integrated into the emerging national Fordist mode of regulation.

Local governance was central to much of this, and was also responsible for some of the local specificity. Among other things, the Fordist period saw a large expansion in public housing. Initially this was undertaken by the local council. Between 1951 and 1959, 10 000 houses were built 'in a continuous belt of new estates on the western edge of the Borough' (Blair, 1988, p. 199) and by the end of the 1960s, council housing effectively 'ringed the Victorian town on all sides' (p. 199). In July 1964, the new town of Washington was designated to the west of Sunderland. Most of the further expansion in public housing was thereafter the responsibility of the New Town Development Corporation. The development of the new town and the institution that ran it, were typical of the Fordist mode of regulation, involving state planning, a degree of social engineering, a social-democratic vision of the good society, a leading role for the public sector and a technocratic approach to management neatly captured by the title of the book that tells the story of Washington new town, written by one of the key protagonists: *Quicker by Quango*.

Superficially, at least, the case of Sunderland also seems to fit well with the idea of a transition from a Fordist to a post-Fordist mode of regulation: The heavy industry of the past has largely disappeared; the jobs lost have been partially replaced by new investment, including a number of plants using so-called 'Japanese' production methods; the services sector has grown in its share of employment; much greater emphasis is placed by local institutions on competition within a global economy; and the City of Sunderland Council has a strategy to make Sunderland the advanced manufacturing centre of the North (hence the significance of the relatively high level of manufacturing employment noted earlier).

Furthermore, the forms of local governance which partly constituted the Fordist mode of regulation, such as the pre-eminence of
elected authorities, the mass provision of public services, and large,
hierarchical and centralised organisation have begun to change, in
some cases quite dramatically. While the local authority (now the
unitary City of Sunderland Council) still plays a key role, it has been
joined by a diverse range of new (or newly influential) agencies of
governance. These include: Tyne and Wear Development Corporation, Sunderland City Training and Enterprise Council, Sunderland
City Challenge, The City of Sunderland Forum, The City of Sunderland Partnership and Sunderland Business Link. In addition to the
city-based institutions, there are also a number of regional organisations which are also involved in processes of governance in
Sunderland, including the Government Office for the North East,
the Northern Development Company and the North East Chamber
of Commerce.

In many cases the traditional single agency approach has been
replaced by various forms of partnership organisation. For example,
the City of Sunderland Partnership, which developed from the City
of Sunderland Forum, brings together the City of Sunderland
Council, the Tyne and Wear Development Corporation, and the
Sunderland City Training and Enterprise Council with the University of Sunderland and the Tyne and Wear Chamber of Commerce.
The high priority placed on the involvement of the private sector is
striking, with considerable influence being wielded by major companies such as Nissan. The reasons for this may be obvious, but the
effects are striking. For example, the local football club, Sunderland
FC, planned to develop a major new stadium on the outskirts of the
city near the Nissan plant. Opposition from the company appeared
likely to lead to a public inquiry. Rather than go through a time-
consuming and expensive inquiry, the football club moved its plans
to a smaller site on the location of the former Wearmouth colliery.
In addition to companies, individual business people also play
prominent roles. Vaux Brewery, located in the city centre, is a key
local employer, with a workforce of over 10 000. The firm was
founded in the mid-nineteenth century by Cuthbert Vaux, and,
although the larger part of the business is now a public company,
his great-great-grandsons, Sir Paul Nicholson and Frank Nicholson
are today the Chairman and Managing Director, respectively. Both
are heavily involved in local affairs. Sir Paul Nicholson, for example,

is the first President of the recently formed North East Chamber of Commerce, a director of the Northern Development Company and Chairman of the Tyne and Wear Development Corporation. Frank Nicholson chairs the City of Sunderland Forum and the City of Sunderland Partnership. In addition, Sir Paul Nicholson chairs the Northern Industrialists Protection Association, an organisation reportedly established to raise funds for the Conservative Party (*Financial Times*, 19 December 1994, p. 8).

Is the local governance of Sunderland becoming post-Fordist?

The growth of a diverse range of new agencies of governance working in partnership, a stress on supply-side and private sector-oriented policies for economic development and a scaling down of the provision of the means of collective consumption by the local state, all appear to match the criteria for identifying a shift to post-Fordist regulation (see Table 2.1).

The detailed case study research we have undertaken, however, tells a rather more complex story. As far as the wage relation is concerned, the local effects of labour market polarisation are clear, and are consequent on the decline of traditional industries. In 1991, Sunderland was the 33rd most deprived district in England (out of 366). The six most deprived wards in the city are among the ten most deprived in the region. Unemployment is heavily concentrated in particular estates and dependency ratios are high. Inward investment has been attracted to the city, in part, by the availability of relatively cheap and adaptable labour pools, and agencies of local governance have been directly involved in the provision of specific training schemes linked to the needs of particular employers. On the other hand, there has been no sharp move towards increasing 'flexibility' within the public sector labour market. The City of Sunderland Council, which remains a major local employer, has pursued a strategy of retaining a substantial core workforce. Council services have been restructured into business units servicing a central 'client', but with the objective of maintaining corporate integration, rather than promoting sub-contracting.

Inter-agency relations strongly reflect a move from hierarchical forms, based on state co-ordination, to partnerships and more networked forms of governance. The City of Sunderland Council recognises the extent to which it is dependent on other agencies in implementing policies and programmes:

> in line with the changing role of local authorities to 'enablers' rather than 'providers' of services, increasing emphasis is placed on using public expenditure to facilitate private investment ... the traditional boundaries between public and private resources are being eroded, with much greater emphasis on co-operation and partnership between the sectors. (City of Sunderland, 1995)

As we have suggested, there has been a significant increase in the number of partnership arrangements in Sunderland. Most of these, however, are instrumental arrangements established for specific purposes, in particularly for bidding for competitively allocated public funds from central government (such as the Single Regeneration Budget) or from the European Union (such as structural funds under Objective 2). City of Sunderland Partnership (responsible for a successful Single Regeneration Budget bid) is typical. While there is some evidence from our research of the development of relations of trust in these arrangement (particularly in improved relations between the City of Sunderland Council and the private sector), their instrumentalist orientation and dependence on central state resources means that they do not (so far, at least) constitute a stable model of governance involving dynamic and self-sustaining inter-organisational relations.

Finally, while some aspects of local governance in Sunderland point to the emergence of a hollowed-out Schumpeterian workfare state, others appear to undermine it. Local agencies of governance demonstrate both a practical and a discursive orientation towards supply-side measures in training and support for business innovation and the attraction of inward investment from national and multinational companies. The aim is to develop the 'advanced manufacturing centre of the North', building on the growth of Nissan and its suppliers and a range of other investments from the Far East and the USA. Innovation and new business formation are supported with premises, funds and advice by, among others, the City of Sunderland Council, the Tyne and Wear Development Corporation, three Enterprise Zones, City Challenge and the Sunderland Training and Enterprise Council. Rates of new business formation remain low by national standards, however. The institutions of local governance are markedly constrained by central state policies in relation to some or all of the following: funding, powers, lifespan and remit. This means that the new local governance in Sunderland has not developed an adequate 'local regulatory capacity', and suggests that the hollowing-out of the state is so far largely formal, rather than substantive.

Conclusion: uneven development and regulation

Our main conclusion is that British local governance is not becoming post-Fordist, because it is not fulfilling the functions which would be required of it to stabilise accumulation in the medium term, enable sustained reproduction and deal with the turbulence of uneven development.

We found a deficit in local regulatory capacity in each of our three case study areas which threatens this medium term stability. Often this deficit arose from an inability to cope with the social and economic problems of uneven development. The relatively stable regulation of economic activity provided by Fordism was premised on the possibility of national modes of growth, which were, in turn, underpinned by a commitment to regional balance and inter-regional resource transfers. In the transition from Fordism, this commitment no longer holds, and we are witnessing the rise of a more uneven mode of regulation. If this is to be stabilised, local governance has a crucial role to play in helping to manage this differentiation. Several key issues follow from this:

- Local governance still depends on national government for its powers. Even where the institutional capacity has been developed to move towards post-Fordist regulation, there is often a lack of authority given to the agencies of local governance. All too often, they are attempting to cope with the specific problems of uneven development in their local areas through centrally prescribed policies.
- This means that despite forces of localisation and globalisation, there is still a key role for the nation state in allocating regulatory capacity and authority to local governance. The hollowing out of the state has not proceeded as far as some would imagine, and, indeed, if local governance is to fulfil its role in any transition to

post-Fordism, the central state will have to ensure that this is possible.

- This, in turn, problematises what we might call the spatial structures of governance. Much more attention needs to be paid to the spatial scale at which various functions of governance are carried out. It can not be assumed that inherited, nineteenth-century boundaries are best placed to deal with a twenty-first century transition to post-Fordism. Even though the emergence of partnerships has begun to overcome this problem, we found there were other problems here of trust and co-ordination.
- In theoretical terms, this means that regulation theory has to be more attentive to uneven spatial development. Indeed, we found that many of the problems of regulation can be traced back to uneven development and a failure to deal adequately with this.

About this study

The research which is described here was part of a research project entitled 'British Local Governance in the Transition from Fordism' undertaken by the authors with Parminder Bakshi, Alan Southern and Michelle Wood. The project sought to evaluate the usefulness of regulation theory as a framework for interpreting changes in local governance in Britain. The research used a variety of research methods including documentary and press research, statistical analysis, in-depth interviewing and theoretical development. Three detailed local case studies were undertaken of Berkshire, industrial south-west Wales and Sunderland. The main results of the research were: (a) the development of a new theoretical model of the relationship between local governance and post-Fordism; (b) the development of the concept of 'local regulatory capacity'; (c) the lack of any clear support in the empirical evidence from the case studies for the idea that British local governance is becoming post-Fordist; and (d) an evaluation of the explanatory limits of regulation theory.

3 Regime Formation in Manchester and Edinburgh

Alan Harding

The rise of urban regime theory (URT)

When it first appeared in urban political analysis, the term 'regime' was used simply to describe 'the circle of powerful elected officials and top administrators' in US city government (Fainstein and Fainstein, 1983, p. 256). Since then, however, the concept of an urban regime has expanded considerably (Stone and Sanders, 1987; Elkin, Stone, 1989), and its popularity has grown to the point where America's major urban journals are now filled with references to regimes (Stoker, 1995, p. 62). A substantial empirical literature has adopted the concepts – or at least the language – of urban regime analysis and claims to find regimes in a wide variety of places and times. These discoveries are not confined to the US. Unlike earlier concepts in US urban social science, particularly those associated with the community power debate (Judge, 1995; Harding, 1995), urban regime theory (URT), along with its cousin, the growth machine thesis (Logan and Molotch, 1987), has had a significant impact beyond North America. The two approaches inform work in the UK (Axford and Pinch, 1994; Bassett and Harloe, 1990; Cooke, 1988; Dunleavy et al., 1995; Harding, 1991; Lloyd and Newlands, 1988), France (Le Galès, 1995; Levine, 1994) Germany (Strom, 1996), Italy (Vicari and Molotch, 1990) and Australia (Caulfield, 1991; Low, 1994; Caulfield and Wanna, 1995) plus cross-national comparisons (DiGaetano and Klemanski, 1993; John and Cole, 1996; Harding, 1997a; Kantor et al., 1996; Molotch, 1990; Molotch and Vicari, 1988).

Before asking why URT should have a growing band of non-American admirers, let us first be clear that we are dealing with a middle-range theory that takes the essential features of capitalist

54

liberal democracy for granted, particularly the basic division of labour between the state and the market. URT adopts a neopluralist position (Lindblom, 1977) which argues that, in liberal democracies, governments depend upon the market to satisfy many human wants and needs. As a result, businesses and business groups have privileged status when it comes to shaping the agenda and actions of governments. Productive assets lie substantially in private hands, therefore state managers lack authority over market decisions. In getting businesses to perform their socially necessary functions – the provision of jobs, goods and services – the state must use inducements, not commands.

Transposing this argument to the local level, urban regime theorists argue that a distinction must be made between holding political power and governing; that is between local government in a narrow sense and local governance in a wider sense. Whilst they monopolise the levers of local political power 'successful electoral coalitions do not necessarily govern' (Stone and Sanders, 1987, pp. 286). In order to achieve anything beyond straightforward statutory tasks, elected leaders need the support of other powerful interests, especially within the business community. *Governing* coalitions regularise these relations of mutual support. They bring together those who have access to, and can deliver, various resources, be they material, such as finance, personnel, and land and buildings, or intangibles, such as political, regulatory, and informational resources. No single organisation or group monopolises these assets and there is no 'conjoining structure of command' (Stone, 1989, p. 5) to link asset holders together. A governing regime must, therefore, be constructed through informal bargaining and the 'tacit understandings' of its members.

Urban regimes work through a system of 'civic cooperation' based upon mutual self-interest. They are 'informal arrangements by which public bodies and private interests function together in order to be able to make and carry out governing decisions' (Stone, 1989, p. 6). They fuse what is otherwise a very fragmented capacity to act, and enable independent social forces and organisations to coordinate their actions over the range of issues upon which they can agree in a way they would not do otherwise. The broader the coalition of forces linked together within a regime, the more resources it collectively deploys and the greater are the chances of its members enhancing its governing capacity by putting 'small opportunities' the way of potential allies and buying-off opponents with 'side payments'.

Regimes are generally talked about in connection with local public–private sector collaboration and the promotion of urban economic and physical change. Both Elkin and Stone identify regime types analogous to the classic American 'growth machine', where, on the development issues which dominate (US) local politics, there are close links between city politicians and officials, local landowners and selected business interests. They also describe departures from this norm in space and time, however. Elkin's 'Federalist political economy', for example, is characterised by a development-orientated regime, but one based upon intergovernmental, as well as local public–private, agreements and coalitions. Stone identifies potential for 'progressive' regimes, which in certain circumstances can pursue redistributive social and welfare goals as well as, or even in opposition to, developmental ones. He also talks of 'caretaker' regimes, in which more limited coalitions deliver only routine services. Both Stone and Elkin nonetheless imply that the growth machine model is dominant in periods of pronounced economic change.

The regime approach: advantages and disadvantages

Why should URT have attracted more significant international interest than earlier US urban theory? In the UK, the answer lies not so much in the intrinsic superiority of Elkin and Stone's arguments, but with the changing context into which they were transplanted, and the challenges it posed for standard urban political analysis. UK urban political science has traditionally focused, more narrowly than its US counterpart, upon three things: local government politics and administration, relations between national and local governments, and the delivery of social and welfare services generally seen as related more to consumption than to production. These institutional and policy-based approaches addressed a crucial dimension of post-war urban politics – the role of local government within the developing national welfare state. They effectively ruled out any distinction between local government and local governance, however. They also played down the significance of the urban politics of production, as opposed to consumption, and of local accommodations between politics and markets. Although criticised on these grounds (Dunleavy 1980), these approaches remained dominant even when the rare empirical research which took a wider view contradicted their assumptions about who wielded power and influence in urban politics (Saunders, 1979). By the late 1980s, however, traditional UK approaches to urban political analysis were becoming untenable. Four interrelated changes in the nature of UK local governance encouraged a widening of conceptual horizons.

The first was fragmentation in the institutional structures of local governance which resulted primarily, but not exclusively, from the 'market-led' reforms of post-1979 Conservative governments (Stewart and Stoker, 1989, 1994). The second was the growing importance of the urban politics of production (Eisenschitz and Gough, 1993); that is, of local economic development as well as consumption issues. This was best illustrated by burgeoning economic programmes run by area-based agencies, be they local authorities, non-statutory bodies or government-appointed quangos. It also reflected concern, in an era of public expenditure constraints, with the economic and employment implications of a broader range of public services. The third change was the proliferation of public–private partnerships, notably as hybrid delivery agencies for local economic programmes (Bailey *et al.*, 1995). The fourth was the steady, government-induced metamorphosis of local authorities into enabling rather than executive bodies. Whilst most discussions bemoaned the constraints caused by the dwindling powers and resources available to local government, some liberating implications were apparent (Wilson and Game, 1994; Clarke and Stewart, 1994). Reforms helped encourage the 'enabling authority' model of local government in which it potentially acted as a strategy-maker and co-ordinator across a broad range of local economic and social affairs, not just as a provider of statutory services.

These changes happened so quickly that much academic energy was devoted to describing them individually rather than conceptualising them collectively. The advantage of URT was that it offered a conceptual framework which linked together many aspects of the 'new' urban governance whilst being sufficiently concrete to form the basis of empirical work. The regime approach effectively enjoined researchers to look for evidence of cross-sectoral and intergovernmental coalition-building for urban development and to assess its importance within the wider politics of localities. It suggested that there can be more to the formulation of development strategies than the formal, bureaucratic processes adopted by individual public institutions. In highlighting informal, as well as formal, agreements and bargaining between the controllers of diverse resources, it encouraged research into public–private *partnership*, as a process, as well as the more standard interest in public–private *partnerships* as institutions (Harding, 1997b). It suggested that bargaining and personal networks between actors at different levels of government can affect the outcomes of intergovernmental linkages as much as formal relationships based on statutes, regulations and formula-based resource transfers. It encouraged analysis of how decision-making difficulties are (or are not) overcome in highly fragmented institutional environments.

Real though these advantages are, URT is not a perfect tool for cross-national research. For one thing, it cannot *explain* the changes referred to above. Critics, even when they are broadly sympathetic to the regime approach (Stoker, 1995; Le Galès, 1995; Stoker and Mossberger, 1994; Ward, 1996), are justified in seeing URT as ethnocentric, in that it assumes not just liberal democracy, but the particular institutional, economic and social forms it takes in the US. There are many factors specific to the US which have traditionally given the urban politics of development there more vitality than they have had in northern Europe (Harding, 1994). Thus any account that tries to 'fit' European experiences into an URT framework needs to look elsewhere for explanations as to why and how far there are meaningful parallels with the US (Lauria, 1996; Jessop *et al.*, 1996; Harding, 1997). Secondly, URT is methodologically underspecified. Researching 'informal arrangements' and coalition-building is inherently tricky but the regime literature, whilst emphasising such phenomena, offers few guidelines to empirical researchers. Stone (1989, pp. 254–60) is methodologically the most explicit, but even he refers only in very general terms to two data sources: a local newspaper and interviews undertaken as an 'aid to interpretation'.

Searching for regimes in Edinburgh and Manchester

URT, then, helps pose interesting questions about the implications of recent changes in the nature of UK local governance for strategy-making processes and outcomes whilst leaving a great deal open to empirical investigation. It can also facilitate broader cross-national comparison, given interesting parallels in the way European systems of local governance are changing (Harding, 1997). As a case study research strategy, regime analysis needs to proceed in three phases which: (a) identify the key players – formal and informal – in the urban politics of production; (b) describe how, and to what extent, they interact and what motivates them to do so; and (c) assess the outcomes and effects of their interactions.

A methodology appropriate to these three phases of analysis was applied in Manchester and Edinburgh (see About this study, p. 00). Its purpose was to contextualise and understand the nature and importance of decision-making on urban development in the two cities since the early 1980s. The first phase generated a snapshot of a small core of 'movers and shakers' (Trounstine and Christenson, 1982; Peck, 1995) in each city; that is, senior decision-makers who were demonstrably interested in strategic urban development issues and able to commit their respective organisations, thereby facilitating (or obstructing) cross-sectoral, inter-agency, and inter-governmental joint-working. In Edinburgh, this group comprised 24 individuals; five from the public sector (three elected leaders and two public officials) and 19 from the business community, the one significant sectoral grouping coming from the city's financial institutions. The Manchester group contained 22 names; nine from the public sector (six politicians, two public officials and one quango board member) and 13 from a diverse range of business sectors.

Such groups do not constitute urban regimes in themselves, but individuals within them were well placed to comment upon the relevance of the key questions raised by URT, including:

- the degree to which the urban politics of production had, and/or was perceived to have, become more important and the reasons why that was so;
- the extent and relevance of cross-sectoral and intergovernmental coalition-building for development within and for the two cities;
- the motivations of key partners in central and sub-national government, other public agencies and the business community and the way they had changed;

- whether there was a consensual development strategy, formal or informal, which acted as a framework within which the -actions of different interests and agencies were located.

A tale of two cities

Edinburgh and Manchester are very different, institutionally, politically, socially and economically. Edinburgh's relative prosperity is underpinned by its capital city status and Scotland's constitutional position within the UK. The city is a 'national' centre for public administration, law, education, religion, culture, arts, entertainment and tourism, as well as a base for businesses, like the major banks, who derive some commercial advantage from their Scottishness. Manchester, by contrast, has long been politically subordinate within the English context. Its prosperity has always been a more straightforward reflection of the performance of its key businesses – particularly manufacturers – in regional, national and international markets. The two cities' experiences of economic and social change in the 1980s and 1990s diverge considerably. Manchester's metamorphosis into a post-industrial, service-dominated regional centre was far more painful than lightly-industrialised Edinburgh's. The way the urban politics of production developed in the two cities is nonetheless strikingly similar.

Both cities began the 1980s with political regimes ill-equipped to deal with the challenges facing them. Neither were especially predisposed to enter into dialogue with local business communities on strategic urban development issues. Manchester's reliance on the municipal socialist route to solving the city's key problems was increasingly constrained by institutional and policy changes imposed by government in key areas of socialised consumption. Local agencies were not remotely geared up to deal with the devastating effects of industrial restructuring – on the environment, the labour market and business confidence – which saw 20 000 local manufacturing jobs disappear in the decade up to 1985. The city council's initial response to economic crisis was defensive. The limited resources available through government urban programmes were used to deal cosmetically with the environmental symptoms of restructuring and it was hoped that the city's pre-eminence in manufacturing would return.

The scale of restructuring in Lothian was less drastic and was mostly concentrated in Edinburgh's more industrialised hinterland. The institutional context was also different. Many of the resources and much of the executive capacity to support regeneration programmes were concentrated within a national development body – the Scottish Development Agency (SDA) as was – which at that time concentrated largely upon the rapidly de-industrialising west of Scotland. Defensive local political responses similar to those in Manchester nonetheless occurred within Lothian Regional Council, which covered the wider urban region. Within the city the crisis was not primarily economic but political. Edinburgh District Council (EDC) was run in the early 1980s by a Conservative administration which had superseded the 'non-political' (i.e. anti-Labour) Progressives who were politically dominant up to the mid-1970s (McCrone and Elliott, 1989). The Conservatives continued the thrust of council policy from the Progressive era; they discharged social and welfare responsibilities imposed by government but minimised rate bills in order to maximise the scope for the party's middle class supporters to spend as they pleased (for example, on fees for the abnormally high number of local non-state school places). In contrast to the Progressives, though, the Conservatives had few organic links into the city's leading businesses.

The Conservative council was not especially respected by Edinburgh business leaders. One who played a prominent role in subsequent development initiatives detected 'a comfortable air of smugness' within the city in the early 1980s. Another, more forthright, declared that 'Edinburgh's Conservatives were...a pretty ordinary bunch of middle of the road nonentities'. The scepticism about the Conservative council felt by the business community paled into insignificance, however, beside that increasingly felt by the city's electorate. In 1984, the gap between the minimalist strategy of the Conservatives and the expectations of voters became apparent when the unthinkable happened – 'Tory Edinburgh' elected not just a Labour administration, but one which bore many similarities to its self-styled 'socialist' cousins in the major English urban areas (Keating, 1984; Gyford, 1985). Lothian Regional Council, customarily less prone to one-party domination, followed suit in 1986, albeit with a less professionally dominated, more blue collar, Labour leadership. Both followed Manchester, where a similar political transformation had already occurred in

1983, as a result of an internal coup within the historically dominant Labour group.

The new, young Labour leaderships initially alienated local business communities with actions which ranged from political symbolism to more serious initiatives designed to promote equal opportunities, irrespective of race, gender, disability and sexual orientation. There was also a measure of symbolism in their approach to economic development. Edinburgh's first post-1984 Labour leader, for example, alarmed business leaders by announcing that employment in the financial services and tourism did not represent 'proper jobs'. Rather than support expanding sectors such as these, all three councils, having emerged from their defensive phase, initially looked to 'radical' alternatives. These included support for cooperatives and community businesses, the establishment of enterprise boards and development agencies offering support to businesses on the proviso that they 'restructure for labour', the promotion of trade union rights and equal opportunities in employment, and vigorous defence of public sector employment (Quilley, 1995; Harding, 1992).

Progress in delivering 'alternative' economic strategies, however, was slow. Local authorities' economic powers were meagre. They remained limited even when, in 1989, a later Conservative government passed legislation to clarify and regulate local government's economic functions. For upper tier authorities like Lothian, in particular, the major services for which they were responsible – social services, education, and transport – were tangential to the concerns of 'alternative' economic policies. Within all three councils, 'radical' economic programmes were lightly-resourced and operated largely in isolation from mainstream council business (and spending). The economic policy field was, therefore, relatively unattractive, at least initially, to ambitious local authority politicians and officers. There was also resistance to new members' preferences from local authority officers who remained committed to existing initiatives which encouraged market activity for the city's benefit. Bureaucratic resistance was particularly pronounced in Edinburgh. Although never articulated as formal policy, EDC's main contribution to economic development had been based upon the selective acquisition and development of property for commercial uses. Whilst viewed suspiciously by the 'radicals', this activity generated a very important income stream for the new council. New initiatives struggled, in practice, to rival land and property programmes as council priorities.

Alternative local economic strategies also ran against the grain of policies pursued by higher levels of government. On one hand, this meant that the rapidly expanding range of policy instruments and resources that supported economic initiatives – through Department of the Environment (DoE) urban programmes and European Commission regional funds in Manchester's case, and the discretionary resources provided through the SDA in Edinburgh's – were, at best, irrelevant to 'radical' council initiatives and, at worst, deflected them from their preferred courses. On the other hand, clashes between central and local authorities over economic policy deepened the government's resolve to reduce the space for local authority manoeuvre and to create a separate policy infrastructure which marginalised local government and was controlled by a combination of civil servants and business leaders. There was also genuine conceptual uncertainty about what alternative strategies should look like (Mackintosh and Wainwright, 1989). For all of these reasons, the economic strategies followed by the three councils in the mid-80s were more radical in principle than in practice.

Symbolism, nonetheless, had significant short-term effects. The approach taken by new Labour groups ensured, in the words of one Edinburgh project-leader, that 'the reality of communication across the sectors was little short of warfare'. These groups' more important medium term achievement, though, was to substantially raise the profile of economic development issues within local government and to pave the way for a more consensual, broader-based approach. The pivotal event is the Conservative victory in the 1987 national election, and the realisation amongst local authority leaderships that further substantive and symbolic resistance to government policies, already counter-productive, would be futile. In Manchester, this 'new realism' caused the existing council leadership to 'wave the white flag', as one senior member put it. In Edinburgh, the change was encouraged by an internal Labour group coup in 1986, which saw the accession of a less abrasive leadership. A similar switch to more pragmatic Labour leadership occurred within Lothian Regional Council in 1990.

From the late 1980s, in both cities there was a clear move to a 'partnership model' of economic policy which fitted more comfortably with government policy and the actions of government agencies, and prioritised dialogue and joint work between public and private sectors. This shift did not represent simple acquiescence by local authorities to government pressures. Experience gained in the 'radical' period served to convince the local authorities that substantial local economic projects could only be delivered successfully if they attracted the support of a broad range of 'champions' amongst other statutory and non-statutory interests. Irrespective of the national political climate, it was always likely that local political leaders and senior officers would eventually do what they did in Manchester and Edinburgh, post-1987; that is, adopt a deliberate policy of informal networking with local business communities, quangos and government officials in the hope of fostering joint initiatives and building consensus on urban development issues. The authorities found a ready audience amongst business leaders, many of whom were independently becoming more interested in playing a role in development initiatives.

Within Greater Manchester, business mobilisation fed upon desperation. A number of business leaders, in the words of one, had 'had enough of dabbing [their] eyes about the disappearance of manufacturing industry', but were sceptical about the marginal, paternalistic contributions the private sector had made to economic development and employment initiatives up to that point. The 'Manchester Mafia' (Cochrane *et al.*, 1996) began to meet informally in a variety of contexts and to explore alternative economic scenarios for the conurbation, the commercial projects needed to realise them, and how the public sector might help. Change occured following these relatively unstructured meetings between key business leaders. In Manchester, 'boosterist' events organised by Granada TV, a company which consciously promoted 'good news' about Manchester and the North West in the later 1980s, brought people together and paved the way for more structured dialogue. In Edinburgh, a trip by business leaders to an Industrial Society event in Liverpool is widely seen as one trigger for greater business activism. Another was the fact that 'we [Edinburgh business leaders] were shamed by Glasgow' and its high profile, partnership-based regeneration activities (Keating, 1988; Boyle, 1990).

Business mobilisation in the two cities was not channelled through established agencies like local Chambers of Commerce or regional branches of the Confederation of British Industry. As one business activist explained, '[t]he Chamber of Commerce is not a great body. It was far better to contact key individuals in the great companies'. That is not to say institutional factors played no part. Government reforms deepened the process of engagement, by encouraging the involvement of business leaders in the delivery of employment and economic development initiatives. In Manchester, there were private sector appointees to the boards of the local Training and Enterprise Council, the Development Corporations in Central Manchester and Trafford Park, and the agency delivering the City Challenge programme in inner city Hulme. The restructuring of the SDA had a similar effect in Edinburgh. Lothian and Edinburgh Enterprise Ltd (LEEL), a local enterprise company, was created to contract to the SDA's national successor – Scottish Enterprise – to deliver publicly-financed labour market and economic development programmes. These quangos enhanced local executive capacity and injected substantial development-related resources. As conduits for business involvement in development programmes they are only part of a bigger story, however. On the debit side, because business representatives rarely imposed themselves upon what are essentially public sector agencies, they did not become unequivocally 'business-led' as Government PR often claimed. More positively, there developed in both cities a variety of public–private partnership which was locally-driven rather than 'top-down'.

Together, these changes meant that local economic policy, from being a marginal activity within local government undertaken for its political demonstration effects as much as its results (Duncan and Goodwin, 1985), developed wider and more practical ambitions with implications for mainstream policy areas. It became a mechanism through which wider development coalitions could be formed, variously bringing together local government departments, other local public sector agencies, and non-statutory interests from both the private and voluntary sectors. Local partnerships were vital in unlocking discretionary resources from higher levels of government because their efforts increasingly followed the grain of government policy. Manchester City Council (MCC), helped by the city's designation under national urban and European regional policies, became particularly adept at winning resources in competition with other authorities. More affluent Edinburgh has never been eligible for the same level of external support but, as a former Scottish Secretary of State explained, 'it is the capital city, and no [central] administration is going to forget that. Edinburgh will always get consideration, and money, if only it can get its own act together'.

In the early to mid-1990s, Manchester was clearly perceived as having 'got its act together' more effectively. It became, according to one quango executive and former civil servant, 'the apotheosis of partnership in the eyes of Government'. Coalition-building and elite consensus on economic development projects became almost axiomatic. A similar path was followed in Edinburgh in the same period, albeit with less enthusiasm and to more muted effect. As regime analysis suggests, change depended upon enlightened self-interest, opportunism, and effective, outward-looking organisational leadership. The capacities of various local and non-local organisations were fused together through a series of joint-projects which grew in their level of ambition and sophistication over time and encouraged a greater sense of trust and shared ownership between partners. A sense of overall strategy *was* expressed through, for example, Manchester's City Pride prospectus (Manchester City Council *et al.*, 1994) and Edinburgh's economic strategy (City of Edinburgh, 1995). Unlike traditional planning documents, these statements concentrated largely upon actions which the councils and their allies felt were realisable relatively quickly.

The project which best symbolises change in the urban politics of production in Manchester is the city's bid to stage the 2000 Olympic Games (Cochrane *et al.*, 1996). The bid rested upon a sports-led strategy to transform east Manchester, the old industrial heartland, and raise the city's international visibility. It triggered unprecedented levels of inter-governmental, inter-agency and public–private sector cooperation which continued into subsequent projects, not least the rebuilding of the city centre after the IRA bomb in 1996. The Olympic bid was delivered by various interlocking partnerships involving MCC, government departments, other local authorities in the region, national and local quangos, and sports organisations. Partnerships also drew in a range of local and non-local businesses which could see substantive and symbolic short-term benefits in being associated with the bid and its regeneration programmes, and longer-term commercial opportunities should the bid be successful.

Although it failed to secure the Games for Manchester, the bidding process brought £70 million worth of direct government investment for sporting facilities and infrastructure at negligible cost to MCC. It played a significant part in expediting further mainstream Department of the Environment investments in infrastructure and cultural facilities. It led directly to Manchester securing the Commonwealth Games for 2002, and to Millennium funding for the new stadium which will host much of it. It also created an image of Manchester as an ambitious, forward-looking, and well-organised city where things got done. Olympics-related projects represent just some of Manchester's partnership-based projects which span policy sectors such as transport, arts and culture, housing, higher education and community regeneration. In Edinburgh, by comparison, consensus was achieved on a smaller range of issues during the same period and there was rather less enthusiastic joint-working.

Inter-governmental and public–private partnerships *were* important in Edinburgh, for example in developing new office space which responded to the growing obsolescence of city centre stock, and in supporting action on social exclusion in some of the city's peripheral estates. Greatest progress was made, however, in the tourism/visitor attraction field, where two long-anticipated 'flagship' projects were realised as part of a consensual inter-agency tourism strategy. The refurbishment of the Festival Theatre as an international standard facility and the development of Edinburgh International Conference Centre were each delivered by partnerships, variously drawing upon new resources from LEEL, the city council's property holdings, capital investment by the two local authorities, support from the Scottish Office and national quangos, and private sector fund-raising.

Local inter-agency and public–private sector relations nonetheless remained more fractious in Edinburgh, as is demonstrated by the Edinburgh Vision (EV) initiative. EV was established in 1990 by the two councils, LEEL, and the Chamber of Commerce to improve local relations and to generate a consensual strategic framework which the partners could support. EV was lightly resourced and able to make headway only if the four partners supported it fully and responded to its ideas – this they conspicuously failed to do. While they viewed EV merely as a convenient symbol of change, they were, paradoxically, also nervous of the fact that if EV was to have substantive implications it might challenge what they each saw as their rightful claim to define the terms of strategic debate. The public agencies, in particular, continued to engage in turf wars and to haggle amongst themselves about who should take credit for particular projects, even when they were nominally based on partnership. These difficult local relations limited the degree of consensus and joint-working. They only began to improve when the unitary local authority for Edinburgh was created in 1996 and LEEL developed a more consensual approach in expectation of a change of government in 1997.

When is a regime not a regime?

Were Manchester and Edinburgh governed by regimes in the period covered here? This question is difficult to answer, given the semantic debate taking place amongst URT followers about whether regimes are found in all cities at all times (Kantor et al., 1996) or are the exception rather than the rule (John and Cole, 1996). Stone, surprisingly, now supports the former position in advocating that regimes be defined, very broadly, as 'the arrangements through which urban communities are governed' (Stone, 1997, p. 7). A contrary view is that 'regimeless cities' are consistent with URT (Orr and Stoker, 1994); indeed, that URT loses its distinctiveness if a regime is taken to cover *any* form of cooperation between local governments and other interests. As Stoker (1995, p. 62) argues, the danger of broadening the regime concept beyond its original scope is that it becomes 'a new descriptive catchword... in place of an explanation of the phenomenon under question' (Stoker, 1995, p. 62).

Let us assume that regimes are present only when there is: (a) predictability and stability to a specific set of informal governing arrangements, (b) continuity of leadership priorities and approaches amongst the agencies and interests that take part in them; (c) coherence in the development strategies and initiatives they promote, and (d) clear overall priority accorded to their strategies. Judged against such criteria, Edinburgh and Manchester in the 1980s and 1990s could not be described as regime-dominated in the way Atlanta and Dallas were when studied by Stone and Elkin. Rather, both witnessed the creation of narrower public–private sector, inter-agency, and intergovernmental development coalitions. As a Manchester banking executive explained, the city does not contain 'a group of people who exercise power collectively in a way that one would not expect from their range of responsibilities, [but] [t]here is certainly a group of people who are interested in doing things'. That said, processes of coalition-formation and consensus-building clearly went further in Manchester than in Edinburgh. These observations illustrate both the limits and the usefulness of URT.

Cities in the UK do not contain regimes in the American sense because the influence of development coalitions is limited to particular production-related strategies and projects rather than the whole range of local political choices. In the US, the heavy reliance by local authorities on resources raised from local citizens and businesses means there is a direct trade-off between the provision of social and welfare services (consumption) and the buoyancy of local incomes and enterprises (production). A UK local authority's ability to provide services, by contrast, generally depends less upon local economic conditions than upon central government cash transfers. National government therefore plays a more important – but not decisive – role in defining the relationship between the urban politics of production and that of consumption.

In Edinburgh and Manchester, the urban politics of production has clearly grown in importance and become characterised by coalition-formation and elite consensus-building. It exists alongside an urban politics of consumption, however, in which difficult intergovernmental relations, characterised by tight expenditure constraints, remain vital to policy outcomes. The emergence of this 'dual polity' at local level has induced strain, and a certain schizophrenia, within local politics. Careful political management has been needed to justify giving priority to development programmes – and the somewhat indirect impact they have on local labour markets and life chances – in an era when established consumption-based policy areas have been in crisis.

MCC was able to manage these strains more easily up to the mid-1990s for a number of reasons. First, the local Labour party is politically unassailable. In contrast to Edinburgh, where the Scottish National Party sporadically had significant influence, it has not needed to share power with other parties. Second, internal Labour party opposition within MCC, whilst sometimes fierce, could not blow the ambitions of the leadership off course. In Edinburgh, two internal Labour party coups, along with the abolition of Lothian Regional Council, militated against political stability. Third, MCC was able to rely primarily on external sources of discretionary funding to finance development programmes. In Edinburgh, greater reliance on local capital receipts meant expenditure choices were far more politicised and consumption-based policies often took precedence over production-related ones. Finally, the small number of key players in the urban politics of production in Manchester exhibited higher levels of energy, trust and co-operation. Compared to Edinburgh, local relationships had stronger regime-like qualities.

Whether both cities will continue along the trajectories described here is an open question. Development coalitions are heavily people-dependent. As one Manchester interviewee put it: '[t]o the extent that cities have been able to achieve sustained regeneration, my impression is that there are five or six people in the right place, at the right time, able to bring key organisations along with them'. The longer-term sustainability of UK urban coalitions is not encouraged by key recent characteristics of the policy environment – short-lived quangos and public programmes, constant institutional tinkering – or by the more enduring tendency for key politicians, public officials and business executives to move in order to enhance their careers. Whatever the future of coalitions in the two cities, however, one thing is certain. A research framework based on URT will be a more appropriate tool for comparing and contrasting their experiences than institutionalist and policy-orientated approaches to urban politics.

About this study

The study methodology had three components: reputational analysis, a review of elite perceptions, and project case studies. The reputational analysis identified key players in civic affairs and the promotion of urban development, particularly in the private sector. (Public sector actors are easier to identify because their formal roles and responsibilities make their broad interests and commitments more publicly visible.) For 1993–95, data were gathered for Edinburgh/Lothian and Greater Manchester on:

- *business elites*, as indicated by overlapping directorships amongst the 25 largest locally-based, publicly-quoted companies;
- *civic elites*, as indicated by appointments to governing bodies of universities, boards overseeing city or regional tourism, arts and

sports bodies, leading cultural institutions and key city events and

- *development elites*, as indicated by appointees to bodies such as Local Enterprise Companies, Training and Enterprise Companies, Urban Development Corporations, enterprise and area development trusts, joint ventures and public–private partnership institutions.

A combination of these elite listings highlighted a number of influential multiple office-holders. The 'master' list, refined and extended after interviews with more objective 'city-watchers' (academics, journalists, Chamber of Commerce officials), defined a pool of interviewees with which to test the main themes of regime analysis. Semi-structured interviews with members of that pool generated data on actual and perceived changes in the processes and outcomes of the urban politics of production. Whilst this phase of the research was largely qualitative – a necessary hazard of regime analysis – opportunities were taken to cross-reference elite perceptions against those of the 'city watchers' and relevant primary and secondary written materials. The narratives derived from elite perceptions and documentary evidence were given more concrete form by case study analyses of particular projects, designed to illustrate how intergovernmental, inter-agency and public–private sector interaction occurred in practice and with what effect. In Manchester, the two projects were the city's bid for the 2000 Olympic Games and Hulme City Challenge. In Edinburgh, they were Edinburgh Vision and the refurbishment of the Festival Theatre.

4 Policy Networks and Local Political Leadership in Britain and France

Peter John and Alistair Cole

In our two-year study into local policy networks in Britain and France we have mapped and researched networks of key actors in economic development policy in Leeds and Southampton, and Lille and Rennes. In the light of the empirical research, this chapter provides some concluding judgements on local governance, policy networks and local political leadership in Britain and France. In the first section ('the traditional accounts'), we revisit traditional Franco-British comparative studies. In the second section ('institutional change and political cooperation'), we consider the changed institutional and political environment within which local networks operate in the four cities. The third section ('the new urban governance') appraises various aspects of the new urban governance, notably the emergence of urban regimes, the importance of locality, and the relationship between governance, networks and democratic accountability. In the final section ('who governs governance?'), we try to locate the centre of gravity of the new urban governance.

The traditional accounts: evidence of continuity

The classic accounts of French and British local government emphasise the differences in the efficiency, accountability and legitimacy of local government in the two countries (Ashford, 1982; Lagroye and Wright, 1979). The thesis of French and British local divergence was pushed furthest by Ashford, who contrasted centralist and inflexible traditions of policy-making in Britain (dogmatism) with a flexible and negotiated style in France (pragmatism). In

72

spite of all the authority delegated to sub-national authorities, the British state imposed a rigid system of central control, whereas the French system benefited from political representation and bargaining between central and local representatives. There were some simple institutional facts behind this analysis. While Britain and France share similar levels of economic development and unitary state traditions, different principles govern their subcentral politics. France's omnipresent central state coexists with powerful local politicians. In Britain, the division of responsibilities between central and local government fosters weak local political leaders. Though French local government is fragmented into over 36 000 local communes, nationally prominent politicians articulate local interests and mediate with the branches of the central state. British local politics, on the other hand, is trapped within large multifunctional organisations where cabals of party elites and professional officers exercise considerable policy autonomy but have little contact with local communities and the central state. For all the complexity and politicisation of French local politics, with its unevenly enforced central policies and corrupting local patronage, comparativists assume that France is better able to deliver well-constructed and long-term policies. The political system provides a mechanism for entrenching local interests in the central state which fosters flexibility in the way in which policy is formulated and implemented. Ironically, for all the claims that the French state is above politics and that it rationally formulates decisions in the general interest, local influence does modify and adapt central policy initiatives, a process more compatible with incremental than rational models of decision-making. Without this interlocking framework, the apparently pragmatic British system produces over-rationalised and inflexible solutions to public problems. Advocates claim the French system is able to produce imaginative, far-reaching solutions to public policy issues through the power, ideas and resources of its key local politicians. Elected mayors are able to initiate local policy in a way their British counterparts could never imagine.

It is important not to take this account of contrast too literally. Accounts of French politics contain a contradiction. Defenders of the French political system often find flexibility when they need it, but strong state power when that is required. Accounts of flexibility run counter to French industrial *dirigisme* of the 1950s and 1960s;

the French state relocated industry around France in the 1950s and 1960s in a highly *étatist* fashion, with prefects coordinating this activity in the localities with little reference to local politicians (Savitch, 1988). In addition, there is a tension in the accounts of the role of deputy-mayors. While representing their local areas, these *notables* are integrated into national politics on account of the practice of *cumul des mandats* (multiple office holding). Their local implantation is part of the strategy of the parties at the centre. Their involvement with the national political scene has implications for local management: how do they find the time to make decisions locally? The portrayal of French pragmatism is a very partial one. The account of cross-regulation, as described by Crozier and Thoenig (1975), drew upon the period of hierarchical, state-centred vision of public policy making before the decentralising reforms of the early 1980s.

Ashford's conceit is neat, but it should not be taken to be the definitive account (Cole and John 1995). His framework over-simplifies the two local political systems in order to make an analytical point. The analysis resembles the many critiques of the British political system which followed from the overpraise of the early post-war years. From being the cradle of local democracy, with imitations the world over, suddenly British local government was thought to be ineffective, less able to deliver efficient policies, and inflexible. The centralised French state, with its thousands of apparently illogically organised communes, seemed much better at making policy than the rigid British system.

This caricature hides the massive complexity of local political systems with their many actors and interests jostling for position. In Lorrain's account (1987, 1993), French local politics has always been very complex, with a large number of private, semi-public and public actors whose role varied according to sector and function. Far from local politicians being omnipotent in the French state, our research confirms the importance of central state actors who were able to block mayoral coalitions. In one of our cities, Lille, the right-wing appointed regional prefect was able to amend urban development schemes and reward Gaullist supporters. With the Socialists' loss of power at the central level in 1993, the influence of the two French political leaders in our study waned as they were not so able to access benefits from the state. This has some similarities to the British political system in the 1980s, where left-wing leaders were marginalised from central government policy and right-wing leaders of 'flagship' Tory councils, such as the leaders of Wandsworth Borough Council, gained favourable treatment from central government and held the ear of ministers.

The British political scene has always been far more complex than that presented in Ashford's account. The idea that local interests do not have power at the centre is an exaggeration. Otherwise how could the reform of local government structure be explained in 1972? Local influence on the amendments to the legislation truncated the neat design of the Royal Commission. In the two English cities in our study, there are plenty of examples to destroy the stereotype. The importance in local politics of George Mudie, the former leader of Leeds, while at the same time being the MP for East Leeds, does not conform to the idea that British local politicians sever their local roots on obtaining a national mandate. The machinations of Conservative MPs and local politicians in Southampton over the 'people mover' (a mono-rail to link sections of the city) is a classic, almost French style, central–local alliance, whereby local politicians deployed their national contacts to scupper the plans of their opponents. Council leader Alan Whitehead's scheme was stopped by Southampton's Conservative MPs, who used their parliamentary privilege to kill the private member's bill introducing the scheme.

It is important not to abandon generalisations, however. The classic analysis captures much of the essence of British and French local politics up until the end of the 1970s, and arguably beyond. Indeed, it can be argued that reforms of the two countries' local political systems have adapted rather than transformed this pattern. As has been persuasively argued, the decentralisation reforms in France since 1982 strengthened the role of the leading mayors by enhancing the powers of the communes and ensuring that they exercised influence in the other new tiers of local government, namely the departments and the regions (Mabileau, 1991). Even though mayors can now hold only two elected offices, they prefer to remain as deputy-mayors rather than as deputy-presidents of either the regional councils or departmental councils. It can be argued that the regions have not become as important as many commentators believed they would (Le Galès and John, 1997). They were part of the socialist government's attempt to introduce regional planning – a state-directed economic strategy which largely failed after the economic crisis of the early 1980s, and had little part in the right-wing government plans after 1986. They are always in the shadow of one of the beneficiaries of the decentralisation reforms, the regional prefects.

Indeed, from studying Lille and Rennes, there is much that remains of the classic pattern of French local politics. Mayor Pierre Mauroy in Lille behaved as a typical French local politician by extracting benefits from the central state when he held high office, and later when his influence was still strong. The freedoms the decentralisation reforms gave to the communes allowed Mauroy to pursue his city centre redevelopment plans. His relationship with the prefect, in this case also the regional prefect, was crucial in coordinating the strategy. Pierre Mauroy exercised strong local political leadership to mobilise the public and private sector actors in support of the massive Euralille redevelopment scheme. The story is similar, if less dramatic, in Rennes, where Hervé, a former Minister, was able to control an economic development coalition. Our sociometric analysis sees mayor Hervé and his associates at the centre of networks, ahead of all the new actors (John, 1998).

The much discussed erosion of elected local government in the UK has not happened as dramatically as the foreboders of woe predicted (John, 1994). In spite of extensive central government reform of the finance, structure and functions of local government during the 1980s, the institution remains as the funder and main policy-maker for most of the services which it administered at the end of the 1970s – environment, social services, transport schemes, street lighting, strategic and local planning, education, homelessness, street cleaning, parks and a host of other responsibilities. Even if contracting-out and the rise of the enabling authority remove the direct provision of services, local government institutions still provide the funds, set the targets, review the performance and determine the policy framework for the services. During the 1980s, local authorities enhanced local economic development policy and European liaison, and central government gave councils new powers over the environment and community care. Confounding central government's attempt to reduce spending, local government expenditure took up the same proportion of Gross Domestic Product and employed the same number of people at the end of the 1980s as at the beginning (Travers 1989, p. 14). The shutting-out of local government from central policy decisions, rather than being the final chapter in a long downfall of local representative institutions, was more the apotheosis of the final years of Thatcherism, and local government regained its influence in the 1990s (John, 1997). Local government's return to favour as participants in urban initiatives, like City Challenge and the Single Regeneration Budget (SRB), signifies a period of normality and the end of the excesses of the Thatcher years.

Local government is far from marginalised in the new community governance. Elected local government takes a key role in policy networks in both Southampton and Leeds. In Leeds, local government was at the centre of the networks and was the agency which made things happen in the city. The city council controls an eighth of the workforce, has extensive land holdings, finance and legitimacy and is likely to be dominant in any public decision. There are no other local government competitors able to challenge its power. The council leader has power which operates through a centralised bureaucracy and the city Labour Party. Provided the leader delivers stable, pragmatic leadership, responds to the demands of the ward Labour parties, and mediates between the left and right, he is free to run policy and to develop his own initiatives without much reference to local interest groups. As an organisation, the council outguns by sheer size the central government agencies, such as the Training and Enterprise Council (TEC), and dwarfs the chamber of commerce and industry. Regional organisations cannot claim to act for the city, so they too tend to defer to the council's leadership. In many ways, Leeds is typical of the old pattern of local government. Its bureaucracy is hierarchical. It has not been subject to the reforms of internal management which have opened up so many other authorities and made them more innovative. In contrast, neighbouring Kirklees, in Huddersfield, has become a byword for new management trends, networking, Europeanisation and good officer–member relationships. Leeds, on the other hand, is a closed authority, driven by bureaucratic conflict, where most policy and implementation decisions are highly political and follow the leader's personal agenda. The council is not well networked into regional and national bodies, and is often slow to take up new ideas. Its inward looking nature, where officers often spend their whole careers in the council bureaucracy, reflects the nature of Leeds as a city.

The very different political system in Southampton also shows signs of continuity. Here too, local government officers and members are central to the network. Even though the economic development partnerships were fragmented and put together by competing local authorities, they were led by local government. Although the projects in Southampton were piecemeal and not part of a strategic plan, at the end of the day it was Southampton City Council which pushed for change and coordinated the decision-makers in other organisations. It can be argued that the central state is relatively weak and ineffective in this local government context. In Southampton, for example, the regional director for the Government Office for the south-east region, at the time of the research, had only made a few, mainly ceremonial, visits. Central government was involved with planning permissions, the development of the port, and the allocation of small amounts of urban regeneration funding, but not much else.

In the view of the leaders of both cities, it is only the elected councils that can pull together the partnerships and mobilise local economic development decision-makers. The council has the legitimacy, the long-term staying power, the finance, and, above all, the professional officer cadre to shape initiatives in each policy sector. In a city like Leeds, it is the elected council which can see the links between the different sectors that impact on policy. The council claims it is able to stand back from the maelstrom of conflicting interests and take the community's point of view and seek to balance out the conflicting priorities which influence policy. As such, it will always be at the central point, seeking to form and guide networks of actors.

The importance of continuity should not be underestimated. It flows from the longevity of institutions which have established ways of processing issues and organisational cultures which do not change rapidly in the face of central government reforms or environmental change. Policy change is inevitably incremental. Radical initiatives, usually announced with great fanfare by central government ministers who are anxious to establish their reputations before moving on to other posts, usually sound as if they are going to reshape the pattern of administration or renenergise the economy. In fact, however, existing initiatives often continue, and local actors adapt their strategies to conform with new urban programmes. In short, local government is able to use its control over many functions and its long entrenched position in localities to maintain its dominance.

Institutional change and political cooperation

But if the politics of continuity allows locally elected government to retain its prominence, there is no escaping the changed environment of local politics in the four cities we studied. While the existing structure of local politics remains, local politicians have to operate in more complex and fluid governing contexts.

In France, the system is far more open and policy is more unpredictable than before 1982. New institutions, such as departments and regions, have real power. The central state has devolved many functions. Regional prefects are important decision-makers. New policy sectors, such as European funding, have emerged. Mayors have to build wider coalitions than was hitherto the case. The vicariousness of changes in party control mean that it is not certain that politicians of the same political hue are in control of the departments and regions. In Lille, the Greens governed the region in an uneasy alliance with the Socialists, and Pierre Mauroy and his allies could not depend on unequivocal support from these decision-makers. Apart from party politics, these new bodies take a different perspective on policy choices. For example, the departmental authorities in both Rennes and Lille tended to articulate rural and small town interests. The established local politicians have to manage and steer their policies through this complex organisational matrix. Even someone as powerful as Mauroy had to manage the quasi-federal urban community (CUDL) by compromising and bargaining. In Rennes too, the mayor had to battle with different interests at the regional level. Although the new freedoms of communes and other elected actors allowed the mayors of Lille and Rennes to exercise more power, they operated within a new set of constraints. Mayors can sponsor their own development projects and initiatives, but they need the cooperation of other public actors and must resolve the many conflicts that arise. Mayors can achieve more than they could in the past; but they have to give up some of their autonomy to do so. French local politics has a more interdependent and networked character than before.

In the UK, much the same thing has happened, if by a different route. In Leeds, up to the mid-1980s, local economic development policy amounted to a series of council planning schemes in only an informal alliance with the business sector. By the late 1980s, new actors appeared (in the form of the development corporation, the

TEC and a Chamber of Commerce), who were more willing to enter into local networks. The property-led economic development coalition that the council fostered in the mid-1980s simply did not work. The economic benefits never materialised and the lack of consultation made the political leadership unpopular. With the opportunities redirected toward many projects aiming to improve Leeds as a whole, rather than just the property developers, the benefits of cooperating with a range of actors was much higher. By the council losing some of its grip on policy and setting up links with other city organisations, the strategic partnership, the Leeds Initiative, was able to create 'feel good' projects which reflected well on those who participated in them. Again, it was a question of doing more through trusting other partners and sharing some of the credit of successes. Rather than projects always assigned to Leeds City Council, the TEC or the corporation, Leeds as a city would benefit. The Royal Armouries project, for example, was part of the Leeds Initiative, and the scheme was partly funded by the development corporation, the city council and central government departments. Many of the key public actors could stand back from economic development projects because at the end of the day they just wanted what was good for Leeds. They could trust the other partners.

In the CUDL, the legacy of inter-communal rivalries ensured that any one commune's benefit could be perceived to be another's loss, particularly when seeking to attract inward investment. This is a classic prisoner's dilemma – there were obstacles to cooperation because each actor believed that they would be worse off if they cooperated, though if they did all cooperate, they would, arguably, all have been better off through higher employment and inward investment. Before the 1980s, the communes did not cooperate much in economic development. There were a series of competitive local economic development programmes in each commune, none of which amounted to much. Mauroy's talent was to overcome the obstacles to cooperation by persuading the other communes to enter into a local economic development coalition with Lille. To create a successful coalition, Lille had to convince the other communes that it was not going to take advantage. It is a measure of Mauroy's success that the other communes did not oppose him more. The logic of the siting of the TGV station in Lille, with the attendant Euralille development, is that Lille becomes the centre of the metropole, the scenario that Roubaix and the other communes feared the most. In part, they cooperated because of Mauroy's brute power. He had the political clout in Paris to overcome the objections of the SNCF (French National Railways) so the tunnel rail link would be re-routed through Lille. He had the reputation to forge the public–private partnership and, in addition, the Lille commune owned the land. What could the commune of Roubaix do but accede to it? Yet the scheme was less an example of the *grand projet* of a *notable* than it might appear, however. The severity of the recession in Lille had convinced local politicians that cooperation was necessary. There was a logic to metropolitisation which drew the sparring communes together. Roubaix's cooperation was ensured by deals on other developments which benefited it directly. The coalition was so important that even though the communes had the chance to ditch Mauroy as leader of the CUDL after 1995, they kept him on. The mayors of the metropole recognised that only Mauroy could keep the coalition together.

Leadership in Southampton shows the contrast between French and British local politics neatly. While Southampton had a polycentric local government structure that resembled that of France, with many tiers of elected and unelected local government, there were only attempts at cooperation rather than successful collective action. The absence of cooperation in Southampton reflected the better economic conditions of the city when compared with northern cities. In these conditions, there is not so much to be gained from imaginative development projects and partnerships. The local authorities, therefore, continued to distrust each other. There was no coordinating structure, such as a large strategic authority or an urban community, which could facilitate cooperation. After the retirement of Alan Whitehead as council leader in 1992, the effectiveness of the political leadership declined in the face of municipal competition and the complexity of the governing tasks.

The new urban governance

Governance is the concept which best characterises the new relationships in policy networks in Britain and France. Governance is not a unilinear end state, but a set of principles of governing that leaves much of government in place and encompasses the continuing variation in countries' political systems. Governance does not mean that the roles of government actors, such as political leaders, mayors, civil servants, state bureaucrats, change out of all recognition, but that the context in which they operate and how they relate to each other alters. Institutional fragmentation and closer interorganisational relationships have transformed the nature of urban politics in Britain in France. Old political systems do not have enough capacity to yield the policies necessary for dynamic local economies in an age of rapid change. The problems are too complex; the solutions are highly contingent upon the actions of others. Political systems must adapt to form more horizontal, cooperative and trusting relationships with the many actors who need to be involved in the policy process. Command and control does not work; networking, bargaining and cooperation are part of the answer. Governance involves political activities that go beyond institutions and encompasses networks of individual and institutional actors.

In part, central governments have recognised the complex nature of policy problems by creating new tiers of elected government, as in the French case, and new layers of the bureaucratic state and quangos as in Britain. On both sides of the channel the centre has restructured local political systems to deal with new policy challenges, whether it is the attempt to introduce consumer-led service delivery in the UK, or the democratisation and deconcentration of functions in France. The result is a plethora of new actors in the respective local scenes, whether they are central government bureaucrats, regional directors or presidents of regional and departmental councils, all of whom wish to share in the making and implementation of policy.

The importance of locality

The comparative approach shows how governance takes various forms in different places and in different countries. There is no uniform pattern. Where there was a variety of political arrangement and practices across and between local political systems in the first place, this is compounded, rather than homogenised, by flexibility, networks and fragmentation. In this sense, our four cities display contrasting approaches to cooperation which reflect the nature of the cities themselves, their political cultures, their levels of social capital, and the balance of costs and benefits of cooperation. Politics has moved toward the new urban governance, but in a way that stresses the uniqueness of place. Thus, in Leeds, networks have appeared with new actors in them, but the council remains as the primary organisation; all decisions have a political edge and are approved by the political leader. In Lille, the communes cooperate, but there is no lessening of the antagonism and competition between them. Southampton struggles to find an identity, but apart from the activities of its leader in the 1980s, cohesion is lost among the shifting networks associated with development projects. The mayor of Rennes dominates his network; others are either part of it or they are opposed.

Urban regimes?

In both Britain and France, businesses have become willing to join cooperative projects because they realise the importance of the public sector and the opportunities and fragilities of a more internationalised economy. Public sector actors realise the limitations of statist economic policy solutions. Economic development projects need the cooperation of the private sector to make them work. In the UK, central funding rules and policy changes have encouraged public sector agencies to find private sector partners and to provide finance. In France, mixed economy societies (SEMs) have become more popular as a vehicle for public–private relationships. From the results of our sociometric analysis we found business representatives in high central positions in all our cities (John, 1998). In three cities, public–private partnerships have taken pride of place, influencing policy. Certain key businessmen have formed close relations with local politicians, and local politicians have modified their positions on key policy issues to be more in line with the views of business. It was in the larger cities where business more readily entered into a coalition with the public sector, whereas cooperation was weaker in the smaller urban spaces. It seems that the costs of cooperation are lower, and the benefits are much greater, in the larger cities.

Governance is about the greater interdependence of the public and the private. In part, the rethinking of decision-making roles is a function of complexity. As policy-makers realise how difficult it is to run a city, they seek to involve those decision-makers whose actions affect the success of a public policy. It is the case, therefore, that stronger networks form between the public and private sectors in an attempt to reduce uncertainty. The exchange between the public and private is highly problematic for social scientists as it implies that public objectives are being superseded by narrow commercial interests. Private power could mean planning for short-term gain, and could lead to a lack of open spaces, a decline in the productive industries and the neglect of the conditions of the urban poor.

The concept of a 'regime' is helpful in illuminating some aspects of contemporary urban governance (Stone, 1989; John and Cole, 1998). In the closer public–private relationships of the larger cities in our study, there was an exchange of objectives and a willingness to cooperate on long-term goals, rather than business domination. Rather than decisional capacity being irretrievably lost from the interlocking of the public and the private, public–private coalitions mobilise resources and achieve more than would be the case if either operated alone. As with networks, such beneficial relationships require trust; they also need selective incentives. In Leeds, the politics–business relationship had long roots which became manifest in the Leeds Initiative, the development partnership created in 1990; in Lille, the hostility between business and the socialists lessened after the economic crisis of the 1980s, when both sides realised the importance of cooperation. While business participated in politics in our other two cities, these relationships did not amount to a regime. In Southampton, the networks were too diffuse and the private sector too weakly organised to create a powerful business–local political coalition; in Rennes, the cosy alliance between the Rennes mairie and the private sector was ruptured by the mayor's ambitions and his costly redevelopment proposals. In all four cities, the regime concept can only explain certain aspects of governance; it illuminates the relationships and exchanges between public and private, rather than defines how a city is governed. Whereas business and politics in Atlanta allied to decide most matters of public importance (Stone, 1989), European central states in their local, regional and national branches are too involved in policy-making for regimes to emerge. Business is one set of actors among many, is itself fractured, and has various allegiances, either to national politics or to parties of various political colours.

Evaluating governance

In each town, many of the good and bad aspects of local government policy-making are replicated or are even amplified in the new networked politics. There is a tendency to think of governance as a better form of politics compared to what went before. The values which make governance work seem opposed to the closed, organisationally driven world of government structures. It is true that to move toward governance there has to be an opening up of politics so that actors have a chance of cooperating. Decision-makers need to set up a dialogue with each other; the basis for the politics of process must be established. To overcome the difficulties of co-operation, regular contact and the involvement of actors in decisions are the bases for the trust needed when an actor fears that it will lose out by making agreements. New networks are a means by which better decisions can be made. Without networks, there would have been no Euralille, no Royal Armouries, no SRB bids (though, in Rennes, Hervé will build a metro even without the support of the business community). There is also a sense in which the openness is a breath of fresh air in closed political systems. There are innovative ideas; and new actors bring their energy to policy-making. For organisations which have a heavy sense of the past and an inward looking mentality, like Leeds City Council, competition and relationships with other organisations can help shake off some of the acquired weight of political conflicts. Participation in a wider decision-making network helps local government to broaden its outlook and to approach decision-making in a spirit of compromise and in a strategic manner.

Yet, if governance is about innovation, it can also exaggerate the tension, competition and conflict in local political systems. In the UK, the presence of new organisations and the activism of old ones creates problems for existing power holders as well as offering challenges. In Leeds, the TEC threatened to undermine the power-base of the chamber of commerce and the council. Rather than a trusting network between them, there was secret warfare which flared up over particular initiatives, such as Business Links and the Single Regeneration Budget. Even the relationship between the council and the chamber of commerce has its problems. In no way can these relationships be characterised as initially trusting, as each organisation believed that the other was going to try to take the credit for development projects. The behaviour of participants was at times belligerent, angry, threatening, obstructive, changeable and disloyal. There was brute politics at work. The same could be said of the relationships between the communes, and between the state bureaus and the communes in Lille. The surprising fact was not that conflict existed, but that the organisations were able to cooperate at all. At the end of the day, bargains were struck with which all sides were able to agree. Cooperation does not require that the participants like each other, or that each party does not try to get the best deal. Cooperation only requires that at the end of the day they agree, which in Leeds they did. The conflicts occurred behind closed doors. At bottom, there needs to be a pragmatism and a realisation that all the factions in a city need to work together.

In all of these conflicts, local political leadership was crucial in their resolution and in bringing together the disparate elements of the local governance system. In Leeds, the leader, the president of the chamber of commerce and the chair of the TEC were able to meet face to face, to sort out the conflicts and to control their subordinates. In Lille, local political leadership was the driving force behind the local economic development coalition. In Rennes and Southampton, in contrast, the local political leadership failed to build governance capacity because of inter organisational competition. Our study shows that it was not so much the contrast between the countries which explained the different levels of cooperation, but the contrast between the types of cities. The larger cities of Leeds and Lille were better able to ensure cooperation than the medium-sized towns of Southampton and Rennes. Large city politics is more brutal, partly because the actors realise the importance of their decisions, but there is more of a tendency to agree policies at the end of the day. In the small towns the conflicts were more internecine.

The quality of political leadership is essential for coordination and the success of policy. The fragmentation of local political systems does not remove the importance of political decision-making. There needs to be a political mechanism able to bring together the fragmented institutions and the array of private actors in a way which leads to better and responsive policy-making. There is only one individual who can perform this task – the elected leader. The question becomes, do leaders have enough powers, legitimacy, capacity and personal qualities to carry out the difficult job of managing complexity? Whereas local government leadership was always difficult, local governance leadership requires almost superhuman skills.

Who governs governance?

In both Britain and France, there has been some improvement of decision-making under conditions of governance. Political leaders have forged new coalitions and they have engaged with the private sector. Yet the more open character of governance poses challenges for democratic institutions. The new way of doing business undermines the existing patterns of chain and command and transfers decision-making into interpersonal relationships and into the semi-institutionalised politics of partnerships. When governing becomes more informal, the patterns of democratic control become less easy to identify. Conflicts occur behind closed doors, rather than in the council chamber or in party organisations. Conflict resolution occurs bilaterally and out of the public glare. Decision-makers conduct relationships with the private sector in a very different manner to that of party organisations. To be accepted by the business sector, political leaders need to appear respectable and to talk some of the language of business. If there is a regime-like politics emerging, then political leaders bargain with business without fear that they have to negotiate and renege on agreements later in the political process.

The sheer complexity of interorganisational relationships means that it is hard to identify who makes decisions. There are many types of actors operating at various territorial tiers across contrasting policy sectors in fast-changing environments. Policy-making becomes looser, more evolutionary and contingent. Corporate strategies tie down actors too much. Policy needs to be made rapidly, with frequent communication between decision-makers to iron out difficulties and to resolve conflicts. The regular pattern of reporting to committee meetings and campaigning on clear manifestos is now not as appropriate. The disengagement of the state from direct intervention in the policy environment, the practice of 'steering not rowing', means that interorganisational relationships have their own life and that they continually mutate. There is no driving force at the centre. In Southampton, for example, Associated British Ports (ABP) could not identify which key actors coordinated state policy on the port, either for it or against it. Because of the complexity and multilayered nature of the proposal, the ABP tried to form networks with decision-makers who had some part of the decision in the hope that all the pieces in the jigsaw – European

Union issues, planning issues, environmental issues and transport maters – would all fall in place. That such important public matters should be coordinated by a private sector actor is a measure of the extent to which the state has retreated in Britain. The implications for democracy of such a role for the private sector are large. Though there are benefits involved in having such a loose structure, there needs to be a more considered relationship between private and public sector actors.

Many of the same processes are at work in France. The retreat from a tight framework of central planning and coordination of industrial activity, the greater number of agencies involved and the new role of the private sector have lessened the ability of the state to coordinate policy. The greater role of the private sector in funding development projects shifts the policy agenda. There was not such a hole in political relationships in our two French towns as we found in Southampton and, to an extent, in Leeds, however. The power of the main locally elected leader in France ensured the coordination of the complex pattern of agencies. It was the leading mayors in Lille and Rennes who pushed for new visions and projects in local economic development policy. They built coalitions of state and local public and private sector actors to prepare their cities for a more European and international role. Though Lille's development depends, in part, on a series of coalitions – public–private, inter-communal and local–state – the role of the mayor at the centre of the networks gave policy-making a coherence, identity and legit-imacy lacking in the UK case.

In part, the mayoral vision is flawed. Euralille could be consid-ered a rather ugly, cheap business and shopping complex in the middle of a beautiful city centre. It is not clear that the development is a commercial success. There was little consultation before the proposal. Pierre Mauroy entered into an alliance with the private sector to knock down a quarter of old Lille, and relocated its poor inhabitants, core socialist supporters, to make way for concrete blocks of banks and shops. Slightly differently, Hervé became convinced that Rennes needed a metro in spite of public and business opposition. It is not clear that Rennes needs an under-ground transport system as it only takes half an hour to walk across the city centre, and business might be crippled by the high taxes as a result. French mayors have much freedom to act as they wish and there are few formal arrangements to hold them to account.

The decentralisation reforms made since 1982 have loosened many of the central controls on their decisions. As national politicians, mayors are often away from their cities and leave decisions to the forceful, and largely invisible, *adjoints* who have the main day-to-day dealings with the other communes, state officials and businesses. The decentralisation reforms have placed a great strain on the system. It is much harder for one person to manage public business, which makes the mayor even more busy and proactive trying to control other decision-makers. Who wants grand schemes and monuments to personal ambition? What is needed is professional, continuous and responsible leadership.

In spite of the apparent lack of control on mayoral power in France, there is no doubt who in the end of the day is responsible for local decisions. Voters had a direct chance to pass judgement on Mauroy's efforts to redevelop Lille in the 1995 municipal elections – and they backed him. They backed Hervé in Rennes too. In spite of the complexity of the new governing relationships, it is still the mayor, with new powers and a new role, who is able to bring some coherence to a more uncertain and unshifting political world. Ironically, Ashford's conceit is reversed. It is Britain which has flexible governance and extensive interterritorial interpenetration of centre and locality; whereas it is in France where enhanced local leadership is able to give a local democratic element to the fragmented framework of governing. Rather than France it is Britain which is overflexible, pragmatic and ever shifting. In France, in contrast, mayors still have a belief in the integrated strategy enforced by personal power. If policy coordination in France is risky, it is better than the more cautious and piecemeal British local policy-making style. French local governance can generate the capacity to govern in spite of the risks of personal power. The conclusion is that UK governance needs more powerful, but accountable, leaders to pull the shifting institutional framework together.

About this study

The research project compared policy networks in two policy sectors – secondary education and local economic development – in four cities in Britain and France: Leeds, Lille, Rennes and

Southampton. The cases were pairs of cities of broadly similar size but with contrasting characters – the research employed the 'most different' systems design to see if there were similarities in policy networks in spite of different geographies, institutions and histories. The research design aimed to compare across three dimensions – country, policy sector and city – to examine the impact of governance trends. The researchers tested hypotheses from the comparative urban government, policy networks and 'new' localism literatures. The research project lasted from January 1994 to January 1996, with six months', field work in each city. Methods were quantitative (sociometric mapping analysis) and qualitative (semi-structured interviewing). The researchers interviewed just over 300 elite actors sampled by the snowball method. The interviewers asked each actor to specify their contacts on policy issues and coded and entered them in a network analysis programme, UCI-NET IV (Borgatti *et al.*, 1992). See John (1998) for the sociometric analysis. The interviewers asked a series of questions about networking, political power, accountability, policy change and decision-making to inform the case studies.

5 Understanding Urban Governance: The Contribution of Rational Choice

Keith Dowding, Patrick Dunleavy, Desmond King, Helen Margetts and Yvonne Rydin

The claims of rational choice

Rational choice is usually greeted with scepticism, and even hostility, by most urban scholars (for example, Keating, 1991; Gray, 1994). Its association with new-right politics and its formalism and abstraction do not appeal to many working on empirical studies in the urban sphere (Dowding, 1996a). In fact, rational choice is not a rival to other theories of urban politics. Rather it is a *method* of study which may illuminate other approaches and provide a dynamic explanation of their descriptive and categorical forms. It should not, for example, theoretically demonstrate whether urban politics is to be dominated by the production of growth machines or urban regimes, or suffused by policy communities or advocacy coalitions. Rather, it provides a way of taking these models and combining them into a general explanatory framework. This broader framework should enable us to understand the conditions and institutions which historically combine to produce differentiation across urban processes in separate communities in the same country, and disparate types of urban processes in different countries. Rational choice is a question-generating methodology, though its deductive and analytic technique also points towards theorised empirical research for answering these questions.

Here, we explore the type of approach implied by rational choice and provide some examples from the Metropolitan Governance and

Community Study (MGCS) of London (for a fuller account see Dowding *et al.*, forthcoming). We explore four areas.

1. Rational choice theory has brought the collective action problem, the fundamental problem, if not the genesis, of politics, to the forefront of modern political science. Understanding the collective action problem enables us to transcend old issues in the *community power debate*, modelling power as a bargaining game and examining the relationship between power, luck and systematic luck (Dowding 1991, 1996b; Dowding *et al.* 1995).
2. If community power begins with study at the microlevel, simple game-theoretic models can help illuminate the processes by which different meso-level actors overcome the collective action and coordination problems they face. In particular it can model *coordination through networks*. These models can help us to generalise across policy networks to understand why certain types of problem are more easily solved, and why some actors dominate.
3. The *nature of state provision* and organisation is examined through a 'collective good' approach to issues of collective consumption, which, together with a bureau-shaping analysis of managerial behaviour (Dunleavy, 1991), explains the new managerial and innovative service-delivery processes which have developed in the post-Fordist urban age.
4. Finally, we examine the *institutional allocation of functions*, and seek to understand how functional requirements structurally suggest behaviour to actors to fulfil roles in the urban setting, no matter what precise constitutional and legal arrangements exist. This is particularly clear in our study of the great metropolis of London which from 1986 to 1997 has operated without any over-arching governing authority.

Collective action and community power

All political activity is the attempt to overcome the problems of antagonistic cooperation and all issues studied in urban politics can be reduced to some form of collective action or coordination problem. Community power can be analysed through the rational choice approach to power and luck. Development is an example of community power involving sets of coalitions, often in mutual hostility; which side is most powerful can be analysed in terms of the resources each enjoys and the depth of their collective action problems. Political parties form coalitions or regimes (Stone, 1989) around a particular ideological or service dimension (Dowding *et al.* 1999), and these coalitions hold together whilst the parties can, when in power, provide benefits for their coalition partners. Each issue area also poses its own collective action or coordination problems. Air pollution is a coordination and collective action problem with stark inter-action and inter-dependency problems; clean air is a diffuse collective good implying massive free-rider problems. Issues such as drugs and prostitution involve externalities between communities within the same local authority jurisdictions. Issues surrounding the relationship between extra-governmental organisations, schools, hospital trusts and local authorities can be seen in terms of club theory (Buchanan, 1965; Cornes and Sandler, 1996). Relationships between local communities, local authorities and the police are a game of antagonistic cooperation. Competition between cities or local authorities within metropolitan areas can be viewed in terms of fiscal federalism and the Tiebout model (Peterson, 1981; Miller, 1981; Schneider *et al.*, 1995; Tiebout, 1956; Olson 1969, Oates 1972). Transport is a coordination and externality problem between boroughs, and so on. Rational choice forces us to examine the balance of costs and benefits of each actor from engaging in collective acts.

The identification of coordination and interdependency problems can provide powerful explanations for policy inaction and the existence of a policy vacuum. Such inaction often benefits specific parties. In such circumstances, the distributive outcomes of the political process produce benefits without the active exercise of power by any party. The beneficiaries may be said to be lucky (Barry, 1991) and when their luck non-randomly attaches to social locations they are said to by *systematically lucky* (Dowding, 1991, 1996b). Rational choice makes a clear distinction between cases where power has been actively exercised involving the use of resources, however varied, to achieve certain goals, and those cases where the incentive structure facing all actors results in an outcome which favours certain parties, who may be described as systematically lucky.

The identification of developers' systematic luck in the growth-machine model (Logan and Molotch, 1987; Molotch, 1990; Harding,

1991, 1994, 1995) is now well attested. Developers tend to be favoured by local authorities, as a buoyant local economy enhances the electoral prospects of local politicians. Whilst local growth may be supported by a large section of the community and local authorities, there is still a battle over the nature of that growth. We can thus divide growth into two games – a positive-sum game over the growth possibilities, and a zero-sum game over where that development is to occur. Developers and landed interests gain even more through growth than does the local community, but if local jobs are created or secured, then many in the local community will gain, leading to positive-sum solutions. If developers agree to provide service facilities for the local community, as a result of bargaining with local politicians for building rights, then many local people may gain more directly. In so far as the developers are able to gain because others gain too, they are pushing at an open door. To that extent they are lucky. What is in their interests is in others' interests too. This is an important aspect of the power structure. In a capitalist society, capitalists are systematically lucky because the welfare of everyone is dependent upon the state of the economy and capitalism is the motor of the economy. This is luck rather than power (as suggested in Lindblom (1977) or Stone (1980), for example), since it attaches to actors in certain social locations even when they do not have to act to achieve their aims, and even when they would not have the ability to achieve their aims despite opposition (Dowding 1991, 1996b). The growth-machine model thus provides a mechanism by which we can see the extra power and luck of developers. The systematic luck of developers occurs because politicians can see the benefits to their community afforded by growth potential. These entrepreneurs pressing for development find themselves able to persuade local leaders easily.

The British case includes a further important actor, central government, and often this is the key actor for the zero-sum game of where development is to take place. The regeneration of Barking Reach in the London Borough of Barking and Dagenham, for example, is recounted by the local authority as a tale of leadership by the council, involving coordination of key actors, the brokering of deals and essential pump-priming investment. Yet, investigation of the context for this urban regeneration project highlights the relationship that key landowners and developers had with central government because of the site's location within a central-government-designated regeneration area – the Thames Gateway, formerly the East Thames Corridor (Rydin, 1998). The proactive role of the Thames Gateway Unit within the Department of the Environment in skewing policy programmes and releasing resources can be shown to be central to the development going ahead, as were the investment strategies of the developer, Bellway Urban Renewal, and a key landowner, National Power. Whilst the borough council undoubtedly did undertake policy action and invest staff time and resources in negotiating and networking on the project, its success in achieving the development on the ground is due to the council's and the developers' luck in being within the central government initiative area the Thames Gateway.

Another example concerns a transport infrastructure project, Thameslink 2000, which sought to upgrade the north–south main-line rail links through central London. It involves no new distribution of positive and negative externalities, no new route construction and only one new station. All parties have been in favour of it. The upgrading will increase capacity on the link; not only will it prove profitable for the rail operators involved, it will complement other planned projects, such as the Channel Tunnel Rail Link (CTRL). Private sector involvement is guaranteed by a good rate of return on investment, and both London Transport and Union Rail are willing to make a contribution as the link helps them avoid additional investment. A consortium of some 140 members was formed to promote the project and to lobby for central government resources (some £650 million) needed up front. Local authorities were involved in the consortium and one such player argues that they

> can legitimately claim that it helped make the case ... Our initial analysis had identified the promising political trends and our technical contacts gave us knowledge of the interconnection issue [with the CTRL terminus]. We were, therefore, ready to take advantage of opportunities as they were presented. (*Planning*, 29.4.96).

This is the resolving of a coordination problem with a state-engendered coalition which was able to form and move quickly, having little opposition as there were no obvious negative externalities.

This is essentially a win–win scenario with identifiable returns however. London Transport, Union Rail and central government saw benefits in terms of cost-avoidance. Rail operators saw benefits in terms of operating profit. A deal could be brokered. Local authorities with stations on the route saw local economic development potential and joined the coalition. Using the resources of information, they identified the synergies between the problems that the CTRL was posing government and the potential solution offered by Thameslink 2000. Central government took the key action to release funds which ensured the deal could go ahead. What the local authorities did was make structural luck work for them.

These two examples should not be taken to imply that all outcomes that local authorities push for on property-led economic development are the result of luck. Other examples of more proactive exercises of power can be identified – the role of the London Borough of Croydon in the Tramlink project is one such case. Croydon remains a good example of an authority-led growth coalition, or growth regime, where the same plans have been promoted by successive Labour, Conservative and Labour administrations.

In London, even more strongly and directly than predicted by the Gurr and King (1987) state thesis, the central state is a key actor in city governance. Its great powers include its knowledge, its power to make threats and promises through its hold upon purse-strings and law-making capacity, its legitimate authority and its ability to change the incentive structure of other organisations. Local authorities differ in their ability to bargain with central government (largely, though not exclusively, through the Department of the Environment, Transport and the Regions (DoETR)) in part due to party links, but also to the extent to which they are seen to be effective in carrying out centre-led policies. The DoETR collects information from the local authorities and looks for best practice. Most of the pressure lobbies, environmental groups, professional groups and economic groups rely upon their informational base and the legitimacy they acquire for speaking on behalf of segments of the population, and local authorities often have no more power than this in many issue areas. Increasingly, even in areas where local authorities once had extensive statutory powers such as planning, they find themselves in an advocacy role, needing to form alliances with other organisations.

Using its superior resources, the central state is able to structure the interests of other actors. In 1991, the Labour council in Lambeth applied for money under the City Challenge project to set up Brixton Challenge. This is a private corporation largely supported by central government funds. Its role is to encourage business to develop in Brixton, which is located within the jurisdiction of Lambeth council. Brixton Challenge tries to encourage development by working with local businesses, the local council, housing associations and other bodies in order to generate redevelopment and to provide jobs in an area of high unemployment and with many social problems. The ruling Labour council in Lambeth was not keen on the City Challenge idea. The councillors believed that it was better to have an integrated plan for the whole of Lambeth, rather than just one area. They did not like the public–private partnerships necessary under the City Challenge concept, preferring, for example, to keep housing policy in the public sector, rather than involving housing associations and private landlords. Nevertheless, despite their ideological objections to the Conservative government's policy, they bid for and received City Challenge money. They did so because the incentives set up by the Conservative government made it irrational for them to do otherwise; most local government funding comes from central government and those areas which received City Challenge money would be advantaged. Councils which did not have a successful City Challenge bid would therefore lose out. The Labour councillors of Lambeth chose of their own free will to bid for City Challenge money, but they did so because the environment in which they made their decisions had been changed by the policy of the Conservative central government.

Power in communities in Britain is diffuse. Central government is able to structure sets of local interests through central initiatives, and then to see that local organisations implement policies it prefers. Capitalist groups can also structure local interests through economic initiatives and can gain both through the power of the purse and through systematic luck where interests are locally structured to provide developers with advantages over any opposition. Coordination of local activities, especially in a London with the lack of a strategic authority, created new sets of collective action and coordination problems leading to overall power loss. This can be understood through the use of game theory to analyse the coordination problems as different types of game.

Coordination through networks

Generalising from the collective action problem highlights problems of coordination. The interplay of groups through bargaining and the lobbying process are usually assumed to bring benefits – to some, if not all. Whilst the fragmentation of a policy area across several different agencies may seem to provide an opportunity for partnership, it also involves transaction costs. These costs are likely to be high in the early stages of establishing partnerships when exchange of information is required and substantial investment in building-up the social capital of trust is needed. Following this, transaction costs fall as trust and information exchange networks are established and contact is routinised. Success and longevity will bring a rise in transaction costs again, however, as new issues are brought within the partnership's remit, new members seek to join and gain the benefits of partnership, easier projects and goals are achieved leaving the relatively more difficult tasks, and turnover in personnel reduces the benefits of routine contacts and raises the costs of information transfer and trust-building again. This shapes the *functional logic* which leads actors to form and maintain partnerships in order to provide governance; it particularly shapes it over time. In this section, we consider how the abolition of the Greater London Council (GLC) created the conditions for metro-level networking at a strategic level. We then go on to look at how specific policy issues can be characterised in terms of the incentive structures modelled by game theory.

There is a functional logic to the governing of large cities, understandable through the nature of the collective consumption demands, and the coordination problems implied in satisfying those demands. With the demise of the GLC, there was a gap in such governance structures. Whilst many networks struggled to coordinate, problems in the areas of transport, development and tourism became obvious relatively quickly. One set of actors, business people concerned with tourism and inward investment, lobbied central government to fill the gap. Lord Sheppard, chairman of Grand Metropolitan, and one-time fundraiser for the Conservative Party, proved to be a key actor in this process, motivating among others Lord Egan, Chairman of the British Airports Authority. Following the general election of 1992, Sheppard led a group of businesspeople to set up London First. At first, Michael Howard, the then Secretary of State for the Environment, opposed them, believing they were setting up a rival to his London Forum. Eventually, Sheppard became Chairman, and Stephen O'Brien Chief Executive, of both organisations, which merged completely after a year, later dropping the name 'Forum'. In the beginning, London First was interested in transport and inward investment, with tourism a major concern. More actors became involved, with 260 businesses putting time and money into London First itself, and another 100 (including many London local authorities) associated with the London First Visitors' Council, which is involved in providing facilities and advice for inward investment. Once established, London First was used by central government, advising John Gummer. When he became Secretary of State for the Environment, he asked London First to draw up a corporate plan for London. Sheppard refused, but helped create the London Pride Partnership, with Toby Harris as co-chair. The London Pride Partnership became a strategic advisor to the Cabinet sub-committee for London. Indeed, when the Joint London Advisory Committee was created, it basically consisted of the London Pride Partnership and the joint Cabinet sub-committee. This met three times a year, with the Government Office for London as observers and later as participants. This is a dynamic story of actors willing to fulfil functions when a gap emerged in London. In this sense, London – post-GLC – is a social science experiment in actors' response to lack of government. The response is to create a government, or governance ... of sorts.

Networking is an important governance function especially in the absence of institutionalised structures, and it enhances actors' power where institutions do exist. A wide body of rival (and perhaps not-so-rival) models examining this has been developed. These are summarised in Table 5.1. Each of the models has merits and problems, but trying to understand the dynamics of coordinative policy networks (understood as a generic term for all the models in Table 5.1) requires a closer look at the structures in which actors behave, and the resources they bring to the bargaining process.

One starting point for this process is to view each network in terms of a game-structure of the important actors, to specify the type of relationship and likely behaviour, given assumptions or empirically determined interests. Table 5.2 schematises the main actors and the types of games, some nested (Tsebelis, 1990) within

TABLE 5.1 Different policy network models

	PC	IN	UC	PDS	ACF	GMM	Regime
Linkages between actors	Close	Problematic	Close institutional	Variable	Variable	Finance dominates	Close formal and informal
Degree of integration	High	Variable	High	Variable	Variable	High dev. Low other	High
Values of actors	Shared	Distinct	Shared	Prof: dominate	Distinct	Develop. dominate	Shared
Rules of interaction	Agreed	Not agreed	Agreed	Agreed	Agreed	Not agreed	Agreed
Type of interest	Shared	Distinct	Shared	Prof: dominate	Distinct	Develop. dominate	Shared
Resources of actors	Equal	Unequal	Unequal	Unequal	Unequal	Unequal	Unequal
Number of members	Low	High	Low	Low	Variable	Low	Low
Continuity of membership	High	Low	High	High	Variable	High	Variable
Policy styles across nations and sectors	Vary	Vary	Same	Same	Vary	Vary	Vary
Levels of government	One	Many	Many	Many	Many	One	One

PC, Policy communities; IN, Issue networks; UC, Urban corporatism; PDS, Professionally dominated subsystems; ACF, Advocacy coalition framework; GMM, Growth-machine model; Regime, Regime theory.

TABLE 5.2 Main actors in London policy networks

Issues	Air Pollution	Child care	Development	Homelessness	Hospital reorganisation	Policing strategies	Tourism	Transport	Waste disposal
Actors	CG	CG	CG	CG	CG	CG	CG	CG	CG
	LA	LA	LA	LA	LG	LA	LA	LA	LA
	PG	PG	PG	LG	Ci	Ci	TAs	LG	LG
	LG	Ci	Ci	Ci	Hospt	Police	LF	Ci	Ci
	Ci				HA				
Type of game	VS	PS	LF	HAT	HA	VS	LF	LF	LF
	ZS	ZS	ZS	VS	ZS		VS	VS	PS
			VS	ZS	VS			ZS	
			ZS	ZS	ZS				
Example	BS	Co-ord	PD or C	PD or C	ZS	PD or BS	BS	BS	Co-ord

Key:
CG, Central government departments; LA, Local authorities; PG, Professional groups; LG, Lobby groups; Ci, Citizens; hospt, Hospitals; HAT, Non-LA housing authorities; HA, Health authorities; Police, Metropolitan police; TAs, Tourist authorities; LF, London first. **Games**: PS, Positive sum game, e.g., Co-ord = game of pure co-ordination; VS, Variable sum game, a game of antagonistic co-operation, e.g., BS = Battle of the Sexes, PD = Prisoners' Dilemma or C = Chicken; ZS, Zero-sum games. Top games are the main game of the issue area analysed, the lower game is a sub-game or nested game (Tsebelis, 1990) which affects strategies in the main game.

broader games, for nine metropolitan-wide issues examined by the MGCS project.

The nature of the power structure varies across different issue areas. It can be explained by: (a) differences in the structure of interests which have been analysed through various game-theoretic models, and (b) differences in the nature of the five sets of resources available to actors in the different policy networks (Dowding 1991, 1996; Dowding *et al.*, 1995).

The convergence or divergence of the interests of major actors structures the nature of the policy game. Three broad game-theoretic models may be used to analyse these. First, a pure coordination game, where there is no (or very little) conflict of interest. Here, the bargaining problem is simply to coordinate activities. It has proved relatively easy for the local authorities to manage waste disposal, since their interest solely consists in where outside London they can dump their waste. Coordinating activity in terms of collection and disposal has worked well.

Secondly, there are games of pure conflict, or constant-sum games, where one actor's gain is another's loss. One obvious example is competition between London hospitals, a game of pure conflict, between organizations which were once in a cooperative situation.

Thirdly, and most importantly, games of both conflict and co-operation. Various games exist in this category (the best known include Prisoners' Dilemma (PD), Chicken and the Battle of the Sexes (BS)). Most bargaining situations can be modelled in terms of these games. These games can either be positive-sum (overall power gain, though some may lose) or negative-sum (overall power loss, though some may gain). The lack of coordination across the boroughs in tourism can be seen in part as a multi-player PD and BS (depending on the sub-issue). Free-riding by one borough on the efforts of others, for example, in the provision of parking for tour buses, is an *n*-actor PD game, whilst tourist-related transport is a coordination game where the authorities all desire the coordination on their own terms (BS game).

The London Tourist Board tries to coordinate these activities but has no authoritative powers and relies upon persuasion and its informational base. It has suffered as a consequence of providing a regulatory role; this brings it into conflict with many of the organisations it tries to coordinate. Following abolition of the

GLC, tourism policy drifted. The individual boroughs have, at best, a patchy record of support for it, some promoting tourism, some indifferent and some seeing tourism as a problem to be managed. The officers in charge of tourism in London's boroughs range from the Chief Librarian, to the Leisure Services department, to the Planning and Development Officer; in all, 26 job descriptions fit the 32 boroughs' tourist officers, demonstrating the boroughs' confusion over the nature of tourism and how to fit it into their organisation. Is tourism part of the borough's leisure complex, is their role the provision of information to visitors, or should tourism be developed for the local economy?

The boroughs' approach to the importance of the tourist industry varies enormously across the boroughs, as Table 5.3, showing the numbers of bed spaces for tourist accommodation, illustrates. This desegregation and lack of overall direction does not help *London* as a product. Neither the London Borough Association (LBA) nor the Association of London Authorities (ALA), now merged into the Association of London Government (ALG), provided any coordination for tourism, neither even having a tourist officer, tourism being one-thirtieth of one officer's time at the LBA shortly before it joined with the ALA. One officer suggested the main reason for this lack of interest is the associations' prioritisation of areas where there are few or no coordinating policy mechanisms at a London-wide level. The associations felt that the London Tourist Board (LTB) fulfilled this role. Most commentators on the London tourist scene believed that the LTB was failing to do this job which, in part, explains the formation of London First, the London Forum and the London Pride Partnership.

The input of the private sector into the LTB has always been important. However, it was not able to develop a corporate structure or to lead the tourist industry in London. LTB itself blames business, complaining that retailers do not seem to understand the importance of tourism to their own economy. The lack of interest of the retail industry reflects a collective action problem, with a large disparate group of actors and with a shared interest in a diffuse collective good (Olson, 1971). It also reflects an ambiguous relationship between the LTB and other potential supporters. As well as an advocacy role for London's tourist industry, LTB has educational and regulatory roles. It is responsible for training in the tourist information offices of the London boroughs (with the exception of

TABLE 5.3   Known serviced tourist accommodation in Greater London

	No. of accommodation providers	Bed spaces
Westminster	381	59 740
Kensington and Chelsea	168	23 261
Camden	105	18 275
Hillingdon	24	10 025
Hammersmith and Fulham	46	3833
Croydon	60	2784
Islington	21	2591
Hounslow	33	1929
Southwark	10	1544
Tower Hamlets	2	1515
Brent	30	1204
Ealing	45	1262
Richmond-Upon-Thames	30	1011
Harrow	19	959
Barnet	31	864
Lewisham	22	849
Hackney	16	832
Greenwich	22	588
Kingston Upon Thames	16	541
Haringey	18	529
Bexley	7	509
Redbridge	16	502
Merton	21	487
Lambeth	24	413
Sutton	9	406
Havering	7	383
Enfield	11	326
Waltham Forest	8	318
City of London	1	314
Newham	8	309
Wandsworth	13	260
Bromley	17	250
Barking and Dagenham	–	–
Greater London	1,241	138,613

Source: London Tourist Board and Convention Bureau

the Corporation of London, whose tourist office does not carry information on events or accommodation outside of the square mile), and it regulates the hotel industry. These roles lead it into a conflictual situation which does not help its advocacy role. The LTB has also been hampered by its corporate relationship with the English Tourist Board (ETB). Before it can provide new initiatives requiring finance, it has to agree these with the ETB; this has led into conflict with the ETB through conflict with other regional boards. The regional boards are in competition with one another, but also have common interests in promoting tourism as a product. Again, an example of the PD game.

Another story of coordination and interdependency is provided by the issue of air quality management in London. This helps our understanding of the policy dynamics, in considering the actions of different government units in tackling a problem where the benefits of policy action are highly dispersed and/or invisible, whilst the costs are highly concentrated and/or visible, and where there are multiple local government units (Rydin, 1997). Any attempt to tackle air pollution, which would benefit many residents, commuters and visitors, but in a largely intangible way, also imposes highly visible costs on selected groups, notably car and other road users. The highly publicised option of road pricing, to internalise the externality of air pollution associated with car use, is rendered unfeasible by the way in which it would impose spatially specific economic costs in the name of an indivisible and collectively consumed collective good – a cleaner atmosphere.

As a result, policy inaction or policy tokenism on air quality management is the norm among the fragmented local government of London. The chief action is being promoted by a single body – the South East Institute of Public Health – which is coordinating an air quality monitoring network of local authorities, bearing the costs of doing so by a combination of using the core budget for the agency and limited charging to local authorities (this representing a very low marginal cost to the authorities). The agency is acting as a policy entrepreneur on the issue in the hope of establishing a larger policy role for itself in the future, possibly a London Air Quality Agency with an expanded remit and budget.

Clean air is a diffuse collective good where everyone loses a little through a polluted atmosphere, but also potentially loses a lot through policies to clean the city's air. Everyone wants to be able to drive their own car, and the distribution of institutional forces, local governments, the Department of the Environment, and the lack of systematic data due to the attitude of the Department of Transport ensure lack of action. Local authorities have started to generate an information base, but they have no power to make their plans work – here the network is in a proto-organisational state.

By analysing these separate policy issues with a small number of simple models, we can generalise across diverse fields within urban politics to see essentially the same problems of antagonistic co-operation and conflictual coordination emerging. Thus, the problems of many disparate areas can be linked and analysed together within the same framework.

State provision and organisation

The 1970s saw a concerted effort to find a conceptual basis for defining the purpose of urban studies, which did not rely upon drawing a line on a map. The result was a focus on socialised or collective consumption within neo-Marxist political economy and subsequent Weberian reworkings within urban sociology. Such approaches posited a specific role for local or urban government in managing socialised or collective consumption, locating it within the relationship between consumption and production processes through reproduction of the labour force. It also sought explanations for instances of collective consumption policy by examining the balance of power between different classes and the contribution that collective consumption could make in any specific time and place.

Its weakness lay in its inability to explain why specific goods and services became the subject of this socialisation process while others did not. It failed to anticipate the restructuring of state involvement following the advent of the New Public Management (NPM) (Dunleavy and Hood, 1994; Dunleavy, 1994; Pollitt, 1993). It proved highly indeterminate in predicting when socialisation of consumption was the result of pressure from capitalist rather than labour interests, or vice-versa. However, it was convincing in its identification of a distinctive emphasis within urban politics, a point which was taken up by those, mainly British writers, working within the Weberian tradition. Indeed, the character of consumption activities and the role of the state in relation to such activities has become increasingly important within patterns of governance, particularly local governance. This is partly due to social shifts from production to consumption determining economic patterns, and the globalisation of economic activity with its consequent spatial distribution of production versus consumption. Within the state, however, it is also due to the adoption of NPM, which transforms many allocation functions of the welfare state into consumer-provider relations mimicking the private sector. Rational choice provides a means of re-examining the collection consumption framework by setting it against the collective goods literature of welfare economics (Cornes and Sandler, 1996). This highlights issues of free-riding and over-or-under-supply due to the balance of costs and benefits facing suppliers of collective goods.

The simplistic dichotomy of perfectly private or collective goods has proved inappropriate to the situation of urban politics in the 1990s, however. The collective goods approach should be developed, therefore, into a differentiated set of categories which take into account the three elements of production, disbursement and consumption, together with the different ways in which the modern state regulates these three processes. This provides a setting for analysing collective consumption processes (Dowding and Dunleavy, 1996). Figure 5.1 combines a modified neoclassical approach to collective goods (in 5.1 b) with a schematic diagram of the new forms of NPM. In Figure 5.1a we see the ways in which government has transformed its regulations and control of public activities beyond the concerns of old public administration (OPA). OPA was concerned with public production, public disbursement (through taxation) for collective and private consumption purposes, though there is also extensive subsidisation of both collective and private consumption. NPM has shifted a lot of public production to the private sector from the public sphere, though this has implied greater specific regulation. NPM has introduced new forms of specific regulation for private production, when disbursement is either collective (contracting-out) or private, through privatisation of the utilities, for example. NPM has also led to greater governmental organisation of non-governmental bodies producing collective and private services once traditionally produced by the state. We can examine NPM through the vision of a modified neoclassical collective goods approach (Savas, 1987) in Figure 5.1b, which recognises the traditional collective/private goods categories but also recognises that they do not fully explain why the state intervenes in production and consumption. The state has traditionally intervened in the production and consumption of both collective and private goods, for normative reasons, or for what Savas calls 'worthy goods'. In Figure 5.1c we see the complex ways in which the goods and services are produced in the modern state.

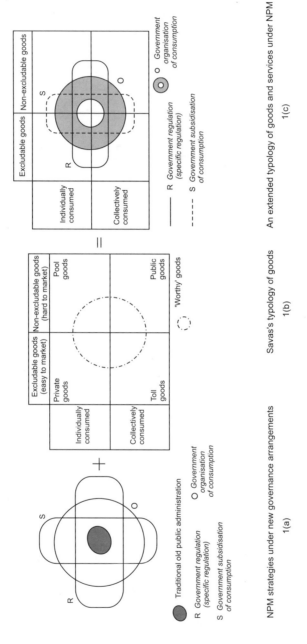

FIGURE 5.1 Goods and services in the modern state

We can see here the basic collective good categories of excludability and non-excludability, individual and collective consumption. The means through which government intervenes in production and disbursement through regulation, subsidisation of consumption, and through government organisation of consumption, giving 32 possible categories. Analysis of each is possible, though perhaps not desirable, but the major ones include: (a) those services directly organised by government, within a legal regulatory framework and with extensive subsidisation or even free provision, such as acute hospital care; (b) those services which may be completely unregulated (outside of general property laws), and unsubsidised – in which case those which are excludable and individually consumed are usually provided by the market, while those which are collectively consumed and non-excludable are not usually provided at all; (c) in between are goods subject to either regulation or government organisation, or subsidisation, and others where the state intervenes in two ways, subsidising and regulating (without directly organising), or subsidising and organising (without specific regulation) or organising and regulating (without paying subsidies). All of the post-Fordist and new managerial service processes such as privatisation, contracting-out, globalisation, creation of quasi-government organisations can be seen as shifting the production of some service or good from one category to another. The basic collective good characteristics enable predictions about the success and later modification of such new managerial practices.

On top of these basic question-generating categories of collective consumption processes we may add managerial bureau-shaping strategies. The very notion of local governance discredits the approach to urban politics based on description of the organisational details concerning local authorities. Governance implies interconnectedness and mutual dependency between a variety of organisations both inside and outside the local authority. This focus requires coordination of activities in order to overcome the multiple collective action problems identified through the nature of collection consumption processes. Local governance does not imply that the organisation of local authorities themselves is of no interest, however, for they remain key actors. Rather, local authorities need to be reconceptualised by reframing local authority organisations in terms of pressures arising from self-interested behaviour by local authority professionals and bureaucrats.

110

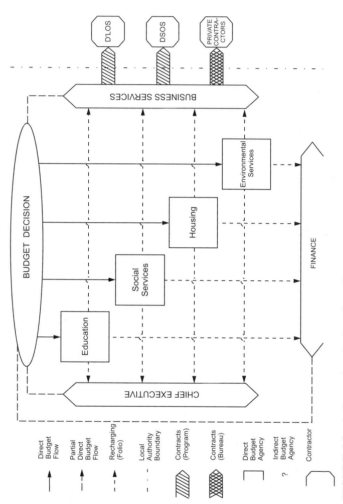

FIGURE 5.2 A three-stage budget flow diagram

The conventional public choice account of state bureaucracies told of pressures for expansion arising from the interests of bureaucrats in a larger department, with larger budgets and a larger staff cohort. Such an account partially fits evidence on the growth of state bureaucracies; these inadequacies have stimulated the formulation of the bureau-shaping thesis (Dunleavy 1985, 1989a, 1989b, 1991). This approach posits the existence of different types of budget: the core budget spent on the agency's own operations; the bureau budget comprising the core budget plus monies paid out by the agency to the private sector; the programme budget combining the bureau budget plan monies transferred to other public sector bodies; and the portfolio elements which add to the programme budget, spending by other bureaux from their own resources over which the agency has some responsibility, control or claim. Agencies fulfil different functions (delivery, regulation, transfer, contracts or control agencies, or a mixture) and in the British urban context we see a complex budgetary flow (see Figure 5.2).

Institutional allocations of functions

Within a metropolitan area, the issue of allocating functions to different organisations and different tiers is highly significant. The public choice approach to this is to emphasise the shifts in demand, the movement of consumers between local authorities with different policy packages, as in the Tiebout (1956) model. Another has been to try to assess the economic efficiency of different allocations and to argue for a tendency towards an optimal distribution (Olson, 1969; Oates, 1972; Bendor and Mookherjee, 1987). The former has little to say, however, on how essential functions are allocated between tiers as opposed to policy options being differentially offered by different local authorities, and the latter tells us nothing of the dynamics by which functional allocation occurs. Rational choice looks for the self-interested decision-making which generates the pressures for allocating functions to different organisations and tiers. The London First story, mentioned above, is an example of elite actors trying to fill a functional gap created by lack of governing institutions at the metropolitan level and feeling the need for central government to step in and create a Government Office for London (GOL); it also indicates this functional logic. Of course, the issues which were taken up first were those to which the actors' own self-interests were most closely tied. Their concerns developed a functional logic as they were taken into other issues which overlapped with their own affairs, and they never took up the more diffuse collective goods, such as air pollution, traditionally recognised as posing greater problems of collective action.

The concerns of London First were primarily the production and consumption issues traditionally associated with the dual state thesis (Cawson, 1986; Saunders, 1984, 1985, 1986). This thesis argued that the difficulties caused by dealing with social consumption, investment and expenditure within the available range of guidance mechanisms offered by the state – that is, bureaucratic, corporatist and pluralist mechanisms – resulted in a separation of functions so that consumption-orientated functions are dealt with at the local level within bureaucratic or pluralist systems, while production-orientated functions are dealt with at the central level by bureaucratic or corporatist systems. In contemporary policy conditions, this thesis has to be modified to take account of the growth of NPM and Quasi-Governmental Agencies (QGAs) and the importance of the supranational tier, the European Union.

Even so, this thesis lacks a dynamic for explaining the allocation of functions. Rational choice suggests that focusing on large-scale business and capital interests provides that dynamic, since it shows why such interests should try to insulate the expenditure and regulation decisions which affect them from the pluralist systems of local government. As well as enjoying systematic luck, business interests include in their rational calculation: the salience of the regulatory or spending function for capital; the vulnerability of the institutions under OPA and NPM, respectively; and the pro-capital asymmetry of political bargaining power between capital and citizen interests under OPA and NPM arrangements, respectively.

If this rational self-interested behaviour of business actors is then set in a policy context which favours business interests due to their corporate discretion, then the dynamic for insulation and upward allocation of functions concerning production is identified. This is modified only by the need to maintain legitimacy of the policy process, deal with the claims of property owners and handle the electoral consequences of distributing costs and benefits of policy decisions at the local level.

Looking at a variety of transport and infrastructure projects in London, the operation of this dynamic is clear. New mass-transit infrastructure such as the Jubilee Line extensions, Crossrail, the Heathrow Express and the CTRL were organised completely separately from the conventional planning process with social investment/ production organisations directly in charge of project definition and sponsoring legislation. Local authority roles were narrowly restricted to the amelioration of the consumption impacts on local environments and amenity levels, to detailed negotiations over construction negative externalities and to the social control of protests. The local authorities faced many of the transaction costs of these capital projects. Councils were fairly marginal lobbies for property holders, with little clout over key policy decisions. The overwhelming policy predominance of central government and now privatised transport companies was clear. Commercial actors needed to identify the potential benefits as measured by profits, and central government then used its funding resources to bring the schemes off, to bridge the funding gap where necessary and, in a few cases, to buy-off potentially significant opposition. Whitehall faced difficulties in legitimating schemes, however, and there were immense procedural overheads potentially involved in conflicts. The dynamic of functional allocation between tiers could not prevent such legitimation complications.

Thus the gap for a form of metro-level government created by the abolition of the GLC and the need to overcome the coordination problems of the numerous local authorities can help explain the moves towards private sector or partnership metro-level governance structures. The models can generate explanation of the divergence and convergence of their forms, though more detailed analysis fills in the detail of how policy develops in each case. This is dependent on the incentive structure involved in each policy issue, the way in which it fulfils production/consumption functions and is therefore subject to imperatives for insulation from pluralist pressures, and the centrality of the issue to the legitimacy claims of the local state.

Conclusion

Scholars in the urban field have tended to examine problems in isolation. Different researchers have used different methods to study decision-making in local governments, the institutional form of local authority, community power, and different types of issues – such as development, crime, air pollution, or relationships between extra-governmental organisations such as schools, hospital trusts and local authorities. The institutional rational choice approach allows us to produce a universal method to study these diverse sets of urban problems and processes. It enables us to use a universal assumption of rational behaviour for all types of political actors, from individuals to government organisations, private institutions, and non-organised or proto-organised groups of individuals.

London, following the abolition of the GLC, has provided political scientists with a ready-made experiment for the consequences of a governance gap in a (post) industrialised democracy. The strategic concerns of the city were left in the hands of disparate and competing organisations. Some problems were relatively easily solved, whilst others proved insurmountable. Various actors, from pre-existing organisations with London-wide remits such as the London Tourist Board, to new organisations such as London First and government creations such as the Government Office for London, slowly emerged to try to fill the governance gaps. In this sense, London at this time has proved to be a good test of the generality of explanatory rational-choice models of governance processes and of the types of functional requirements of a large international city.

The logic of explanation of rational choice is not well understood. Many people still insist that rational choice produces methodologically individualistic explanation (Green and Shapiro, 1994; Udehn, 1996), not understanding that the major variation between models, for example game-theoretic models, concerns their structural form. Thus, the major explanatory variable is structural at least as much as it is individualistic (Dowding and King, 1995; Grafstein, 1983, 1992).

Institutional rational choice concentrates upon the regularities of behaviour to be found under similar institutions, and the divergences of behaviour occasioned by diverse institutional forms. In this chapter, we have suggested the ways in which the different metropolitan-wide issues of the governance of London can better be understood by using rational choice methods. In doing so, we hope eventually to persuade the community of urban scholars that all aspects of urban politics can be analysed through institutional rational choice theory and, thereby, help provide a universal method of study which will enable us to have a deeper understanding of the societal forces and contingent historical circumstances which lead to the institutions and the political outcomes which we see in urban societies around the world today.

About this study

The study examined London at three levels:

- a general analysis of London governance through the development of a database of London elites in all London boroughs, major quasi- and non-governmental organisations with over 2500 entries;
- a detailed study of eight London boroughs with distinctive regimes;
- a detailed study of eight metropolitan-wide strategic issues.

The study developed a new set of theoretical models including:

- the institutional rational-choice incentive approach to the study of community power;
- the development of the bureau-shaping analysis and its first application to the changing forms of British local government;
- the development and use of regime theory and network analysis;
- a new approach to the study of collective consumption;
- the refinement of 'reputational' analysis;
- the examination of the ways in which the above are conceptually and empirically 'gendered' in London's urban bureaucracies (in cooperation with the sister project, Gender and the New Urban Governance, directed by Professor Joni Lovenduski).

The study used a multiple set of complementary methods:

- the development of the database used online media sources to generate an 'outsiders' view of the power elite, as well as primary written sources, reports, published information and information gleaned from elite interviews;

and, for the eight metropolitan-wide issues:

- Semi-structured interviewing of key actors in the eight London boroughs (81 interviewed), organisations involved in the eight metro-wide issues (48 interviewed), and small set of central elites (20 interviewed). The total number of people interviewed was 140. As several people were interviewed under 'two hats', the total number interviewed is lower than the sum of those interviewed under the three headings.
- budgetary analysis of seven of the eight boroughs (it proved impossible to analyse Wandsworth from the information given to the team);
- examination of documents and primary published sources;
- use of online media methods systematically to glean information for the relevant time period for the eight boroughs and eight metropolitan-wide issues;
- computer-generated network analysis using insider and outsider sources for the eight metropolitan-wide issues.

6 Local Governance in the Shadow of Juridification

Davina Cooper

The period from the mid-1980s until early 1990s has been characterised as one where law played a more forceful role in local government. Both local authorities and other actors became more aware of
the legal context in which they were acting and central government
became more willing to use law to impose its will on local authorities.
The term juridification has been used to describe this process
(Loughlin, 1989).

It is often assumed that juridification causes actors to grant law a
more prominent role, but this does not tell us what that role is, nor
does it recognise law's capacity to hide its own power. In this
chapter, I wish to explore the complex, contradictory nature of
legal consciousness-how law is understood, utilised, and responded
to by local government actors-within a context of juridification. In
my discussion, six overlapping images of law stand out: (a) a colonising force; (b) a game; (c) a facilitator/resource; (d) a discourse; (e)
an environmental nuisance; and (f) a means of conflict resolution/
expresser of social consensus.

Six images of law

Colonising force

> [Our council] is exhausted by legislation. As a tool to dismantle
> local government, it's produced a bunker town hall. Because we
> can't do what communities want, it's led to a defensive atmo-
> sphere...*Legislation has led to the emasculation of local politics.*
> [Labour councillor, North London, Labour administration]

Municipal actors' depiction of law as colonising expresses a dominant narrative of juridification. The image of law as a powerful,

external force, increasingly displacing more domestic forms of organisation and regulation became almost a truism within local government during the late 1980s. Law as a colonising force merges two ideas: first, law as a foreign entity, with alien methods and goals, that imposes itself on a distant locale, changing the latter's character in accordance with its own principles (Teubner, 1987). Second, law functions as the coloniser's tool – a means of promoting policies decided upon elsewhere (see generally Sarat and Kearns, 1993, pp. 24–6). Thus, instead of law itself exercising agency to promote its own agenda, it functions as a mechanism through which others maintain control and pursue their goals.

Actors I interviewed drew on both sets of images. Identifying law instrumentally, they emphasised the importance of new rules which reduced local discretion in line with conservative central government dictats. At the same time, law itself became reified – as a gaze that rendered bare all within its path, a truth only temporarily evaded. Indeed, initial avoidance law would simply unleash an escalating series of judgments against the municipal penitent. Law was also hailed as generating more subjective effects. While consciousness of this differed, several interviewees claimed law incited them to action through its ever increasing demands. One primary school teacher described being wound past breaking point as a result of the requirements of the Education (Schools) Act 1992 for new, intensive, external inspections coming on top of earlier education law:

> It's a very daunting process that within the next couple of years we shall have [an inspection], and there's absolutely no doubt they will hit us hard in very many areas [where we aren't complying with the law]...So part of you says, 'Well we must at least make an effort', the other part of you says, 'Oh, sod it'...because you can only do so much. This is in the context that everyone is working very hard, and really pulling out the stops. Teachers work very, very hard, and we can't do everything. We're producing policies. Writing policies is hard going. We're producing them as fast as we can...and legally you've got to do these policies, you've got to have a policy on everything....[Primary school teacher, West Midlands]

The depiction of law as colonising local government is often associated with a left critique. Surprising political consensus existed on this point, however. The main line of divergence concerned its normative and strategic implications. Conservative local politicians tended to perceive colonisation as *necessary* during the 1980s to control 'extreme' Labour politicians: 'it's frustrating that the only good things that happen in terms of running the council properly are done in response to government legislation' [Conservative Group Leader, North London, Labour administration]. Labour moderates and some officers, in contrast, voiced their dissatisfaction with the extent and substance of legal regulation, yet saw no alternative to compliance. A West Yorkshire mayor declared, 'We can slow down the process, but we can't totally ignore the law. We are bound to operate within the legal framework whether we like it or not'. In adopting this approach, Labour moderates focused their critique on the identity of those making law rather than on law itself. Indeed, they saw the colonising capacity of law as an important tool in the hands of a future Labour government.

Pitted against them, left-wing Labour councillors and union activists drew on colonisation rhetoric to argue for non-compliance and defiance; to the problem of legal content, they posed the solution of (resisting) legal form. Deploying discourses of local democracy, they argued law had overstepped the mark, thus forfeiting its right to be obeyed. Their opponents argued this position both fetishised law and contradicted the interests of a Labour government. Yet, such attempts to arrive at generalisable conclusions missed the highly situated nature of the left's response, which for the most part did not pathologise 'law in general', but rather the particularistic character of 'capitalist law'.

Law as a game

> Law is a double-edged sword. If you've got confidence and ingenuity, you won't beat it every time, but there's always a chance that you can, and the fear that central government has that you can. It worries them. [Ex-leader, West Midlands, Labour administration]

Images of law as a game of strategy and skill were expressed by a range of interviewees. According to one trade union official, law had replaced other methods of political contestation. Thus, juridification had not only colonised local government policy agendas, but, in addition, the very way in which local disputes were argued and settled.

Depicting law as a game decentred both normative goals and substantive legitimacy. Interviewees identified law, first, as a positive framework with rules, tactics, and positions that could be effectively deployed by a range of players (see generally Febbrajo, 1986; Ost, 1988);[1] second, as a terrain whose contingency and open texture made a range of tactical readings possible; third, as an umpire whom players would incite to speak. Law-games were not only framed in different ways, but also played according to different strategies. The London left, for instance, were criticised during the mid and late 1980s by party members for adopting a provocative, high-risk approach that teased the boundaries of legality. This was not only likely to fail, but also drew opponents' attention to the game. As one provincial Labour councillor put it, 'the point is not to let the other side know you're playing the game, or else they'll play it too'.

Nevertheless, politicians from both parties emphasised their opponents' right to compete, and the legitimacy of tactics adopted solely to win. Indeed, respect was often expressed for resourceful opponents, providing they adhered to the rules and acknowledged the outcome. Being a 'good loser' was characterised by several politicians as a crucial game norm. One Conservative councillor interviewed related his anger and subsequent revenge towards a trade union official who 'wrongly' claimed victory in an industrial dispute with the council.

In describing play, role and party politics made little difference. Political experience did affect game objectives, however. Less experienced, 'one-shot' players tended to emphasise the final win/lose outcome, whether arrived at in the court room or through internal municipal deliberations. Repeat players, on the other hand, drew attention to other, seemingly more tangential, effects, for instance, the way law-games could generate an interrogation of law itself, revealing its undemocratic nature. Publicity and delay were also identified as reasons for playing (see generally White, 1987–8; Herman, 1994):

> We took action in the High Court.... It didn't win, but it was actually very useful because I think it meant they had to hold off, and while they held off we basically sorted out most of the

problems in terms of cuts. [UNISON Branch Secretary, North London]

While juridification can be seen as generating a greater focus on law's ambiguities and possibilities, what this meant for different actors varied (see Cooper, 1997). Conservative politicians, not surprisingly, were more likely to see the law as 'fair'. Labour councillors, in contrast, tended to locate their game-playing within what they saw as the political context of colonisation. Whether playing defensively or offensively, Labour councillors and trade unionists presented themselves as engaged on a terrain skewed against them. Legalistic manoeuvres offered one, risky, tactic through which to respond to an increasingly combative and restrictive political environment.

Law as facilitator and resource

We couldn't have done what we wanted without the legislation. [Conservative councillor, West London, Conservative administration]

Law as game-playing brings to the fore a more 'positive' image than the victimology of legal colonisation. Its centring of political agency emphasises law as a resource and facilitative structure. In the legal economy generated by juridification, the value of law, as a resource, intensified. Law's value was both foundational and strategic. In identifying the former, several interviewees drew attention to law's status in enabling local government activity to take place. They drew on a conventional discourse that local government gets its powers from the state, its permission and 'goal posts' from law. To function with legitimacy local government needed to draw on its *legal* role and authority.

Yet, given the explicitly political context of local government law in the late 1980s, more strategic benefits were usually ascribed to law. Conservative councillors, for instance, described how compulsory competitive tendering legislation had facilitated their political objectives (see Ascher, 1989; Walsh, 1989). As one councillor declared, 'CCT legislation helped because it made it impossible for ... the unions to say you're just doing this because you're anti-union' [Conservative councillor, West London, Conservative administration]. Statutory validation provided a green light, enabling councils to outpace the legislation and shake up established interests and hierarchies. It facilitated major organisational and cultural changes that would have been hard to push through simply as local policy development.

Not only Conservative politicians described legislation as resourceful. Labour councillors too drew on legislation for legitimacy, albeit often older statutes, such as the Race Relations and Sex Discrimination Acts. This use of law highlights the multi-layered character of juridification. Law's increased normative importance to demonstrating responsible government led progressive actors to seek legal justification. Yet, the legislation relied on largely did not emanate from central government's juridificatory agenda. Nevertheless, post-1979 legislation was used tactically by Labour authorities in some instances; on such occasions, they, like Conservative councils, deployed statutory interpretation as a gate--keeping technique to resist the incursion of more marginal actors onto the municipal stage.[2]

In discussing law as a resource, officers and boundary actors highlighted the capacity of law to bestow power, confidence and status on those who understood it. Juridification's gaze did not simply colonise, but offered visibility and illumination. In the field of education, several teaching advisors/inspectors identified this benefit to regulatory law:

> I think [the Education (No. 2) Act 1986] is important because it commits schools to thinking about sex education, which is important, and by making it law, one assumes that it means it has importance. [Health Education Coordinator, North London, Labour administration]

Legislation put sex education 'on the map', bestowing formal status and inclusion on a previously marginal discipline. Despite professional ambivalence regarding the content of much late 1980s legislation, the health coordinator and other educators I interviewed, perceived themselves as able to pick and choose. Law's capacity to dictate was mediated by their capacity to exercise professional judgement:

> Some schools were a bit concerned about [moral values and family life within the Education (No. 2) Act 1986]. . . . I tried to

steer them away, to say, 'Well look, it's just about what you want it to be about. So don't get caught up in making assumptions about what [the government] wants our lives to be'. [Health Education Coordinator, North London, Labour administration]

Within the wider socio-legal and theoretical literature, law's resourcefulness is often closely linked to rights (see Fudge and Glasbeek, 1992; Herman, 1994; Bakan, 1995). In the interviews I conducted, however, empowerment from pursuing rights claims received little attention. Reflecting a, perhaps characteristically, British perspective, rights were identified as the *effect* of government reforms rather than their cause. Conservative interviewees, for instance, highlighted the way government legislation had empowered boundary actors, such as school parents. Yet, such empowerment remained contingent on, and contained by, government policy. Thus, the very process of bestowal emphasised the reliance and dependency of local actors on public decision-making.

Law as knowledge/discourse

One of the effects often associated with juridification is the profusion of legal discourse as legal concepts and actors come to dominate, and legal knowledge becomes an increasingly valuable commodity. In the context of British local government, perceptions of law as knowledge took different forms. For instance, while some politicians and officers perceived law as a state truth to be uncovered, others described law's meaning as contingent and fluid. The dominance of this second perspective, particularly in relation to financial legislation, problematises the notion that juridification strengthens municipal legal hierarchies. Whilst the increased prominence of law might be expected to empower council lawyers, most interviewees identified the effects as more complex (see also Stallworthy, 1992). First, within the highly politicised, highly legalised context of central–local relations, creative, specialist, politically-nuanced advice was crucial. Leaderships consequently sought legal opinions from a range of external bodies, even minority factions sometimes obtained independent legal advice. Second, lack of confidence in municipal lawyers and an increased emphasis on legal creativity had the somewhat paradoxical effect of placing councillors – at least in their own eyes – on a more equal footing with in-house professionals. Interviews suggested that where the area of law was perceived as highly politicised and controversial, councillors and officers proved much more ready to challenge local government lawyers' advice.

The growing importance of legal knowledge also impacted upon other municipal discourses. Several actors interviewed stated they could no longer rely on common sense or professional knowledge to carry out their work. As one London headteacher put it, 'in learning to be a head, the law is crucial, especially in relations with teachers'. Yet, such incorporation, particularly given law's constant modifications, did not offer coherence. As a result, professional practice required repeated 'grazing' of legal norms and technicalities: 'Before, we knew what we could and couldn't do; now we always have to check' [Senior Education Officer, West London, Conservative administration].

Yet, any easy assumption of legal discourse's increased prominence also needs interrogating, and with it the relationship between legal discourse and juridification. First, several interviewees queried the extent of law's permeation, claiming the language and concepts of finance and accounting had become far more integral to the character of restructuring, and to the depiction of municipal problems and solutions (see also Radford, 1991; Stallworthy, 1992; Cochrane, 1994, pp. 147–9). Yet, even if this is a convincing picture of municipal discourse, it does not necessarily indicate an absence of juridification; rather, it gives flesh to law's increased importance. In other words, the character of juridification, in this instance, centred on financial legislation as a governing technique.

Second, there is a problem in assuming a shared understanding of legal discourse. Several interviewees queried what I meant, perceiving elements, such as contract – treated by lawyers as paradigmatically legal – quite differently. Within the shifting discourse of local government, interviewees associated contract with bargaining, autonomy, and lateral accountability (see also Arrowsmith, 1990; Vincent Jones, 1994); a way of *facilitating* relationships in a context of formal division. Legal frameworks were associated, in contrast, with coercion, hierarchy, relationship breakdown and conflict.

Third, law was not only seen as colonising other discourses; it was also described as something that itself could be colonised by the norms and imperatives of competing disciplines. Law's vulnerability to capture was explicitly expressed by one Conservative housing chair. He described how he and his chief officer attempted to monopolise implementation of particular provisions in order to stop social services' more liberal interpretation.

Law as an environmental nuisance

> The bulk of local government activity has been unaffected by legal change. [Local government] is so vast, it would take several lifetimes to get around to doing it all. [Conservative councillor, West Yorkshire, Labour administration]

So far I have focused on those forms of legal consciousness which appear to confirm or at least not challenge the juridification thesis. More controversial are those perceptions which deny law's (increased) centrality. Clearly, these can also be seen as an effect of juridification. Indeed, we might argue that certain forms of juridification are effective *because* their naturalised status renders them invisible. At the same time, disputation of the juridification thesis should be taken seriously on its own terms. If participants do not perceive law as particularly central, maybe they are offering a useful antidote to an overestimation of law's power and importance.

Amongst interviewees, rejection of juridification tended to take one of three forms. First, several older Conservative and Labour councillors argued that law's role had not suddenly intensified. They drew attention instead to historical continuities, claiming central government under Labour in the late 1960s and 1970s had deployed law in similar ways. The second form of rejection entailed a political refusal to give law importance within the policy implementation process. As one left-wing councillor I interviewed declared, '[When I started] law didn't mean much and still doesn't. We have a healthy antipathy. Law's an obstacle or pain' [Labour councillor, North London, Labour administration]. For officers and boundary actors, unpopular or troublesome law could be ignored because the power to compel compliance was absent. Areas of professional practice might be becoming legalised, but without adequate coercion techniques, juridification remained inconsequential.

The third rejection of juridification resonates with autopoietic theory in identifying law as an environmental nuisance. This might be seen as failed colonisation – law being unable to impose itself on its object domain. Alternatively, where successful, it can be understood as law precipitating change through irritating its object domain into action. Either way, the common features of this approach are a perception of law as marginal and external. Officers and politicians who treated law as a nuisance tended to be less ideologically orientated, identifying their own role in non-political terms. For instance, several older, back-bench Conservative councillors identified the law's nuisance value in impeding their ability to support and negotiate effectively with the private sector. In such instances, differentiation between local and central government became largely blurred. Instead, both were articulated together as part of a wider state framework whose restrictions and interventions hindered 'private' sector decisions, and the regulatory capacity of the 'free' market.

Law as conflict resolution/expresser of social consensus

One nuisance ascribed to law concerned its tendency to aggravate rather than resolve conflict. While several actors saw legal challenges as a useful way of obtaining secondary objectives (delay, publicity, etc.), there was less confidence in law's ability to settle disagreements. In one authority, where parents were challenging the council's allocation of school places on grounds of racism, several interviewees suggested the conflict would have been better resolved through municipal rather than juridical procedures. Whilst their dissatisfaction may be unsurprising given that they were officers and councillors in the challenged authority, their comments reveal a more widespread perception that the process of judicial review can structure municipal behaviour in antagonistic ways, deflecting attention from potentially more effective resolution mechanisms.

Clearly, this is not always the case. Particularly in authorities with a strong aversion to litigation, legal challenge may precipitate attempts to settle. Indeed, even in the school admissions' case, the possibility of judicial review drew attention to a problem otherwise largely ignored. At the same time, the council's desire not to lose and, thus, be construed as racist, was identified as delaying policy revisions that could be interpreted in court as acknowledging the validity of the parents' case.

Pessimism towards law, or rather adjudication, as a means of dispute settlement was principally verbalised in relation to specific incidents. In response to abstract questions about law's role and function, interviewees tended to be far more idealistic:

> The law should be the direct result of society asking questions and passing laws to protect itself.... The law is there to try and hold it all together.... Now we all break the law, I think, every day, possibly unwittingly sometimes, and there are stupid little laws that perhaps shouldn't be there, but it's a kind of embodiment of what you would like the world to be. [Conservative councillor, West Yorkshire, Labour administration]

This response by a Conservative councillor was largely echoed by Labour councillors and other municipal actors. Its general pervasiveness highlights an important finding: particular legal experiences may affect consciousness of law within a given domain, but may not necessarily impact on people's more general or abstract legal understandings which continue to be drawn from dominant, hegemonic ideologies (see Merry, 1986, pp. 253–70). Thus, while law in particular may be criticised, law in general remains largely protected.

Conclusion

In this chapter, I have examined perceptions of law amongst local government actors during the late 1980s and early 1990s. My aim has been to explore the relationship between juridification and legal consciousness. My starting point was the notion that the legal consciousness of local government actors was not principally that of powerful subjects. Despite their state location, the majority of actors I interviewed depicted their relationship to law in ways that resonate with other research on the powerless. By revealing the ways some state actors, including politicians and policy-makers, experience state law, my analysis affirms a more fragmented view of the state (see Cooper, 1995, 1998).

Second, I have contested the notion that juridification leads simply to an amplified awareness of law. Rather, I explored how juridification, embedded within, and articulated to, a range of social and institutional relations, produces varied and contradictory legal images. Loughlin (1989) argues juridification in local government in the 1980s revolved around two strands: (a) the turn to law by local and central government as other normative/conflict resolution frameworks were undermined; (b) the explicit deployment of law by central government as a means of enforcing their municipal agenda. Linked to these trajectories are two interrelated, but also competing images, of law. The first highlights law as a game of strategy and skill which all can play; the second shows law as a colonising force bent on achieving central government's will. Yet, despite their differences, both images centre on law. Juridification can, however, focus attention elsewhere onto other discourses, such as finance and accountancy. In addition, certain forms of municipal legal consciousness (e.g., law as social cohesion), while possibly affected by the juridification of public services, may principally be constituted by other, wider ideologies. Municipal actors do not live isolated lives. Their consciousness of law is thus not simply, or even primarily, shaped by their local government experience of juridification.

One of my motives in writing this chapter was to explore how municipal actors' comprehension of law impacted upon their decisions. As I have argued elsewhere, the right and centre within municipal Labour Parties mobilised legality's boundaries to constrain the range of policy options (Cooper, 1996). Despite engaging in law-games that highlighted the open, albeit skewed, nature of legal possibility, Labour moderates claimed that 'the law was the law' – a normatively closed tool of government policy. My aim in highlighting the discrepancies and contradictions between different envisionings of law is to challenge the political closure legality is often granted. Law may be a technique of state power, but it is also subject to local interpretations and responses, in other words to agency. In the legal consciousness literature, writers explore the impact of location and class on perceptions and engagements with law – a process that can reinscribe agency as an effect of social power and history. In this chapter, my focus has been on the role of political ideology. This was principally because ideology formed a major determinant in how municipal actors engaged with and understood law. However, it may also prove a less static variable opening up possibilities for municipal actors to comprehend and engage with law in different ways.

Yet, political ideology and legal consciousness are historically specific. As a result, their character during the late 1980s and early 1990s does not tell us what form they will take in the aftermath of Labour's 1997 general election victory. Yet, while not predictive, the experience of the last 15 years does generate interesting and important questions in this area: what form will future juridification take? Will the legal consciousness of local government actors change as a result? What factors, other than juridification, will explain differences in perception and engagement with law within the local government field?

Notes

1 For judicial critique of the game analogy within the local government context, see Templeman in *R. v. Secretary of State for the Environment, ex. p. Nottinghamshire County Council* [1986] AC 240, 267.

2 In one of the authorities studied, this strategy was adopted several times by the head of legal services. In one instance, provisions of the Education Reform Act 1988 were utilised to stop Humanists from becoming members of the Standing Advisory Council on Religious Education (SACRE), and, in another instance, S. 28 of the Local Government Act 1988 was used to stop a lesbian group from meeting on council premises.

About this study

The research for this chapter was part of a larger project on the impact of legal change on urban power relations, co-organised by myself and Ann Stewart. We focused on four urban unitary authorities across the country, and through interviews, council documentation and press coverage explored the impact of law on education, housing, and political relations. Our aim was to focus on the unexpected and contradictory effects emanating from statutory reforms. Our interviews were semi-structured, and conducted with approximately 100 municipal actors. These included local politicians, officers, and community activists. This chapter is a revised and shortened version of an article which appeared in the *Journal of Law and Society*, vol. 22, no. 4, December 1995.

7 Local Governance: The Assessments of Councillors, Quango Members and the Public

Bill Miller and Malcolm Dickson

Introduction

Changes in local government since 1979 have raised such serious questions of democratic accountability that even the term 'local government' has been replaced by the term 'local governance' – a change designed to emphasise the increasingly limited and constrained role of elected 'local government' councils in the much wider process of 'local governance'. Local public services had long been provided by national organisations, such as the NHS, as well as by local government councils, but increasing emphasis in the 1980s on the use of appointed boards and private companies diminished the role of elected local councils still further, and in the process diminished the role of local democracy.

Do the public care whether local services are run by private companies, appointed quango boards or elected councils? How do appointed board members differ from elected councillors – on their commitment to the locality, on their views about the proper objectives for local governance, and on the different institutional structures and mechanisms available to achieve those objectives? We shall use our own survey of the public, elected councillors and appointed board members to answer these questions.

Both elected councillors and appointed board members are part of the local governance elite. As such, they can be expected to differ from the general public. They owe their place to different processes of selection, however, so they are at least potentially rival elites within the overall structure of local governance. How do these rival local governance elites differ from each other?

It would be surprising if appointed board members did not have an unusually positive 'insiders' view of appointed boards. Whether they have a negative attitude towards elected councils is a more open question. Appointed board members may see their boards as a superior replacement for elected councils; the way of the future. On the other hand, board members may see their boards more as a useful adjunct to elected councils, useful only in limited areas where there is more need for specialist technocratic expertise than for democratic representation.

In particular, board members may see their own particular board as 'exceptional', and take a positive view of it, without a wider commitment to the general principle of appointed boards. So we shall look in detail at the opinions of two different non-elected local elites – those who had been appointed to the boards of TEC/LECs (Training and Enterprise Councils in England and Wales or Local Enterprise Companies in Scotland); and those who had been appointed to the boards of DHA/HBs (District Health Authorities in England and Wales or Health Boards in Scotland). How these two non-elected elites view each other may prove as interesting and enlightening as the way they view the old democratic elite of elected councillors.

Our CATI survey method

Right at the start, it is necessary to say something about our CATI (*C*omputer *A*ssisted *T*elephone *I*nterviewing), otherwise some entries in our tables will be incomprehensible. Each interviewer worked with a desk-top computer. The questionnaire appeared, question by question, on the computer screen. Many of our questions came with two or more variants of question wording however, and, during an interview, the computer would randomly select one form of words to put up on the screen, silently recording which form of question wording was used on that occasion, along with the respondent's answer. For example, the first question in Table 7.4 was:

Local councils like the council in [council district] generally take decisions that [represent / do not represent] the views of local people. Agree/disagree?

In this example, the actual district name was automatically inserted instead of [council district]. More important, a randomly selected half sample was asked to agree that the local council 'did represent' local views; while the other half were asked to agree that it 'did not represent' local views. No one was asked to choose between these two alternatives. In a situation where people had no strong views but tended to be generally agreeable, we might find – as we do with the public in this case – that two-thirds would agree to the proposition no matter which way round it was put. When the percentages agreeing to such directly contradictory propositions together exceed 100%, it indicates a lack of clearly formed opinions amongst the public, not an error in our table. Wherever we report findings that are based upon such randomly divided subsamples, rather than on a choice offered to all respondents, we indicate it in the table by means of an asterisk. It is a revealing way to ask questions provided we interpret the answers properly.

Identifications: with party, ideology and locality

In terms of national voting preferences, appointed board members were somewhat more Conservative, less Labour and less Liberal than elected councillors – and, of course, far less Labour than the mood of the public at the time of our survey. In terms of ideological self-images, appointed board members were far more right-wing than councillors, while the public placed themselves somewhere between councillors and board members (Table 7.1).

The findings shown in Table 7.1 do *not* suggest that appointed board members were such Thatcherite placemen as journalists and politicians on the left sometimes claimed, but they undoubtedly had a degree of Conservative and right-wing bias compared both to councillors and the public.

By every objective measure except the location of their workplace – though that is a very significant exception, however – board members were less local than the public; and TEC/LEC board members especially so (Table 7.2). Quango board members were significantly less likely than elected councillors or the public to be born in the region or the district where they now lived, to have all their relatives or friends living in the region, or to find all their shopping and leisure facilities within the district.

TABLE 7.1 Party and ideology

	Public (%)	Elected Councillors (%)	TEC/LEC Boards (%)	DHA/HB Boards (%)
Voting choice in an immediate parliamentary election:				
Conservative	25	33	44	44
Liberal Democrat	17	23	15	18
Labour	59	44	41	39
Labour lead over Conservative:	+34	+11	−3	−5
Ideological self-image:				
Left	26	33	19	19
Centre-left	22	24	18	21
Centre	14	9	17	14
Centre right	21	16	23	23
Right	17	20	24	24
Left (incl. centre-left) minus right (incl. centre-right)	+10	+21	−10	−7

Note: Votes as percentages of those who opted for one of the three main parties.

TABLE 7.2 Identification – a sense of belonging

	Public (Mean score)	Elected Councillors (Mean score)	TEC/LEC Boards (Mean score)	DHA/HB Boards (Mean score)
Strength of feeling of belonging to:				
Family	3.9	4.3	4.1	4.1
Britain	3.0	3.6	3.4	3.5
Circle of friends	2.8	2.9	2.2	2.7
Region	2.7	3.3	2.5	2.6
Home neighbourhood	2.3	3.9	2.5	2.5
District	2.0	3.7	2.3	2.3
Birthplace	1.8	1.9	1.1	0.9
A social class	1.0	1.1	−0.1	0.4
Work neighbourhood	0.5	2.1	1.8	1.5
Europe	−0.1	1.2	1.3	1.0
A religion	−0.2	0.4	−0.6	0.4
A political party	−0.4	3.3	−0.9	−0.4

Note: All scores measured on a scale from minus 5 to plus 5.

Board members, councillors and the public were very similar to each other in terms of their strength of identification with family, friends and religion. Board members identified less than councillors with local areas, however – their region, their work neighbourhood, their birthplace, and especially their district and their home neighbourhood. In addition, board members identified much less than councillors with a social class or a political party.

The proper objectives of local governance

Appointed board members differed relatively little from elected councillors or the general public in their support for local government provision of special services for the needy, or even on the provision of universal services. Board members were noticeably more favourable than elected councillors towards the provision of extra chargeable services, however, though still not so favourable as the public. TEC/LEC board members, in particular, were 17% more favourable than councillors towards such extra services. At the same time, TEC/LEC board members were also almost as favourable to 'quality of life' subsidies as councillors, and 14% more than the general public. Despite their relatively right-wing ideology board members certainly did *not* tend towards a minimalist view on local council services.

Despite their self-confessed right-wing ideology, appointed board members were just as insistent as councillors that local services, in the abstract, should be funded mainly by taxation rather than by user-charges. When asked whether 'most local services' should be funded mainly by user-charges, local taxation, or national taxation, board members were only 5% more inclined than councillors – and 9% *less* than the public – to opt for user charges.

Boards members were as willing as the public, and almost as willing as councillors, to agree that 'local government should actively encourage local business' and not 'leave economic development to market forces'. They were slightly more favourable than the public towards local government helping to develop individuals' personalities and capabilities through participation, though far less favourable than councillors – though board members, like the public but unlike councillors, were more favourable to encouraging personal development through participation in self-management than through political campaigns.

TABLE 7. 3   A mission to mobilise

	Public (%)	Elected Councillors (%)	TEC/ LEC Boards (%)	DHA/ HB Boards (%)
Develop people's capabilities and personalities by participation:	47	72	53	56
• *in elections and political campaigns*	42	72	48	51
• *in self-management of services*	52	71	49	61
* *Set up support committees:*	51	46	34	35
• *for women's groups*	55	48	33	33
• *for racial and ethnic groups*	62	59	52	50
• *for gays and lesbians*	35	31	15	20
Encourage those in need to demand more services	78	61	56	55
Local councils should stay out of national politics	78	53	77	71

Note : * means the different versions of the question were put to randomly selected subsamples: no one was asked to choose between these options.

Board members, however were much less favourable than either the public or councillors to setting up committees to support social minorities – about 12% less favourable than councillors and 17% less than the public. Understandably, councillors were less inclined than the public to agree that 'local government should encourage those in need to demand more services'; and board members even less than councillors.

Images of local governance

Appointed members of quango boards had a somewhat less favourable image of local councils than did councillors themselves. That might be expected. Much less obviously, although their image of local councils was less favourable than the image held by elected councillors, it was still remarkably favourable: generally speaking, appointed board members held a positive, sympathetic view of local councils.

Conversely, appointed members of quango boards also held relatively favourable images of their own boards. Again that might be expected. Again, however, there was a rather less obvious qualification: appointed board members held considerably less favourable images of quango boards other than their own.

Representation and responsiveness (Table 7.4) of local councils

By margins of two or three to one, board members thought local council decisions did represent the views of local people. That was less than the margin of four to one amongst councillors, but quite different from the public, who were as likely to claim that council decisions were *un*representative as that they were representative.

Board members were almost identical to councillors in terms of personal efficacy – their feeling that the people they met in everyday life generally took account of their views and opinions – and their

TABLE 7.4　Representation and responsiveness

	Public (%)	Elected Councillors (%)	TEC/LEC Boards (%)	DHA/HB Boards (%)
*Local councils like the council in [council] generally take decisions				
• *that represent the views of local people*	60	85	71	61
• *that do not represent the views of local people*	66	19	26	35
People I meet in everyday life generally take account of my views	68	89	91	85
The local council doesn't care about the views of people like me	41	8	8	16
The local health authority doesn't care about the views of people like me	46	46	22	4
The local enterprise company doesn't care about the views of people like me	48	24	7	28
The local police force doesn't care about the views of people like me	26	14	12	7

Note: * means the different versions of the question were put to randomly selected subsamples: no one was asked to chose between these options.

TABLE 7.5   Too much or too little influence?

	Public (%)	% = % 'too much' minus % 'too little' Elected Councillors (%)	TEC/LEC Boards (%)	DHA/HB Boards (%)
Central government	54	74	65	64
Senior local government officials	35	31	24	39
Elected councillors	3	−36	−1	5
Women's groups	−49	−28	−24	−22
Ordinary council workers	−63	−37	−27	−32
Racial and ethnic groups	−30	−31	−29	−32
Those who pay most in local taxes	−32	−20	−32	−30
Those who vote in local elections	−60	−43	−46	−48
Local businessmen	−10	−17	−49	−35

Note: Although the question only asked whether each group had 'too much or too little influence', large numbers of respondents replied 'neither too much nor too little – about right', or words to that effect. Excluding the question about central government, on which opinion was more one-sided, the numbers replying 'neither' ranged from 21% to 32% amongst the public; from 45% to 68% amongst councillors; and from 38% to 68% amongst appointed board members. Consequently, in this table, we have not excluded such answers from our calculation of percentages, and report the difference between the 'too much' and 'too little' percentages, calculated as percentages of all three responses – 'too much', 'too little' and 'neither'.

views about the extent to which the local council or the local police took account of their views closely mirrored the views of councillors themselves. Both felt much more self-confident and respected than the public.

Councillors and board members parted company, however, when asked whether quango boards, such as the local health authority or the local enterprise company, cared about their views. They distinguished very sharply between TEC/LEC and DHA/HB boards. It is particularly illuminating to compare the views of board members towards other boards, with their views about their local council. Let us take TEC/LEC board members first: 22% of them alleged that the local health authority did not care, but only 8% that the local council did not care. Conversely, 28% of the DHA/HB board members alleged that the local enterprise company did not care, but only 16% that the local council did not care. So members of each appointed board were more critical of the other appointed board than they were of the elected council. There was no community of interest or ideology between members of different appointed boards in this respect: their own board excepted, they each held a significantly more favourable image of *elected* than *appointed* local governance.

Special interests (Table 7.5)

When asked which groups had too much or too little influence on decisions about local services, the pattern of board members opinions were remarkably close to those of elected councillors – with only two obvious exceptions. Board members, unlike councillors, did *not* think councillors had too little influence. Conversely, board members complained more than councillors about local businessmen's lack of influence – though even councillors agreed local businessmen had too little influence. Board members, like councillors, were most critical of central government's excessive influence and of local voters' lack of influence.

Self-interest (Table 7.6)

Compared to councillors, board members were more critical of self-interested councillors and less critical of self-interested board members. By itself that is hardly surprising. What is far more surprising is the extent to which councillors and board members held positive attitudes about each other. The mutual sympathy was not perfectly symmetrical, but it was impressive nonetheless. Over 90% of board members agreed that councillors had the 'good of the community at heart' and were motivated by 'a sense of duty towards their fellow citizens'; and only 30% of board members agreed that councillors were motivated by a desire for prestige, much less that they were 'in it for personal gain'. Conversely, only around a quarter of councillors made such criticisms of appointed board members, and around two-thirds of councillors agreed that board members had 'the good of the community at heart' or were motivated by a 'sense of duty'. Councillors were no more critical of board members, but somewhat less positive about board members than vice versa.

Though a majority of appointed board members refused to accept that local councils were any more or less corrupt than private business, those that would discriminate felt, by a margin of around

TABLE 7.6 Self-interest

	Public (%)	Elected Councillors (%)	TEC/LEC Boards (%)	DHA/HB Boards (%)
* *Local councillors:*				
• *have the good of the community at heart*	79	98	90	90
• *are in it for personal gain*	42	7	15	21
• *have a sense of duty towards their fellow citizens*	80	96	93	92
• *just want people to look up to them*	44	13	33	27
* *People appointed to DHA/ HBs:*				
• *have the good of the community at heart*	66	69	87	97
• *are in it for personal gain*	31	32	11	3
• *have a sense of duty towards their fellow citizens*	73	67	83	98
• *just want people to look up to them*	31	25	18	5
* *People appointed to TEC/ LECs............*				
• *have the good of the community at heart*	73	70	93	81
• *are in it for personal gain*	41	22	3	17
• *have a sense of duty towards their fellow citizens*	70	66	94	78
• *just want people to look up to them*	37	23	9	16

Note: * means the different versions of the question were put to randomly selected subsamples: no one was asked to chose between these options.

22%, that local councils were *less* corrupt than private business. Indeed, amongst the business-orientated TEC/LEC boards the margin was 28%; amongst the public it was only 16%.

Efficiency and waste (Table 7.7)

Appointed board members were far more critical of *waste* by central government than by local councils, but, compared to councillors, they were much more critical of council waste, and slightly less critical of central government.

TABLE 7.7   Efficiency

	Public (%)	Elected Councillors (%)	TEC/LEC Boards (%)	DHA/HB Boards (%)
* *Parliament and the government waste a good deal of taxpayers' money*	92	77	76	67
* *The council in [council] waste a good deal of taxpayers, money*	61	17	29	46
* *Local councils like the council in [council]:*				
• *are generally more efficient than private businesses*	22	43	10	9
• *are generally less efficient than private businesses*	66	29	65	69
* *Local councillors:*				
• *are good at organising things*	57	82	34	40
• *are not very good at organising things*	45	16	55	47
* *People appointed to DHA/HBs:*				
• *are good at organising things*	55	52	56	84
• *are not very good at organising things*	50	50	35	13
* *People appointed to TEC/ LECs:*				
• *are good at organising things*	69	56	89	75
• *are not very good at organising things*	38	37	8	35

Note: * means the different versions of the question were put to randomly selected subsamples: no one was asked to chose between these options.

Board members differed sharply from councillors in their perception of the relative *efficiency* of local councils and private businesses. By a margin of almost 60%, board members thought councils less efficient than private business, while councillors thought the exact opposite by a margin of 14%.

There were similar differences in perceptions of whether councillors and appointed board members were 'good' rather than 'not very good' at organising things. By a margin of 66%, councillors thought their fellow councillors were 'good' at organisation; but by a margin of 21%, TEC/LEC boards thought councillors were 'not very good' at organisation, and DHA/HB boards agreed with them, though by a smaller margin. Conversely, by a margin of about 56%, board members thought their fellow board members were 'good' at organisation; and while councillors did agree with them, it was only by a small margin of 11%.

Institutional preferences

Central versus *local control* (Table 7.8)

Board members were about 17% less willing than councillors or the public to back local government in a confrontation with central government; and they were also a little more inclined than councillors (and much more inclined than the public) to opt for 'national government inspectors' as the best way to ensure proper standards in local services. They were scarcely any more willing than councillors,

TABLE 7.8   **Local versus central control?**

	Public (%)	Elected Councillors (%)	TEC/LEC Boards (%)	DHA/HB Boards (%)
Local rather than central government should have the final say	86	84	66	70
Best way to ensure proper standards in local services:				
• *National government inspectors*	39	59	64	66
• *Voter power in local elections*	32	30	22	23
• *Go to court and claim compensation*	29	11	14	11
* *Proper rights for local minorities:*				
• *to campaign against the decision at the next local election*	83	95	95	95
• *to appeal to central govt to over-rule the local council*	54	64	64	68

Note: * both these propositions were put to the entire sample.

however, to accept that it was 'right and proper' for the minority in a district to appeal to central government over the head of their local council. Overall, the similarity between board members and elected councillors in their attitudes towards central control of local government was more striking than the differences.

Popular control (Table 7.9)

Board members' support for mechanisms to give the public more direct say in politics was at least consistent, albeit weak – that of the public was consistently strong. The position of elected councillors was inconsistent and paradoxical: they were at least weakly favourable on balance towards referenda, but deeply opposed to directly elected council leaders.

TABLE 7.9   Populism

	Public (%)	Elected Councillors (%)	TEC/LEC Boards (%)	DHA/HB Boards (%)
* *Support referenda:*	65	51	43	50
• *in national politics*	69	58	45	51
• *in local politics*	61	45	40	48
Council leader should be				
directly elected	78	18	38	37

Note: * means the different versions of the question were put to randomly selected subsamples: no one was asked to chose between these options.

Rating rival institutions of local governance (Table 7.10)

There were some sharp differences between board members and councillors on the best institutions for running local services. Board members, especially DHA/HB members, were much more favourable than councillors to single-purpose, specialist bodies rather than multi-purpose authorities. On this, the preferences of board members reflected their personal situation to a degree that the preferences of councillors did not. Board members were also much more inclined than councillors – though much less than the public – to agree that it 'really does not matter whether local services are run by elected councils, appointed boards or private businesses as long as they keep the quality up while keeping charges and taxes down'.

TABLE 7.10 Best form of control?

	Public (%)	Elected Councillors (%)	TEC/LEC Boards (%)	DHA/HB Boards (%)
Does not matter who runs local services if quality is right	70	28	51	43
All-purpose local authorities are better than specialist bodies	30	53	34	21
	Mean score on +/-5 scale	Mean score on +/-5 scale	Mean score on +/-5 scale	Mean score on +/-5 scale
Best way to organise and control local services:				
• *Elected council*	2.6	4.1	2.9	2.9
• *Providers, e.g. teachers running schools*	0.7	−1.1	−1.5	−1.2
• *Users, e.g. parents running schools*	0.1	−0.1	−0.1	−0.3
• *Experts appointed by central government*	−0.1	−2.3	−1.0	−0.3
• *Businessmen appointed by central government*	−0.5	−2.3	−0.7	−1.2
• *Private companies charging for use of service*	−0.8	−2.0	−0.6	−0.9

When asked directly to rate various alternative ways of organising and controlling local services, however, there was a remarkable degree of support even amongst *appointed* board members for *electorally* based methods of control. Both TEC/LEC and DHA/HB board members rated elected councils as the best; and both gave negative ratings to all other forms of organisation. It is interesting to compare the ratings given to elected councils and appointed boards. On the plus/minus 5 scale, board members rated elected councils 3.8 points higher than appointed boards – less of a margin than amongst councillors who rated elected councils 6.4 points higher than appointed boards, but more of a margin than amongst the public who only rated elected councils 2.9 points higher than appointed boards.

Across all sections of the public, elected local councils were universally seen as the best way to organise local services. Support for elected local councils failed to correlate either with local identity or ideology because even those with a weak sense of local identity or a right-wing ideology still gave elected councils very high marks as a way of organising and controlling local services. Right-wingers were clearly more inclined than left-wingers to give higher ratings to private companies and quangos run by 'businessmen'; people with a strong sense of local identity were more inclined than others to give higher ratings to self-management by local service-users and service-providers; but they all still gave by far the highest ratings to elected councils.

This combination of findings suggests that the essential appeal of elected local government councils may be that they were *elected*, rather than that they were *local*, or that they represented more or less *government* intervention. That is, support for elected local government councils was based upon a pervasive public commitment to democratic procedures that was relatively unaffected by localism or left-right ideology.

There was clearly an element of complacent self-satisfaction about the fact that councillors rated elected councils so highly. It might be argued that the general public's support for elected local councils was merely an expression of their ignorance, or conservatism (with a small 'c'). But that argument cannot explain the views of quango board members: they rated elected councils even more highly than the public; they rated their own kind of quango slightly lower than the public; and they rated other quangos far lower than the public. Appointed board members might be accused of many things but they could not be accused of ignorance about the alternatives to elected councils, or a timidly conservative disposition to avoid them.

Monitoring quangos (Table 7.11)

For members of appointed boards, the issue of whether quangos should be monitored and, if so, by whom, came very close to home. When we focused upon non-elected bodies like Health Authorities (boards in Scotland), NHS Trusts, Training and Enterprise Councils (Local Enterprise Companies in Scotland) and School Boards, appointed board members were only around 10% more inclined than councillors to say they should be left to run their own affairs. They differed sharply from councillors in their views about the

TABLE 7.11   Monitoring quango boards

	Public (%)	Elected Councillors (%)	TEC/LEC Boards (%)	DHA/HB Boards (%)
Non-elected bodies like Health authorities, NHS Trusts, TEC/LECs and School boards should:				
• *be responsible to central government*	20	18	42	55
• *be responsible to local councils*	68	76	39	34
• *decide their own affairs, like private companies*	12	6	19	11
Local councils should:				
• *have powers to control these non-elected bodies*	26	38	14	12
• *have power to investigate, but not control them*	57	51	44	42
• *leave them to get on with managing their own affairs*	18	10	42	46

proper line of responsibility, however: 76% of councillors, but only 37% of board members said these non-elected bodies should be responsible to local councils; while only 18% of councillors, but 42% of TEC/LEC board members and 55% of DHA/HB members said these bodies should be responsible to central government. The public sided with the councillors.

When we put the question in a different way, focusing upon the powers of local councils to investigate and/or control appointed boards, we again found board members very resistant to local council control – so much so that 44% of them now said that appointed boards should be left to manage their own affairs, compared to 18% of the public and 10% of councillors. Of course, they were no longer offered the option of submitting to central government control this time.

Elected regional assemblies (Table 7.12)

DHA/HB members were the least inclined to support the idea of elected regional assemblies, yet the most inclined to complain that

TABLE 7.12   Regions and districts

	Public (%)	Elected Councillors (%)	TEC/LEC Boards (%)	DHA/HB Boards (%)
District council area:				
• *too big*	18	4	7	3
• *too small*	38	53	57	63
Elected assembly for [your region]				
• *support (unconditionally)*	56	57	51	37
• *support, if locals want it*	4	3	2	1
• *oppose*	40	40	47	62

the area represented by their district council was too small for effective provision of public services. Perhaps they feared – probably rightly – that elected regional assemblies would either take over health authority functions or at least insist on monitoring them.

In our survey, both the public and elected councillors in Scotland, Wales and London were particularly favourable to the concept of an elected assembly for their own region. Inevitably, these regional subsamples were relatively small. Nonetheless, we did find a remarkable degree of support amongst quango board members in London for an elected London authority – more even than amongst Scottish and Welsh board members for elected Scottish and Welsh Assemblies.

Conclusions

To a remarkable and surprising extent, the views of the non-elected local governance elites were similar to those of elected councillors; but not in everything. Moreover, the views of those appointed to one kind of quango differed from those appointed to another.

What made non-elected elites different from elected councillors, insofar as they were different at all? They had far less objective connections to their locality. They were far less likely to be long-term local residents than elected councillors; far less likely to have all their relatives or friends living locally. Psychologically, too, they were far less local. In particular, the non-elected elite identified much less than councillors with their region, their district or their home neighbourhood – though almost as much with their work neighbourhood. They were much less inclined than councillors to see participation in local government as a means of developing citizens' capabilities and personalities, and, insofar as they recognised this possibility, they emphasised participation in self-management rather than in elections and political campaigns, while councillors gave equal weight to both.

Appointed board members were also much more likely than councillors to claim that councils did not take enough account of business interests or that local businessmen had too little influence over local services – though councillors, on balance, agreed with these criticisms, if to a lesser extent. Board members were twice as likely as councillors to allege that councils were inefficient – though councillors, on balance, agreed with that too.

Conversely, councillors were far more likely than appointed board members to say that councillors themselves had too little influence on local services. They were twice as likely as board members to claim that councils were less corrupt than private business – though board members, on balance, agreed with them.

Appointed board members were largely willing to accept that boards should be monitored in some way, but much less willing than councillors to advocate monitoring by the local council, still less control by the local council. Faced with the option of varying the degree of local council control, with no mention of direct responsibility to central government, almost half the appointed board members were inclined to demand freedom from monitoring or control of any kind, while 90% of councillors demanded local council monitoring of some kind.

There was an imbalance between the opinions of councillors about appointed boards and the opinions of board members about councillors. Councillors were more likely to claim that board members ignored their views, than vice versa; and more likely to criticise board members for being out for personal gain, than vice versa. Councillors were less likely to trust members of appointed boards than vice versa. Most significant of all, the non-elected elite joined councillors in rating elected local councils as by far the best way to organise and control local services, while councillors rated private companies and appointed boards as by far the worst – and appointed quango boards even worse than private companies!

There is also evidence that the elite defended the very particular institution in which they themselves served: thus, for example, councillors were the most likely to claim that their fellow councillors were good organisers, TEC/LEC board members were the most likely to make that claim about TEC/LEC boards, and DHA/HB board members about DHA/HB boards. Elected councillors rated their fellow councillors as the most effective channel of protest for citizens' individual or collective grievances; but the non-elected elite did not agree. Councillors gave top marks to fellow councillors for trustworthiness, TEC/LEC board members to their colleagues on TEC/LEC boards, and DHA/HB board members to their colleagues on DHA/HB boards.

There was surprisingly little community of respect between the members of different boards, however. Far more members of TEC/LEC and DHA/HB boards alleged that members of the other board did not care about their views, than made the same criticism of elected councils. TEC/LEC and DHA/HB board members rated the trustworthiness of people on their own kind of board much higher than that of councillors, but they rated the trustworthiness of people on the other kind of board at about the same level as that of councillors. When they came to rate alternative institutions as the best way to organise and control local services it was noticeable that, although both TEC/LEC and DHA/HB boards put elected councils far above all other institutions, and gave negative ratings to appointed boards of all kinds, TEC/LEC board members rated boards of 'experts' even lower than boards of 'businessmen', while DHA/HB members rated boards of 'businessmen' even lower than boards of 'experts'. It is difficult not to see that as a reflection of each board's own composition and self-image.

Whatever their partisanship, their left/right ideology, their commitment to efficiency, or their service in an institution of non-elected local governance, members of quango boards remained committed to the principle of elective democracy in local as well as national politics – indeed, more so than the public. The non-elected elite might perhaps be more committed to elective democracy in principle than in practice, some time other than now, some place other than in their own backyard. They were reluctant to submit to monitoring and control by elected local councils, and DHA/HB members were distinctively opposed to setting up elected regional assemblies which would, no doubt, want some role in the control of the Health Service. Nonetheless, although appointed board members had a star role in the system of non-elected local governance, they remained committed in principle to the general concept of local democracy. That principle requires them to accept either direct or indirect local electoral control of local quangos – monitoring by elected local councils, monitoring or control by elected regional assemblies, or direct election to the boards of the quangos themselves.

The public, too, are generally supportive of the principle of local democracy, yet they remain willing to support provision through specialist bodies, appointed boards and even private companies as long as service standards are high. They have a fairly jaundiced view of the way local democracy works at the moment and give strong support to measures to increase the direct say of people in decision-making.

About this study

During 1994 and 1995 we interviewed 2200 members of the public, 794 elected councillors, and 899 appointed members of quango boards – 570 members of TEC/LEC boards, and 329 members of DHA/HB boards. All our samples were spread throughout Britain. All the interviews were done by telephone, using our own system of CATI (Computer Assisted Telephone Interviewing).

8 The Changing Nature of Local Labour Politics

Declan Hall and Steve Leach

Introduction: the Labour Party and local democracy

One of the consequences of the overwhelming victory of the Labour Party in the May 1997 general election is that for the first time since the mid-1970s (and then only briefly) there is a congruence of party dominance at national and local government levels. Labour dominates the world of British local government in which it controls on a majority basis 43% of the 430 local authorities (including 90% of metropolitan districts, 60% of London boroughs, and 43% of shire districts, where traditionally the Conservative Party has been dominant). In the 33% of authorities which are currently hung, there is a predominance of Labour/Liberal Democrat cooperative arrangements, whether formal or informal. Thus, the true extent of Labour dominance of the world of British local government becomes apparent when it is realised that they control, or share the control of about three-quarters of all local authorities.

That situation is, of course, likely to change over time. However, the fragmented sequential pattern of local elections means that any decline is likely to be gradual rather than spectacular; over 2–3 years at least. For that length of time, at least, the quality of central–local relations is likely to be transformed.

Since the early 1980s, the quality of central–local relations has been marked by misunderstanding, mistrust and overt conflict, reflecting the difference in party dominance and ideology at central and local government levels, particularly during the Thatcher era. In the new situation, there is an unprecedented opportunity for a new style of central–local politics, emphasising a genuine sense of partnership based on shared values, the re-opening of atrophied communication channels, and the wealth of local government experience to be found within the Parliamentary Labour Party (of which around 40% have relatively recent experience as local councillors).

150

This new world of central–local relations raises some interesting questions about two key areas of concern in the authors' ESRC research project 'Changing Forms of Local Politics': How is the pattern of influence of local Labour parties on Labour Party groups in local authorities likely to change, now that Labour is in power nationally? How is the relationship between the national party and local party networks (including party groups on council) likely to change?

The national Labour Party may wish to influence – or, in extremis, control – the activities of a local council party group for two primary reasons: policy and procedure. In relation to procedure, apart from with the various minor disciplinary disputes which occur from time to time, where the regional party will normally make the judgement (or at least do the spadework), the national party will be particularly concerned about activities of local parties and groups which have broken the party rules, particularly in the context where an internal party conflict is taking place in public. In relation to policy, the national party will be concerned about party groups which are clearly flouting national policy priorities, through omission as well as commission (see Shaw, 1994). In either case, the national party will be concerned and take an interest in local parties and groups which are perceived as a embarrassment to the party, and hence as a potential influence on electoral success in a local constituency or (if the embarrassment is great enough) nationally.

In understanding intra-party relationships it is helpful to bear in mind the distinction between three concepts of democracy (and accountability) which are currently influential within the Labour Party. At the local level there is the familiar tension between *representative democracy*, which underpins the legitimacy of the party group on council, and *delegate democracy* which underpins the legitimacy of the local party to mandate the party group. Both these concepts have, however, been challenged recently by a growing interest in and commitment to *participatory democracy*, admittedly stronger within the national party than in local party networks. This view of democracy is manifested in a concern to develop a wide range of ways of involving local stakeholders, local pressure groups and local residents, through greater use of public–private sector partnerships, decentralised decision-making committees, local referenda, citizens juries, community forums and similar devices. To understand the possible pattern of changes in local Labour politics, the changing balance or emphasis within the party between these three concepts of democracy/accountability has to be appreciated.

The recent history of local Labour politics has centred around negotiations and sporadic conflict between two structural elements in the Labour Party – the party group and the local party – underpinned by two different sources of legitimacy, representative democracy and delegate democracy respectively. The different areas of responsibility are spelled out in the Labour Party rules, but there remains a good deal of scope for interpretation and manoeuvring. Occasionally, the national or regional party machinery is drawn into the local arena, either at the request of a local actor, or by a choice to intervene on the part of the centre. In making such interventions, the national party is in effect overriding the local democratic mandate with the national mandate.

Tensions within the party machinery and between different conceptions are best examined through a range of 'critical issues' in which the potential for tension between party group and wider party network exists (see Gluckman, 1940; Stoker and Brindley, 1985) Set out below are three mini-case studies which illustrate different aspects of the relationship between national party, local party and party group on council: the Dave Church saga in Walsall, the decentralisation initiative in Rochdale and the manoeuvring in connection with local government reorganisation in the Chesterfield area. There follows a more general analysis in which these and other examples are used to develop a composite picture of the balance of resources between party group, local party and national party. In the final section we return to a more speculative analysis, introduced in the previous paragraph, of possible future changes in such relationships.

Walsall: decentralisation and the heavy hand of Walworth Road

Issue

In May 1995, Labour took control of Walsall Borough Council. Moreover, due to the surprising size of the win, the left wing was able to form a broad alliance with the centre of the group and become the controlling faction. The leadership of the Labour group, under Dave Church, was committed to a policy of radical decentralisation. The previously dominant right wing of the Labour group had never felt comfortable with radical decentralisation and, over the years, had resisted the policy although it was official Walsall Labour Party policy as laid out in a succession of manifesto commitments. In this way, decentralisation became a defining issue between the left and right in Walsall Labour politics. The cleavage was between a left-wing faction controlling the group, supported by the local district, or borough party (BLP) as it is called in Walsall, wanting to implement decentralisation versus right-wing group members and a local Labour MP who were opposed to radical decentralisation proposals.

Role of borough labour party

The left in Walsall had previously used its control of the BLP to keep decentralisation on the agenda and to protect left-wing councillors from expulsion from the group when they voted against group decisions. It was able to do this because the decision to expel someone from the group is made jointly by the group and the BLP executive committee, at least as long as the national party was not involved. Ironically, although the left wing had long controlled the BLP it was unable to use the BLP to directly affect group policy. In Walsall, as elsewhere, there is little the local party can do if the group is indifferent to it, and *vice versa*. Despite the formal hierarchical structures, the Labour Party component parts are relatively free to operate within their own spheres of responsibility. It is very difficult for a dominant group faction to get rid of dissidents if the dissidents retain support in a district party and individual branches. Each are dominant within their own domain.

Role of national party

Ostensibly, the national party suspended the local party in August 1995 because of allegations of intimidation at party meetings, but in reality it was because the national party had no other means to deflect a radical policy of decentralisation (see Hall, 1996). It was the threat of negative publicity impinging on Labour's run up to the general election, rather than the policy principle, which the national party was trying to smother.

The intervention of the National Executive Committee (NEC), as the party's constitutional custodian, at the behest of the local Labour

MP, was to investigate alleged infractions of party rules and make definitive rulings on procedural issues. The MP's action shows how MPs have little formal influence over local government, however. Formally, Labour MPs are kept out of local politics by the organisational distinctiveness of having separate district (or Local Government Committee, as they are now called) and constituency Labour parties with separate responsibilities. The local MP may not have liked Walsall Labour group's decentralisation plans, but he was only able to indirectly affect local group policy by acting as an intermediary between discontented local party and group members and the national party, and the latter was only able to intervene on constitutional rather than policy grounds as local decentralisation is an accepted Labour Party policy

Herein lies the dilemma for the Labour Party. The party leadership, where it takes a view, may disapprove of policies advocated by a particular local Labour group but it has only very limited direct means of affecting what individual groups on council do, as long as the policy under question does not clearly contravene national party policy; and even where it does, such as local Labour groups forming ruling coalitions, it often chooses to ignore it. There were few options available to the national party. The most common way for the national party to get a local group to revise its policy is to consult, listen, debate, argue, apply some gentle pressure and engage in some classic behind-closed-doors wheeling and dealing. A local group, however, will only be persuaded to the extent that it wants to be or if the national party can offer a local group something it needs, like extra support in the next elections. The Dave Churchled faction of the Labour group had no reason to be persuaded to drop, or tone down at least, its decentralisation plans.

In Walsall, the national party eventually used an indirect and very blunt strategy by utilising its ultimate power in party constitutional affairs. The left-wing BLP lost its ability to act as a shield for left-wing councillors when the NEC suspended it. Thus, all Walsall BLP functions were transferred to centrally appointed West Midlands regional party staff. This simultaneously fractured the Labour group's majority on Walsall council within 4 months of it regaining control. Out of 60 seats in council, Labour had controlled 34, but by the end of August 1995 the Labour group had 19 official group members, leaving a 15-strong left-wing unofficial Labour group faction free to vote as they pleased.

The Walsall saga highlights the limitations of the national party to influence local group decision making. There are inherent problems in any attempt to impose a national blueprint upon local Labour groups and parties despite the oft perceived view that local groups operate in accordance with national rules and direction. Moreover, as the Walsall affair shows, the national party does not have the direct mechanisms to rein in local groups without resorting to the blunt, and potentially counter-productive, instrument of suspension.

Rochdale: decentralisation and the role of the DLP

Issue

When Labour took control of Rochdale council in 1986, it was based on a general commitment to empower the community, operational-ised in the form of a wide-ranging decentralisation programme. There was also a general local party commitment to the programme. There was some foot dragging, however, which developed into out-right opposition, especially among senior Labour chairs of local authority committees who felt that decentralisation was a threat to their own political interests. The latter were also supported by their chief officers who felt decentralisation posed a professional threat.

In response, the leadership formed a chair's panel which was essentially an informal cabinet to give decentralisation a high-level priority, e.g. by providing money for decentralisation in a budget, and to provide a counter resistance to the opponents of decentralisation. This eventually became a sub-committee and thus decentralisation was firmly on the council agenda. Nevertheless, the political attacks from some chairs continued and they attempted to use the local party networks to de-legitimise decentralisation as a policy. The battle over decentralisation was largely fought out in the DLP; if the opponents could get the DLP to drop its commitment to decentralisation they would have removed the legitimising stamp the DLP provided for the Labour group's policy.

The role of the DLP

The role of the DLP in Rochdale Labour politics was historically a strong one. There was an electoral college to elect the group leader, with half of the votes going to the group and the other half to the DLP. This gave the DLP an important voice in the leadership of the group. Decentralisation as a policy originated with the DLP, so it was a policy which was central to the DLP; the DLP owned it, which then made decentralisation automatically important for the leadership.

Opponents of decentralisation were unable to sway the Labour group so they used their power bases in the branches to send resolutions to the DLP attacking the group's decentralisation plans. Many in the group supported decentralisation on the urging of the group leader (usually by citing it as local party policy) and the chair of the DLP was also a councillor and vice chair of the neighbourhood services sub-committee. Both these key supporters of decentralisation were careful to make sure decentralisation commanded broad party/group support by holding joint meetings packed full of councillor delegates to ensure wider consensus on decentralisation. The resolutions, which reappeared in many various guises, were always defeated, or, alternatively, if it looked as if an anti-decentralisation resolution might not be defeated at the DLP, it would be the last item on the DLP agenda and there was never time for a discussion and a vote.

Role of other party units

There was no role for any other party unit in this particular dispute. The constituency parties (CLPs), of which there were three, had little direct input into the DLP, but when a DLP and CLP are 'co-determinous' then the CLP might have a bigger impact as the delegates are usually mostly the same people (see Wainwright, 1987). Nor was there any impact from the national party. The only role played by the national party was that it was cited by supporters of decentralisation to buttress their case for decentralisation, by arguing that decentralisation was national party policy, but, because decentralisation was never as radical as in Walsall, the national party was not involved in the conflict nor did it take any interest.

Legitimising function of the DLP

The few chairs who opposed decentralisation could never get past the DLP. As the DLP supported decentralisation it was, therefore, official local party policy and that argument was presented to the group whenever a chair tried to propose an alternative in group meetings. Although the DLP never dictated group policy, because of group/party relations decentralisation became a flagship policy of the Labour group leadership and the party. If it was defeated at the DLP it would have meant loss of face for the leadership and opened up a doorway for other group members who may have had second thoughts on how the process was developing. In this way, the DLP was a battle ground by proxy for the decentralisation debate, and proponents of the policy were able to use the local party as a reference point in group discussion.

Chesterfield: local government reorganisation and the mobilisation of local party networks

Issue

Local government reorganisation in Derbyshire, 1994–95, pitted the political interests of local Labour politicians from Chesterfield against Labour Party interests across Derbyshire. The majority of the Chesterfield Labour group supported the proposed unitary North East Derbyshire authority despite the opposition of not only the county party and county group, but also the local party and the unions. The Chesterfield group leadership saw a unitary North East Derbyshire as an opportunity to develop their political careers, while the Chesterfield-area county councillors saw such a proposition as a threat to their own political careers. The majority of the Chesterfield council Labour group were generally supportive of their leadership, although there was a hard core of resistance within the Chesterfield group who had the full backing of the local party and unions in resisting any change to the status quo.

Networks, reorganisation and political careers

In Derbyshire, the party networks and the membership of the various components of the Labour movement within the county meshed, particularly in the North East, to produce county-wide pressure on the Labour group on Chesterfield council. This is highlighted by looking at some of the key players in the party in

Chesterfield. One local Chesterfield councillor was secretary of Derbyshire UNISON, which supported the status quo; he was also vice chair of Chesterfield CLP and the DLP. Another district councillor who supported the status quo was also treasurer of the Chesterfield DLP and the CLP. In addition, the ex-DLP secretary was a county councillor and later became chair of the Chesterfield CLP. Another DLP chair through part of the period and observer to the Chesterfield Labour group was also a delegate to the County Labour Party (CoLP), which was pushing the status quo line. Thus, the local party in Chesterfield was infiltrated and dominated by activists who had close ties with the county and who saw Matlock (the centre of county government) as a political good in itself, as well as seeing that was where their political career interests lay. The DLP was largely dominated by county councillors and union activists who supported the status quo. The DLP was putting county interests first because of its strong links with the county party, and county unions.

The CoLP used its links with the Chesterfield CLP and DLP (which was largely co-determinous) as one of the ways to maintain pressure on the Chesterfield group. It was not a direct or heavy-handed pressure, as that was not necessary. The Chesterfield CLP and DLP were supporting the county-wide view in any case, so there was not a large role for the CoLP to play. The way one supporter of a unitary North East Derbyshire saw it, CoLP did not have to be conspicuously active as it 'had troops on the ground' (Interview with authors).

The overlapping networks stood out even more when looking at the political careers of the union activists. The Derbyshire UNISON secretary and Chesterfield councillor argued that the interests of the county-wide unions in Chesterfield were represented 'through me'. The local Chesterfield unions were not that active in local politics. It was the county unions and their spokespersons who most used the DLP to put pressure on the group. A pro-unitary authority councillor supported this view by arguing the position of the DLP could largely be explained by county influence: 'I think it was very much to do with the fact that we have, within the structure of the DLP, members and prominent officials of the District Party, who are employees of the County Council' (Interview with authors).

The locally-based county union spokespersons were not alone, however. Once the Chesterfield Labour group had come out in favour of a unitary authority, the county unions were active in backing-up the supporters of the status quo. The trade union liaison committee (for workplace unions at the county council) at Matlock supported the county through not only helping to swing the Confederation of Derbyshire Unions behind the status quo, but also in providing administrative support to its supporters by framing resolutions for CLPs and DLPs and by providing the arguments against unitaries in general.

Yet, as many councillors pointed out, the group could ignore the DLP if ultimately it wanted to. For a while, the majority of the Chesterfield Labour group did so as it was perceived to be in their best political interests that Chesterfield should become part of a unitary authority for reasons of increased status, power and expenditure. In particular, it was the leadership who were 'pivotal' in keeping the group in favour of unitary authorities as they were the councillors who would be the greatest beneficiaries of a new unitary authority in North East Derbyshire.

The Chesterfield DLP, however, began to threaten deselection for any district councillor who did not support the CLPs/DLPs' line, and the 'frighteners was put on them' (Interview with authors). As the County party/local party network swung into action, largely in an informal manner through, *inter alia*, telephone calls and one-to one-meetings, then the career trajectories of many of the group in Chesterfield started to change. When the wards (especially those wards with high levels of CoLP/DLP delegates) found out about the divergence between the DLP and the group then they put pressure on their councillors to support the status quo and a change in the attitude of some councillors came about through this pressure. It is at this point that many councillors came to see that their interests did not necessarily lie with a new unitary authority because of the possibility that they may not have been part of it. Although their territorial orientation may have been towards the unitary option, it suddenly became an all-or-nothing strategy and, for many, the maintenance of the status quo was the safest way to protect their political careers.

The change in preference of Chesterfield Labour group *vis-à-vis* local government reorganisation could, therefore, largely be seen as the realisation that, ultimately, their interests would not be served by a unitary North East Derbyshire authority; in fact, they could lose everything in the long run, whereas opting for the status quo at least preserved what they had. In this way, the operation of the county/union/local party network in Chesterfield can be seen to affect the career trajectories of the political activists amongst the Chesterfield Labour group. It also provides an example of the type of conditions under which a local DLP can influence group policy – if enough interests converge through party networks, (and the networks are in place), and if an issue becomes serious enough for the branches and the DLP to threaten deselection, then it is difficult for a group on council not to bow to that pressure.

Understanding intra-party relations within the Labour Party

Our case studies – and other evidence – show that the scope for effective national party action is much greater in relation to procedural than policy matters. Indeed, sometimes procedural opportunities are the only way to deal with policy aberrations; the Dave Church/Walsall saga well illustrates this point. The national party were concerned both about the 'extreme' form of decentralisation policy adopted by the Walsall Labour group and by some aspects of the way it was behaving in implementing the policy. In dealing with the 'problem', the procedural aspect was challenged rather than the policy itself, and disciplinary action – of a particularly heavy-handed nature – taken to minimise the influence of the key protagonist. In Rochdale, a few years earlier, no action was taken in relation to a similarly radical decentralisation initiative, mostly because, in that case, no coverage occurred in the national press and, therefore, the spectre of 'loony leftism', which the national party wanted to suppress, was not raised.

In relation to the Local Government Review 1991–7, it was noticeable how little action the national party took to influence party groups to follow the national party line of support for unitary authorities, or how little was done to challenge those which did not do so. The national party took action to try to limit public conflict between party groups in Cleveland, but that was an isolated example.

A further element of research looked at inter-group cooperation in hung authorities, where there has clearly been a perception that national party electoral interests are affected, showed that there has been little in the way of decisive action from the centre despite the national party issuing guidelines forbidding inter-group coalitions. We are not aware of any Labour Party group which has been prevented by Walworth Road from entering into a preferred form of co-operation by either the threat or imposition of disciplinary action (certainly since 1993). The reality is that, although formal sanctions on the behaviour of party groups are stronger in the Labour Party than in the other major parties, the influence of the centre is largely contingent upon local party group acquiescence. This contingency certainly applies to policy issues and, except where there are clear breaches of party rules, to many procedural issues also. Interestingly, this analysis would seem similar to the one postulated over 30 years ago by Bulpitt (1967, p. 97), who concluded that local politics and group policies and behaviour had not been 'nationalised' through control by party central office and the 'picture presented was one of diversity'.

In understanding the limits and circumstances of influence of district or county parties on party groups, the very different composition and climate of local parties have to be appreciated. There is a spectrum of activity, at one end of which the local party is moribund or dormant (county and metropolitan parties are particularly prone to this condition). At a somewhat higher activity rating are those local parties which, although operational, are acquiescent in relation to party group activities, often because they have become dominated by party group members. An additional case study in the research, of the Coventry District Labour Party, highlights an example of this acquiescent genre. On the only major issue on which the local party took a stand during a year's meetings – the establishment of a Coventry Labour Club – the DLP was tactically outmanoeuvred by the party group representatives (and their allies) on the District Party.

At the other end of the spectrum are those local parties which are both active and which have a policy view which differs, at least in part, from the party group view. There are two variants of this position. First, the local party and party group may behave cooperatively, debating and resolving disputes in a fraternal way (even where 'resolution' involves agreeing to differ). Alternatively, there are local parties which have become the base of a Labour Party faction which, though represented on the party groups on council, is marginalised within it. The Walsall District party/party group relationship before Dave Church was returned to power illustrated this situation, and also illustrated the fact that whilst a party group can ignore a district party with which it is in conflict in the short term, there are dangers in so doing. The influence of the district party on candidate recruitment and selection processes, means that there is always the potential for the factional view on the district (or county) party to become the majority view on the party group after the next election (a process exemplified in Manchester in the early 1980s (see Wainwright, 1987). The Rochdale case study provides an example of an active but co-operative district party, whilst the Chesterfield case study depicts a local party which was ultimately influential on a key policy outcome, despite the fact that the party group leadership was resistant to its view.

The most typical situation, on the basis of our research, is of the active/cooperative model, where there is

1. A significant overlap of membership between party group and active local party, but a strong sense of the distinctness of the two pieces of machinery;
2. An acceptance that the local party should take the lead in manifesto preparation, but with input from committee chairs into relevant manifesto working groups to ensure a sense of realism in manifesto proposals;
3. A leader who takes the local party seriously, reports back regularly, and who tries to generate local party support for, or at least acceptance of, proposals from the group on council, but who will ultimately resist pressures from the local party if it is out of line with a legitimate interpretation by the party group of its brief;
4. Considerable use of informal channels between key actors in the local party and the party leadership, and a recognition that most problems can be resolved in this way rather than by the passing of formal resolutions.

Labour and local governance: A reform agenda

As argued earlier, the recent history of local Labour politics has centred around negotiations and sporadic conflict between two structural elements in the Labour Party – the party group and the local party. The legitimacy of the former is underpinned by its representative democratic status. The legitimacy of the latter is underpinned by its delegate democracy status amongst local Labour Party members.

Both elements have caused problems for the Labour Party nationally, particularly when a general election is approaching and concerns about the potential impact of 'bad news' associated with the activities of either local party group or local party is paramount. But the Labour Party, as we have illustrated, has often found it difficult to intervene in local matters, particularly in relation to local policy.

As the Walsall example illustrates, although intervention is sometimes inspired by disagreement over *policy*, it is often the case that it is *procedural* malpractice which are used as the grounds for disciplinary action, rather than attempts to impose or restrict policy per se.

As we have also demonstrated, however, any dispute between local party and party groups on council normally takes place within a relatively closed and restricted community. Membership of the Labour Party may have increased in the mid-1990s, but there is little indication yet that this increase has been translated into a significantly greater level of local activism, of the kind that manifests itself in the affairs of local constituency, district or county parties. The conclusions we reached about levels of activism (see also Seyd and Whiteley, 1992) are likely still to be valid (cf. Game and Leach, 1996, p. 148):

> The numbers of party activists and members will vary considerably, depending on local circumstances. Typically, however, the number of political careerists – those members sufficiently committed to party activity that they are prepared to stand for local council election or local party office – may well not exceed 40–50, of which perhaps around 20 might be considered 'key influentials'.

There are, therefore, serious problems of justification and legitimacy both for Labour Party groups citing the principles of representative democracy and local parties citing the principles of delegate democracy. In the case of the former, local electoral turnout remains at an obstinately low level of under 40%, and the anomalies of the first-past-the-post electoral system contribute further to the lack of legitimacy ('one party states' in which Labour hold over 90% of the seats on less than 50% of a popular vote of under a 40% turnout have become increasingly common in recent years). In relation to delegate democracy, it is not uncommon for policy to be made and reviewed by at most, 20–30 local activists (several of whom will typically be councillors) a number which will typically represent around 5–10% of the individual party membership locally. The potential in both arenas for 'factional' domination has been apparent in the recent history of the Labour Party at local level. The closed circle of party group and local party in many areas co-exists uneasily with the vision of democratic renewal on the New Labour agenda.

It is not always been so. At different periods in the history of the Labour Party the roots of the local council and local party have been much stronger. Even today there are exceptions to the picture of limited active membership painted above (for example, the Norwich Labour Party described in Game and Leach (1995, p.1)). However, the overall trend is unmistakable:

> Parties used to be in a class of their own as the main agencies of political participation as locally-grounded, mass-membership organisations. Today's parties reflect the dramatically changed nature of our political system: severely depleted memberships, increasing dependence on limited numbers of activists, and their relevance challenged by ever-proliferating numbers of single-issue groups...Yet they dominate the operation of our local councils as never before. (Game and Leach, 1996, pp. 148–9)

The challenge for the Labour Party if 'democratic renewal' is to become a reality at local level is thus threefold. It is a challenge more widely recognised at national level than locally:

1. To strengthen the legitimacy of local representative democracy by increasing electoral turnout and improving the fairness of the voting system (the recent debates about elected mayors (see Hodge, Leach and Stoker, 1997) and changes in the electoral system are relevant here);
2. To improve the legitimacy of local delegate democracy by increasing the level of consultation and debate about local party policy (the possible extension of the scope of activities covered by 'one person, one vote' is worthy of consideration in this context);

3. To supplement both forms of democratic logic with a strong input of participatory democracy, in which the legitimacy of forms of public consultation and participation, going well beyond the periodic right to vote, is recognised and actively encouraged. Much that is included in the recent Labour Party policy documents on local government argues for this trend: the emphasis on stakeholders; new forms of democracy, such as citizens juries and increased use of referenda; the devolution of power to local communities; and greater consultation with users and carers.

To the extent that this vision of a strengthened participatory democracy is implemented (and it is more likely to be implemented through the growth in enthusiasm for it of local Labour councillors than through the ability of the national party to impose it), then it is likely to reduce the significance of party group/local party power battles and the capacity of either element to dominate. Both elements – and the concepts of democracy which they embody – will remain important. Party groups will still have hard decisions to make, whatever the results of public participation, which will sometimes be inconclusive and in opposition to group priorities. Party groups will continue to wish to present manifestos to the electorate as a basis for their policies and actions if elected, and it is difficult to see an alternative legitimate source for such manifestos other than the local party. By introducing or strengthening a third force of democracy into the equation, however, there is the possibility that other forms of democracy will gradually be enhanced and both party group and local party will themselves be revitalised.

About this study

This chapter is based on an ESRC-funded Local Governance project by Professor Steve Leach and Declan Hall on 'The Changing Forms of Local Politics'. The principal focus of the research was on the impact of the three major political parties on decision-making in local government, and in particular on the influence of the party outside the town or county hall on the behaviour of party groups within local authorities. This local focus was also supplemented by analysis of the national party networks on local party and group decision-making processes.

9 The Conservative Party in Local Government, 1979–1997

Ian Holliday

Local government was so much a part of national politics in the Thatcher-Major years that Conservative Party activity in the local sphere itself has been rather overlooked. Although there have certainly been studies of Conservatism in specific local authorities and distinct local policy areas, few synthetic analyses have been written. This chapter does not pretend to fill the gap. Instead, it provides a brief summary of Conservative Party experience in county and district councils in the years 1979–1997, focusing on ways in which local Conservative conceptions of local government changed in those years.

Analysing the Conservative Party in local government

Many problems confront an analysis of this kind. How to deal in a short chapter with the wide variety of Conservative experience witnessed in the 1980s and 1990s is one. How to place boundaries around a party which at its margins flows almost seamlessly into and out of Independence, Ratepayerism and other such movements is a second. How to handle the interview material on which this chapter is partly based is a third. None of these issues can be debated in the space available here.

Instead, all that can be set out at the start is the basic approach to local government Conservation adopted here. Because the core interest of the chapter is in ways in which that Conservatism changed in character in the Thatcher-Major years, the chapter focuses on a series of broad Conservative doctrines about the nature of local government in British society and looks at how they altered in 18 years of Conservative rule at the national level. The diversity of doctrine and belief which characterises the Conservative party naturally makes this a slightly reductionist exercise.

The three main doctrines on which the chapter focuses are:

- *Apoliticism.* The Conservative interest in British local government has long contained a strong tradition which holds that politics should not be allowed to intrude in local matters. Instead, the community should come together to decide issues on their merits rather than on the basis of entrenched political positions, and councils should focus on prudent administration rather than on political conflict (Bulpitt, 1967, p. 19). Needless to say, this tradition has always been most vibrant in those (rural) parts of Britain where aristocratic modes of behaviour have been most enduring and the memory of social leadership by a local elite has not been entirely erased (Lee, 1963). Apoliticism has also found expression in the more reactive and indignant ratepayer movements which have sought to insist that the expensive welfare politics practised by many twentieth-century governments have no proper place in local politics (Bulpitt, 1992). It is clearly stretching a point to say that such a view is apolitical, but in practice it has fed into a form of Conservatism that abhors political initiative. Although it is less firmly tied to place than traditional apolitical Conservatism, it has tended to be a suburban phenomenon (Grant, 1977). These strands of Conservatism have frequently spilled over into the non-Conservative modes of representation which exist on the party's fringe.
- *Mainstream Conservatism.* The mainstream strand in local government Conservatism combines both the small and big 'c' variations on this theme. It is small 'c' to the extent that it tends towards incrementalism and consensus, believing that step changes are on the whole inadvisable and that reform on the basis of a broad coalition of support is to be welcomed. It is big 'c' in the sense that it espouses the party loyalty which is such an important part of the parliamentary party. This aspect of this strand holds that the Conservative Party must engage in overt political activity and 'fight its corner'. Circumstances dictate whether these two aspects of mainstream Conservatism are in tension or not.
- *Radicalism.* Radicalism has always been something of a rarity in the Conservative tradition, chiefly because it depends on

a level of abstraction with which Conservatives are usually uncomfortable. Radicalism, however, relies on that abstraction to generate an alternative to existing conditions. It is explicitly political, in that it holds political change to be essential to realisation of its vision. It is, therefore, not mainstream Conservative because it is not incrementalist, consensual or reliably loyal.

On the basis of this three-fold division, this chapter examines the experiences of local government Conservatism in the Thatcher-Major years. Some experiences were, of course, common to all Conservative councils. The devastation which befell local government Conservatism in the 1990s, resulting in unprecedentedly low levels of representation throughout the UK, and notably its Celtic fringes, is one example. Another is the change forced on all local councils – whether Conservative or not – by the Thatcher-Major governments. These shared experiences are not, however, the central interest here. Rather, the chapter focuses on ways in which distinct Conservative doctrines about local government fared when faced with the many challenges of the 1980s and 1990s.

Apolitical councils

The apolitical strand of local government Conservatism is extremely hard to pin down, chiefly because it straddles the frontiers of Conservatism, Independence, Ratepayerism and related movements. Which of these labels a given individual chooses to fight a particular election under is often determined by local circumstance as much as by anything else. Electoral labels have been less confusing since 1974, when reorganisation prompted a step change in party politicisation of local government. Since then, apolitical Conservatives have increasingly tended to stand for the party, and the number of apolitical councils has fallen substantially: from 50% in the mid-1960s to 16% in the mid-1980s (Secretary of State for the Environment *et al.*, 1986, 2.39–2.40). Many Conservatives nevertheless continue to stand under non-Conservative labels. In the mid-1980s, 26% of Independents were in fact Conservative Party members (and 62% were genuinely independent) (England, 1986, Table 4.4). In these circumstances a choice must be made between the inclusion and exclusion of formally non-Conservative Conservatives. Inclusion is the choice made here.

Conservative apoliticism has often been a strictly local phenomenon; party politics are perfectly acceptable at national level, but have no place in local politics. Its underlying philosophy has always tended towards financial rectitude and prudent adminstration, with committee structures prioritising resources over spending and focusing on clear identification of costs. Organisationally, the officer lead has always been strong. Policy making has been incremental and reactive. This remained the case in apolitical councils in 1979. For many reasons, however, apoliticism was challenged by the election of successive Thatcher governments. One reason was simply that the spirit of the times, for at least the length of the 1980s, was very much against apoliticism: in the confrontational political atmosphere of those years it was hard not to take a well-defined position. Secondly, the financial squeeze imposed on local councils by national governments from the mid-1970s onwards meant that hard choices had to be made about service cuts, rather than service growth, which had hitherto been the post-war norm. Thirdly, specific government interventions altered the way in which local government worked to the detriment of apoliticism. Notable in this regard was one of the few Widdicombe proposals on which the Thatcher government chose to legislate, which provided for the formation of political groups and their representation on committees. A fourth (consequential) reason was that these changes contributed to a situation in which non-Conservative elements on apolitical councils simply refused to play by the old rules any longer.

In this context, a series of local experiences was nevertheless played out. One clear change witnessed in the 1980s and 1990s was further extension of the frontiers of party politics. In 1985, Cornwall County Council became the last county council to switch from Independent to party political control. In some, but not all, rural districts a similar change took place in the Thatcher-Major years. A Conservative government in Westminster was only one reason for this, however. The rise of the Liberal Party as a local electoral force in the 1970s and 1980s was also a key factor. The increased assertiveness and political consciousness of local electorates was a further influence. Once it had taken place, formal party politicisation often had an important effect on local council operations.

This can be seen in the case of North Kesteven District Council (Lincolnshire), which was formally politicised during the Thatcher-Major years. The trigger for this change was the creation at the end of the 1980s of a formal group of Liberal Democratic councillors who, exploiting the Widdicombe legislation, sought pro rata representation on council committees. The response of Conservative forces was not to form a Conservative group – a move seen as too confrontational – but, instead, in 1991, to form a '1994 group' to bring together all those councillors who wished to avoid either Labour or Liberal Democrat control. Distribution of committee chairs became defined by political affiliation, with groups meeting to agree a line before committees convened. The council's central political drive was substantially enhanced by a shift towards a more prime ministerial mode of operation, and the power and influence of both backbench councillors and officers were eroded. A reorganisation of the council's structure on the basis of an outside consultant's review followed. In policy terms, the council became increasingly defined by a clear service orientation and customer focus. It also prioritised decentralisation issues, through community audits and a '100 flourishing communities' programme, all of which were part of a programme to build coherence and identity.

A more striking instance of change is Braintree District Council (Essex), which shifted from a considerable degree of apoliticism in the 1970s to a cutting-edge profile in the late 1980s and 1990s. In some ways the apoliticism of Braintree District Council in the 1970s was artificial, being generated chiefly by the stitching together of the authority which took place in 1974 and the consequent loss of coherence. Once, however, a measure of identity had been developed (chiefly through the conscious decision to build a central office complex), the council took on a strong political drive under a Conservative leader and his chief executive. Together, these two spearheaded a set of reforms which took Braintree District Council to the forefront of service-orientation and gained it an international profile. This reform programme was extended in the 1990s by a four-party coalition formed in 1991 and underpinned by a formal power-sharing agreement.

One key example of Braintree District Council's initiatives is its attainment of the quality management standard BS 5750/ISO 9000 across the full 70 sections of the council in the 14 months to September 1993. More generally, the council has a highly developed consumer orientation, based on a quality assurance policy with four main elements: (a) setting the right standards (aided by consumer research conducted through opinion polls, customer panels, complaints procedures and satisfaction cards); (b) making sure those standards are met on each and every occasion; (c) guaranteeing quality to customers (through individual customer contracts which set precise standards); (d) using an industry-model complaints system (whereby all complaints are logged, scheduled and monitored). Whilst this programme started life as a Conservative initiative, it gained bipartisan support through Labour Party adherence to its central themes. Whereas Conservatives were able to support it for managerial efficiency reasons (as part of their good value to customers/consumers programme), Labour was interested in the consumer democracy aspects (which fitted with its local citizenship programme).

It was also possible, however, for apoliticism to survive the Thatcher-Major years. East Lindsey District Council, a Lincolnshire neighbour of North Kesteven, was under Independent control in the late 1970s, and remained that way in the mid-1990s. By 1997, the extent of central direction of local government as a whole had obviously had an impact on the council, but in terms of internal structure and operation East Lindsey experienced only limited change in the Thatcher-Major years. Politically, the situation altered only minimally. Structurally, the council had moved away from a management team made up uniquely of chief officers to one which also brought in committee chairs. The officer lead nevertheless remained strong and, in policy terms, the council was still largely reactive.

Apoliticism in 1997 clearly did not stand where it had stood in 1979. Some formerly apolitical councils were politicised, and even those which were not had had to make some changes. That said, the 1979 cohort of apolitical councils had not been moved significantly from its starting point, for the changes some parts of it underwent in the 1980s and 1990s did not greatly challenge its heritage. The reason for this is that apolitical Conservatism was often highly receptive to the politicized Conservatism which Thatcherism represented, chiefly because those councils which were apolitical after reorganisation tended to be those which had missed out on the entire tradition of municipal enterprise which emerged towards the end of the nineteenth century, and which affected many Conservative councils in the twentieth. As such, they were something of a political vacuum waiting for Thatcherism to happen. Crucially, their core tradition of financial rectitude made them peculiarly susceptible to some of Thatcherism's central themes, such as value for money (VFM), efficiency and rolling back the state. In some sense, they provided a form of latent resistance to the entire constructivist trend which Conservatism took from the 1930s to the 1970s. When a more classical Conservatism was recreated in the 1980s, many apolitical councils found themselves in tune with its central themes, a large number of which were strikingly apolitical. The service orientation, of which Braintree District Council is a foremost exponent, has been found attractive by many formerly apolitical councils precisely because it is devoid of significant political content.

In one sense, apoliticism fought a losing battle in the 1980s and 1990s as formal politicisation extended its frontiers. In another, it remained vibrant, for formal politicisation often made little real difference to the underlying policy orientation of apolitical councils because the reformist agenda around which they converged stressed VFM, customer focus and devolved management structures. The first of these themes was practised in apolitical councils long before it became a watchword of Thatcherism. The other two could easily be neutralised in a political sense and restricted to the administrative sphere.

Mainstream Conservative councils

Almost by definition, the mainstream strand dominated local government Conservatism in the late 1970s. It was of an increasingly odd character however, for the tension which exists in mainstream Conservatism between incrementalism on the one hand and party loyalty on the other was revealed more clearly by Margaret Thatcher than by any other twentieth-century Conservative leader. Before the 1979 general election victory the extent of Thatcherite radicalism was unclear, with the result that Conservative local government could remain committed to Heathite beliefs in the post-war consensus and welfare Conservatism – Whitelaw with local – rather than to Thatcherite critiques of it without exposing itself to evident charges of disloyalty. After 1979, when Thatcherism became increasingly radical, tensions within mainstream Conservatism were fully revealed. Then Conservatives in local government were forced to choose between their often innate conservatism and their often equally instinctive party loyalty.

In those councils where this choice was managed most effectively, it was largely through a negotiated return to something akin to a ratepayers' culture, that is, by prioritisation of the very themes of financial rectitude and VFM which linked Conservatism's apolitical tradition into Thatcherism. Sometimes the ease of this transition was enhanced by a long-standing, but recently-superseded, tradition of apoliticism in a particular locality. Good examples are those county councils which had a strong Independent tradition until reorganisation in 1974, but were then transformed by the incorporation of more politicised areas into their new boundaries. Classic cases are the incorporation of county boroughs into counties: Brighton into East Sussex, Southend into Essex, Gloucester into Gloucestershire, and so on. In each of these cases a clash of cultures – between sets of values which were often diametrically opposed (Jones, 1975) – was still being worked out when Thatcher came to power in 1979. It was to remain a theme of the early years of the Thatcher government as the rise of the Liberal Party to local prominence gave a further impetus to politicisation by local government by treating local government as a mirror of central government, with highly political debates. The response of Conservative groups was often to unite around themes with which they felt comfortable in the context both of their traditions and of the Conservative Party's Thatcherite orientation. On the basis of a strong finance drive Conservative groups found it relatively easy both to fall in line with (most) government policy and to retain their own unity. They may have had some radical Thatcherite elements on their fringes, but not to a destabilising degree. In many mainstream Conservative councils, then, the Conservative group sought unity in running a tight ship, pursuing cost effectiveness in all things, and by not spending (quite) up to SSA.

A different pattern was, witnessed in other mainstream Conservative councils, however. Instead of making a largely negotiated and seamless transition to the new local government world of the 1980s and 1990s, some took the route of confrontation and turmoil. The degree of constraint on Conservative councils in the 1980s – both formal (legislation) and informal (Conservative Party links and culture) – was such that very few openly opposed Thatcherite measures (though many sought to make representations to ministers through intra-party channels). Instead, most turmoil was experienced in those councils that were captured by radical forces pursuing an explicitly Thatcherite agenda. In Lincolnshire County Council, a palace revolution in the early 1980s saw aristocratic monetarists displaced by self-made types determined to take a more activist stance. The council was often ahead of the government in subsequent years, particularly in the educational sphere. On marketisation issues, it was always well to the right of the government. It also recognised something that most Conservative councils came to acknowledge; that running a tight ship and not spending up to SSA was in many ways an irrational response to the funding regime which dominated local government finance in the Thatcher-Major years. The result was a certain degree of internal conflict, real frustration with central government constraints on local government and, ultimately, an accommodation based on efficiency and VFM.

A more extreme transition was made by Arun District Council. Here, a difficult experience of reorganisation meant that building both council and party group identity was the major task facing Conservatives in the 1970s. In the 1980s, however, efficiency became the central theme, and was ruthlessly driven through the council's structures by a determined Conservative group leader and chief executive, both of whom were exponents of Thatcherite ideals. External agents – such as the Audit Commission and INLOGOV (the University of Birmingham's flagship local government training and consultancy department) – were used as a means of reinforcing the case for change. The high tide of Thatcherism in Arun District Council, as in Lincolnshire County Council, lasted no more than a few years before a further transition to a more consensual 'Majorite' orientation was made. In other councils the flirtation with Thatcherism was even more passing. Essex County Council experienced something of an 'Essex man' revolution following the 1989 local council elections, but forces of resistance within the council (notably the chief executive) ensured that the extent of policy change was limited. In 1993, 'Essex man' lost control of the council.

Mainstream Conservative councils and councillors found the 1980s and 1990s rather difficult. One of their central objectives has always been exercising power, and in this sense the Conservative years were clearly a disaster. Beyond this, the direction in which mainstream Conservatism should point was clearly contested, and caused a number of councillors to fall back on the financial rectitude which has always been a part of their tradition and which was also used by apolitical councils for regrouping purposes. By 1997, mainstream Conservatives had largely fallen in with the moderation and service orientation forced on local government by successive Conservative governments. In many ways, mainstream Conservatives viewed this as no bad thing.

Radical councils

There were very few radical Conservative councils in 1979. One or two had already taken the plunge and embraced nascent Thatcherite ideals: Dudley Metropolitan Borough Council is an example (Hall, 1995). Others were on the verge of doing so. They include what were to become very visible Conservative authorities in the 1980s, such as Solihull Borough Council and Southend Borough Council in the early part of the decade, and the two flagships of the latter part, the London boroughs of Wandsworth and Westminster (Holliday, 1991). On the whole, however, Thatcherism had made little impact on local government in 1979, in large part because it was in a highly under-developed state and was no more than a minority perspective within the Conservative Party as a whole. Nevertheless, radicalism did develop in Conservative councils in the 1980s and 1990s.

In the late 1970s and early 1980s the Solihull Conservative group was marked by an important Thatcherite presence, and became a pioneer of educational reform. Its first significant initiative was an attempt to reintroduce grammar schools into the borough, an attempt which ultimately failed chiefly because of opposition from within the Conservative Party itself. Locally, pressure from leafy suburbs with well-functioning comprehensives slowly undermined support for the proposal among Conservative councillors. When, in 1984, an Independent stood against Peter Tebbit (brother of Norman) on the single issue of opposition to risk introduction of selective education, and won, the initiative was fatally undermined. It had, however, already been weakened by the failure of the Thatcher government to support the Solihull Borough Council initiative, even though it did nothing formally to obstruct it. Also in the 1980s, Solihull was at the forefront of promoting (along with councils like Cambridgeshire County Council and Lincolnshire County Council) of local management in schools and of experimenting with city technology colleges (CTCs). Indeed, Britain's first CTC, sponsored by the Hanson Trust (in a deal brokered by the Conservative Party national elite), was opened in Solihull. Like many other Conservative councils, Solihull Borough Council was not permanently radical, ultimately falling in line behind a mainstream figure.

At Southend Borough Council, the policy area in which the council became a pioneer was refuse collection (Evans, 1985), which was put out to competitive tender in the early 1980s and awarded to David Evans' Exclusive Cleansing. This issue arose on the dominant Conservative group's agenda as a result of a long-running battle with the council workforce – including go slows, working to rule, strikes and a generally poor service – and substantial resentment and protest amongst residents. Southend's initiative generated widespread interest and imitation. Privatisation of refuse collection was also a starting point for radicalism when the Conservative Party regained control of Birmingham County Council in 1982 and consciously followed Southend and Wandsworth councils (Coombs, 1983). Elsewhere, however, Conservative councils were dissuaded from radical action by local resistance. In Aylesbury Vale District Council (Buckinghamshire), the threat of joint industrial action was sufficient to persuade the council quietly to drop a proposal to invite tenders for refuse collection (Minogue and O'Grady, 1985, p. 38). In other councils, of course, officer or member resistance meant that initiatives of this kind never even saw the light of day. There is some evidence that Conservative local government experience in the educational, competitive tendering and, more generally, VFM fields fed into Conservative government legislation (Byrne, 1996) but it is rather partly.

In the later 1980s and in the 1990s the Conservatives became, in many ways, less political and more administrative in focus. Prudent administration was, of course, a theme throughout the Thatcher-Major years, with VFM a prime example. In the late Thatcher years, however, when government policy became increasingly conflictual in a political sense, Conservative local government radicalism contented itself chiefly with administrative reform. Central to most change were customer orientation and devolved structures, both of which were capable of drawing cross-party support (as has been seen in the case of Braintree District Council). In the Wrekin District Council, customer orientation was made central to council operations (Hancox *et al.*, 1989). Similar initiatives were taken in Buckinghamshire, Westminster and Arun (Gyford, 1991). 'Making use of complaints' was how one key official at Braintree District Council described it (Atkins, 1992).

There is, then, something of a paradox here. Instances of Conservative local government radicalism actually became increasingly apolitical as the Thatcher-Major years progressed, driven away from high-profile political spheres into spheres of internal organisation and administration. Moreover, in areas of headline politics, local government initiative was always difficult to sustain and only rarely travelled well. Part of the reason for this was limited government interest in anything other than its own reformist initiatives.

Conclusion

What happened to the Conservative Party in local government between 1979 and 1997 is both easy and hard to say. It is easy to say in the sense that local government Conservatism suffered, mightily, from association with an increasingly unpopular government and was generally in a poor shape by the mid-1990s. The feeling of demoralisation among Conservative councillors by this stage was palpable, being generated both by the extent of Conservative defeat at the local level and by a feeling of betrayal by a Conservative elite which had little or no time for the party in local government. By the mid-1990s, many Conservative councillors were only too ready to pin responsibility for the collapse of party representation at local level on a party hierarchy which was not interested in local government even, in some cases, when it had direct experience of it. Others put that collapse down to the vagaries of British electoral politics, and the now established tradition that governing parties do badly in by-elections and local elections. Prospects for a revitalisation of Conservative local government fortunes are heavily contingent on which of these two competing views is correct. Uniting both camps is a hostility to the quango state, which those Conservative councillors who retain seats tend to view with deep suspicion.

It is hard to say what happened to the Conservative Party in local government between 1979 and 1997 in the sense that one picture of diversity was replaced by another. To be fair, though, the extent of diversity in 1997 was considerably less than it had been in 1979. This is partly due to the massive amount of ground lost by the Conservatives during those 18 years. It is partly due to the general boxing in of local government by successive Conservative governments and also to changes within Conservative local government itself, notably a consolidation over time around VFM, efficiency and 'good government' themes. The strange thing is that these themes have more in common with the apolitical strand of local government Conservatism than with either the mainstream or the radical. Although apoliticism was formally undermined (still further) in the Thatcher-Major years, it actually fared rather well in those years as its central tenets were impressed on local government by Conservative administrations which sought to depoliticise local authorities and impose market rationality on them (Gyford et al, 1989, p. 327). Two further points need, however, to be made in conclusion.

First, for a number of reasons, mapping changes in the diverse nature of Conservative government between 1979 and 1997 is an inherently tricky exercise. One reason is that the extent of volatility in local elections means that big swings are possible. This, when linked to the difficulty the Conservative Party has of getting people to stand for local office, means that local parties often have little control over the character of the Conservative group that emerges in any particular council. In consequence, marked shifts in party character can take place, see-saw change can be witnessed, and little is available to explain any of what has happened except strictly contingent factors, including the roles played by key individuals. Indeed, given that many – perhaps most – ruling Conservative groups are run by no more than a handful of people, unexpected shifts become very possible. It is certainly not feasible to place territorial or socio-economic boundaries around patterns of change. Indeed, the only general points that can be made are negative rather than positive. It can be said that formal apoliticism is not now found in county or non-rural district politics, but the reason, for instance, that North Kesteven District Council went down the road of formal politicisation in the Conservative years when its neighbour, East Lindsey District Council, did not, is almost wholly explained by contingent local factors. Equally, Braintree District Council's international reputation for customer orientation cannot be explained other than by specific local factors. One important consequence is that in an analysis of the 1980s and 1990s some Conservative councils appear in more than one category. To take just two examples, Arun District Council and Solihull Borough Council were both mainstream Conservative and radical in the course of the Thatcher-Major years.

The second concluding point is that it would be misleading to end a survey of local government Conservatism between 1979 and 1997 on anything approaching the positive note that identification of Conservative government success in depoliticising and marketising local authorities might suggest. Clearly, a high price was paid for this success, and much of it was met by the party in local government. The importance of rebuilding this element of Conservatism has been recognised by many, from academics (Whiteley *et al.*, 1994) to the party leader, William Hague. Unless voters return to the Conservative Party in reaction to a Labour government in Westminster, this will not be readily accomplished, however. Even if this were to happen, the task facing the party is substantial. On the one hand, many broadly Conservative individuals who were once happy to serve on local councils are no longer prepared to do so, chiefly because of the openly political nature of most councils and the reduced range of local government responsibilities. The days of disinterested public service are largely over, which is a problem for a party which has long relied on it. On the other hand, it is genuinely hard in many parts of Britain to identify the communities to which local councils purportedly relate and thus difficult to persuade them that local government is something worth caring about. The Labour government's devolutionist drive and Conservative Party opposition to it may finally persuade the party again to take seriously the localist philosophy which was once so central to its identity. The problem for the Conservative Party at the end of the 1990s is that it has few ideas about how that localist philosophy might find practical expression in contemporary circumstances.

About this study

This chapter draws on a wide-ranging programme of largely unstructured interviews conducted with officers and members from Conservative-controlled councils in the 1980s and 1990s. This programme was funded by the ESRC (L311 25 3004) and carried out chiefly in 1994 and 1995. The author is very grateful to all his interviewees, and to the ESRC.

10 Participation Strategies and Environmental Politics: Local Agenda 21

Stephen C. Young

During the late 1980s and early 1990s, several factors combined to push a range of environment-related issues up the political agenda at both the national and local levels in Britain (McCormick, 1991; Robinson, 1992; Young, 1993). These factors included external events like the Chernobyl accident, growing media interest, group campaigns on many issues, and local controversies. Increasing public concern about the environment was reflected in opinion poll findings. In producing the 1990 environment white paper, *This Common Inheritance* (Department of the Environment, 1990), and the subsequent annual reports on the environment, and in focusing to a greater extent on environmental issues, Whitehall was also responding to local authority concerns (Stoker and Young, 1993, chs 4 & 7; Ward, 1993); and to pressures from Brussels (Commission of the European Communities, 1992; Collins and Earnshaw, 1993).

These British developments took place against a background of growing international interest in the concept of sustainable development which had been popularised by the Brundtland Report (World Commission on Environment and Development, 1987). In essence, sustainable development is about charting a new course which reconciles economic demands and pressures with social needs; and with the continuing capacity of the environment – of the planet – to cope with discharges of pollution to land, air and water, and to support human and other forms of life now and in the future (Baker *et al.*, 1997, Introduction). Concern about the environment thus relates to much more than tidying-up and cosmetics like countryside issues, wildlife, tree-planting, pollution control and cyclepaths. The sustainable development agenda at the local level covers a much wider range of issues, including waste, transport, energy, pollution prevention, planning, housing, tourism, anti-poverty strategies, and economic development (Haughton and Hunter, 1994; Selman, 1996; Wild, 1996; Local Government Management Board, 1994, Appendix).

At the Rio Earth Summit in 1992, following on from the publication of the Brundtland Report, governments of the world signed up to Agenda 21 (Grubb et al, 1993). Agenda 21 is the name given to the action plan to promote sustainable development – and thus to safeguard the planet for future generations – during the twenty-first century.The main consequence for sub-national governments everywhere is that they have to draw up their own Local Agenda 21 (LA21) strategies showing how they will apply the principles set out in the main Agenda 21 document and promote sustainable development at the local level (Lafferty and Eckerberg, 1997). From the perspective of this project, the breadth of issues raised by sustainable development had important implications. When councils began to focus on their LA21s they found local groups wanted to discuss a huge range of topics.

Interest in the participation dimensions

A number of factors contributed to the post-Rio growth of interest in the participation aspects of LA21. First of all, Chapter 28 of Agenda 21, as agreed at Rio, stressed the need to involve all groups in society when preparing LA21s. Particular mention was made of drawing in women and young people, involving all groups in society and not just the more articulate ones, and of trying to generate consensus. Participation was thus promoted as being an integral part of the LA21 policy-making process. In the LA21 context it was no longer – as so often in contemporary politics – an optional extra. Rio elevated community involvement to a new status.

Interest in participation was further promoted by two other factors. To begin with, the Local Government Management Board (LGMB) played an influential role in promoting LA21. It continually stressed, in its publications about LA21 and its monthly mailings to environmental co-ordinators, the importance of promoting community involvement. This encouraged individual councils to give it more attention and to be more innovative (LGMB, 1994, 1995, 1997).

In addition, those within individual councils involved in promoting the participation aspects of LA21 have brought new approaches to the task. They have come in with experience of community development, running adult education programmes and directly involving people in countryside and recreational projects, as via the Groundwork Trusts. There has also been an influx of people from Non-Governmental Organisations (NGOs) with detailed ideas about how to promote participation. Collectively, the attitudes of all these people towards participation reflects much more of a bottom-up, people-centred perspective than that of planners who have previously been running top-down structure plan consultation programmes. The views and values of these people have decisively influenced the nature of the participation programmes followed by the more innovative councils.

The period after Rio also coincided with two broader contextual developments. First, there was a change of attitude towards community involvement amongst some policy-makers. The resulting exploration of new ideas was not just directed at LA21. It also found expression in the contexts of housing renewal and estate regeneration; City Challenge; and the Single Regeneration Budget (SRB) programmes (Department of the Environment, 1995a; DoE, 1995b). The attempts to promote bottom-up style strategies reflected a growing recognition of the need to move on from the top-down, bureaucratic paternalist approaches that predominated during the 1960s and 1970s (Gyford, 1991). The process of imposing projects with minimal consultation programmes created schemes that did not work – like the high-rise flats and the Hulme crescents in Manchester. A range of subsequent inner city regeneration programmes did promote economic renewal and make a physical impact in terms of new buildings and landscaping projects. They did not produce social renewal and tackle local unemployment, housing deprivation, crime and other dimensions of urban poverty, however (Stoker and Young, 1993).

As a result, a small but growing number of policy-makers began to argue the need for a new approach. Their starting point was that top-down solutions do not relate effectively to peoples' perceptions of what is wrong. They argued that the lesson from previous decades was that it was important to start with a blank agenda, and to ask local people to define the problems as they perceived them (Taylor, 1995). It then becomes possible to produce relevant and creative solutions. These have more chance of working because they draw from local peoples' knowledge and experience. The solutions that emerge are promoted and supported by local people; they are not just more acceptable to them. They are also more likely to be protected by local people. These arguments are reflected in the discourse of estate regeneration, City Challenge and the SRB in the early 1990s, about the importance of drawing in all the stakeholders, and empowering local communities.

This new emphasis on bottom-up approaches has also found support from another constituency. The early 1990s produced a debate in the media and amongst academics about social exclusion, alienation, a loss of trust in local government, and a loss of faith in the capacity of local political institutions and processes (Macnaughten *et al.*, 1995). Despite attempts to communicate more effectively with local people and experiments with decentralisation and neighbourhood offices, many were increasingly concerned about the growing disillusionment with local democracy. Discussion amongst media commentators, academics, politicians and leading local government figures focused around the need to regenerate local democracy (Commission for Local Democracy, 1995; King & Stoker, 1997; Pratchett & Wilson, 1996; Lafferty and Meadowcroft, 1997). These people were not specifically interested in the environment or LA21. They were drawn to the bottom-up approaches to participation because of the opportunity to experiment with ways of communicating with the public and with promoting community involvement. These new approaches thus offered a way of breathing new life and vitality into the institutions and processes of local government itself.

In the period after Rio, LA21 and its participation dimensions were only a concern to a minority of councils. However, by the mid-1990s interest in the participation aspects of LA21 was growing not just because more were involved in LA21 activity, but also because of their relevance to these wider debates.

The four different LA21 participation strategies

One of the most widely used distinctions in discussions about participation is the difference between top-down and bottom-up approaches. The top-down approach is a one-way consultation process dominated by the council. In contrast, the bottom-up approach is a two-way process that develops into a genuine dialogue between the council and local communities. The reality is, of course, more complex. In the context of LA21 in the 1990s, British local authorities have used four different strategies to promote participation (Young, 1996, Part 1).

With the *top-down strategy* the authority remains firmly in control. It sets up a one-way process. Its attitude is that participation is mainly concerned with passing information about what the council is doing down to the public and interested parties. It sets and controls the agenda during the participation process. It determines the direction of policy proposals and the choice of priorities. It dominates the participation process itself; and it ensures there is no real scope for change to its position after the participation process has finished. This top-down strategy generally is used where the authority wants to publicise what it has been doing and what it is planning to do. This strategy helps to legitimise its activities. It is always widely criticised for structuring the participation stage in such a way as to prevent any real input from local communities. As a result it is often referred to as consultation. In the LA21 context, it undermines both the detail and the spirit of Chapter 28.

The *bottom-up strategy* is the polar opposite of the top-down strategy. The authority takes a quite different approach, giving participation contrasting features. It conceives of participation as a genuine two-way dialogue based on a sharing of information. It aims to reach out beyond the groups that were usually involved in participation exercises in the 1970s and 1980s, in order to involve all local stakeholders and minority groups, as envisaged in Chapter 28 of Agenda 21. The council aims to give people a real role in shaping council decisions. The authority takes a hands-off, listening and learning stance, and seeks to empower people. It leaves the agenda open, to be set by local people. It leaves the direction of policy and the choice of priorities open to discussion. It shares power with the participants, thus enabling local communities to own the participation process itself. The authority therefore ensures that there is plenty of scope to change its position after the participation process is over. Crucially the participation programme comes at the start of the policy-making process, and is not grafted on to a process that is already well advanced. The empowering approaches inherent in the bottom-up strategy have a lot in common with the ideas at the top of

Arnstein's ladder (Gyford, 1991, pp. 52–3) and in some of the analysis of the decentralisation schemes of the late 1980s/early 1990s (Burns *et al.*, 1994).

Probably about 50 or 60 councils have aimed at something like a bottom-up strategy. These include Kirklees, Reading, Gloucestershire, Derbyshire, Vale Royal, Nottinghamshire, Mendip, Croydon, Merton, and Leicester. Others have tried similar approaches in the context of the SRB and estate regeneration programmes. In practice however, councils have fallen back on a *'Yes... but...'* strategy.

This occurs where the council adopts the rhetoric of the bottom-up strategy, but finds it difficult to let go of the participation process and carry that strategy right through. The main problem is that the council is committed to some policies and projects that are widely seen as being environmentally damaging – like open-cast mining or a big road scheme – so the authority's approach changes. What happens can be summed up as follows: 'Yes let's aim at a bottom-up strategy, but the issue of the ring road/opencast mine/landfill site is too important to compromise on'. The council thus changes the nature of its approach as the participation programme develops. It evolves into a more limited and controlled exercise.

The council establishes a two-way dialogue. It *aims* to open things up and get away from simply passing out information, and to give groups and communities a real role in shaping decisions. It sets much of the agenda, but relinquishes control and welcomes additions. It opens up the direction of policy and the choice of priorities for wider discussion, but, in reality, it remains committed on some issues and cannot compromise. It aims to promote power-sharing, but in fact remains in control. There is scope for change at the end of the participation process, but there are some positions that the authority is committed to, and will not budge from. These may only become apparent after the participation process. The strength of the authority's commitment is such that some inputs from the participation process are vetoed. This strategy seems to emerge as it develops. What happens is that those setting up the participation process present it as a bottom-up strategy. The reality, however, is that some senior officers and/or committee chairs are strongly committed to broad policies like promoting economic development, or specific projects like a major housing scheme or developing a specific landfill site. Bolton is an example here.

The final variant is the *limited dialogue strategy*. This arises where the authority is drawn to the top-down approach, but, seeing the problems with this, wants to be more flexible, as in the case of Cheshire for example. The authority conceives the dialogue with the public as being a two-way process but within limited parameters. It aims to get beyond pushing out information to the public and to get some feedback on what it is proposing – mainly over the details. It sets the agenda. It determines the direction of policy and the choice of priorities. It holds the balance of power and controls the participation process. It is prepared to amend its proposals at the end of the participation process. Although significant issues may be affected, changes mostly relate to details. This is a common strategy, especially in areas that have been relatively unaffected by the new approaches to participation that emerged during the late 1980s. It is also being adopted in places where the council's approach to planning does not lay much emphasis on participation.

The nature of LA21 participation

The features of the LA21 participation programmes that stand out are those of variety and imagination. Traditional approaches based around leaflets, exhibitions and public meetings have been submerged in a riot of experimentation with empowering approaches (Bell *et al.*, 1994; Church, 1995; County Planning Officers' Society LA21 Task Force, 1995; Department of the Environment, 1995a, 1995b; Kirklees MBC, 1995; LGMB, 1995; Whittaker, 1995, pp. 48–52; Wilcox, 1994; Wood, 1995; Wild, 1996; Young 1996, Part 1). The visioning technique, for example, is used to get people to discuss in groups how they would like their neighbourhood to be in 20 years' time. It is then possible to work backwards, constructing programmes that lead there. The small group discussion technique is used to tackle a range of issues in a relaxed atmosphere with neutral chairs. Focus groups bring together individuals on a regular basis to discuss a pre-set agenda. Socio-economic criteria are used to pick individuals from a common background – rural professionals, or Asian women, for example (Macnaghten *et al.*, 1995). The 'planning for real' technique brings local people together for short, intensive periods to produce consensus about future developments. With village appraisals, local people do detailed surveys to identify the scope for action. Another widely used technique is to get residents to design questionnaires around local issues and to conduct the house-to-house interviews. With these approaches councils aim to draw in all local stakeholders; and to share information with them as part of a wider attempt to empower local communities.

A different approach has been to forge stronger links with local environmental groups so as to draw their expertise into the policy-making process. Some councils – Croydon, for example – have coopted group representatives onto new and existing committees and environmental working parties. A more common approach though, as in Lancashire, has been the creation of Environment Forums (LGMB, 1997, Appendix, Figure 12). These have been based on the Canadian Round Table principle of bringing together all the stakeholders from the public, private and community sectors with the aim of generating consensus-based approaches (Whittaker, 1995, p. 132). Practice varies with regard to the details on composition, organisation, functions and links to the council's committee structure, but the main aims have been to promote discussion and to give the Forum a role in preparing the authority's LA21 document, and commenting on its approaches to sustainable development.

Evaluation

This section argues that it is too early for a full assessment of the LA21 participation programmes. It evaluates them in terms of three criteria, before relating them to a broader discussion about participation in the mid-1990s.

Changing policy?

First, there is the criterion of the impact of LA21 participation on policies – the outputs from the participation processes. Here it is important to identify the perspective from which a programme is being judged. A council promoting a top-down strategy, for example, would judge 'success' in terms of its out-of-town industrial estate proposal not being irreversibly damaged. On the other hand, a council pushing a bottom-up strategy would focus on the extent to which it was empowering local communities and putting their views at the heart of policy-making processes. With the small number that had been completed by the end of 1996, though it is too soon to assess the outputs – the impact of the LA21 participation programme on the LA21 document itself; and that document's influence on the revision of a council's statutory plan and the restructuring of its budget in ways that reflect sustainable development principles (Young, 1997a).

One big problem is that the LA21 participation programmes have been proceeding under a serious handicap. People have been asked about the promotion of sustainable development and about priorities in a situation where the extent of future resources is not clear. A shift to better and more extensive public transport, for example, requires substantial capital investment. With regard to urban traffic congestion, participation programmes have produced extensive calls for change, but it was very difficult for councils to react positively because of the Major government's lack of response to the urban traffic agenda set out in the Royal Commission on Environmental Pollution's report (1994). In addition, privatisation led to the fragmentation of public transport undertakings and made it much more difficult to promote integrated investment programmes.

Better processes?

Second, with regard to the processes themselves, the participation programmes have certainly had an impact. Councils which adopted the more innovative approaches seem to have had positive responses and a wider range of people getting involved than the usual self-presenting groups (Wild, 1996; Tuxworth, 1997; Young, 1997B; LGMB, 1997, Appendix, Figures 10–12). In retrospect, however, the LA21 participation activity of the mid-1990s can be seen to have taken place during a period of great enthusiasm for community involvement, before the more difficult stage of evaluating the inputs and producing the documents themselves (Young, 1997a). In some respects this may turn out to be a case of raised expectations leaving participants disappointed in the longer term. Already, in the short term, some councils have found it difficult to maintain momentum. Some of the early enthusiasm for the Environment Forums, for example, has ebbed away amidst criticisms that they have become fossilised talking shops. In some places it has proved difficult to draw lower income groups and young people into the participation programmes.

Two factors affect the nature of the process in ways that constrain outputs. First, business has been involved to only a limited extent. The firms that have given their views tend to be committed to sustainable development anyway. In addition, chambers of commerce and local branches of the National Farmers' Union can speak for their members, but cannot commit them to action – sending more goods by rail or using less fertiliser, for example. The problem of business disinterest will limit the effectiveness of LA21s at the implementation stage.

The other main problem is that it has proved difficult to integrate the experiments in participation with the need for strategic planning. Many of the pioneering councils' participation programmes have focused on the micro-level – the level of the village and the urban neighbourhood. Work on LA21s, however, has also clarified the need for a strategic level of analysis. On waste, for example, a council needs to decide the balance between landfill, recycling, and incineration (including the Combined Heat and Power option) within its programme for the next decade. Promoting recycling, reuse and waste minimisation can help, but this does not remove the need for new landfill sites. Transport also has to be planned at the strategic level. Similarly, a city-wide or county-wide approach has to be taken to identifying land that needs to be released for housing or industry or a new site for a major football club. The use of vacant urban sites can help reduce, but not remove, the demand for land release. In practice, many LA21 participation programmes have been taking place in something of a vacuum, with key strategic dimensions being omitted.

Towards partnership?

The third criterion for assessing LA21 participation programmes is the positive impact they have had on the growth of partnerships between local communities and other agencies (Wild, 1996; Tuxworth, 1997). These were picked out at Rio as having a significant contribution to make to the implementation of LA21s. There are lots of these community-based partnership organisations (Young, 1996, Part 2), examples include community businesses, recycling schemes, housing co-ops (see Chapter 12), Local Exchange Trading Systems (LETS), credit unions, self-help user groups in social

services (Barnes *et al.*, 1999), traditional voluntary sector organisations, environmental improvement schemes, community co-ops,
heritage trusts, wildlife organisations, small housing associations,
community arts projects, and a variety of local development trusts
(Thake, 1995).

One of the problems of writing about this myriad of different
organisations is that there is no commonly understood term to
describe them. The phrases used include community enterprise,
community action, third sector organisations, community regeneration organisations, voluntary sector bodies, community-based
organisations and local NGOs.

A path through the confusion is offered by writers like Cattell
(1994, Appendix 1) and Welch and Coles (1994). They have brought
the concept of a 'social economy' into the English language from the
languages of southern Europe. In France and other parts of Latin
Europe, the concept is well-established and clearly understood. All
these different community-based partnerships are seen as belonging
to a social economy. This social economy operates as a third force
between the mainstream public and private sectors. The European
Union's DG23 in Brussels is focusing on ways of expanding it
(Young, 1997b).

These community-based partnerships take many forms; there is
no space for a detailed discussion here. They have three main
features in common (Cattell, 1994, Appendix 1; Young, 1996, pp.
34–8; and Young 1997c). First, they operate on a not-for-profit
basis. Second, they focus on the level of the local community. This is
usually meant in the geographical sense of the village, the estate or
the urban neighbourhood, but it also refers to communities of need,
interest and experience across a wider area – as with ethnic groups
across a city, for example (Haughton and Hunter, 1994, p. 113).
Finally, these organisations emphasise local democracy and the
involvement of local people in defining their needs, shaping programmes, and controlling the development of the organisation. The
contrast with the private sector is important here. Capital is free to
move, but these community-based partnerships are closely linked to
place, to improving conditions where their members and stakeholders live.

LA21 participation programmes are creating opportunities to
identify potential projects in the social economy, and have thus
scored well on the third criterion. The significant point here is

that the establishment of these not-for-profit organisations represents a practical response to local needs as a result of visioning
exercises. These 'Third Force Organisations' provide another
means of tackling economic and social problems (Stoker, 1997b,
pp. 37–9). They offer a way of linking sustainable development,
community, participatory democracy and place, at the micro level
of the village, the estate, and the urban neighbourhood. In sustainable development terms they can combine the social, economic and
environmental dimensions in one organisation rooted to locality
(O'Riordan, 1995).

Competing interpretations

Looking more widely across British local government in the 1990s, it
is not possible to draw clear conclusions about the impact of the
participatory experiments. Some writers take a positive, optimistic
view, seeing gains and benefits from attempts to promote community-based partnerships, and 'Yes…but…' and bottom-up strategies. Wilcox (1994) and Skinner (1997) are examples here, as is
Chapter 12 of this book. A monitoring report on Hulme City
Challenge, based on extensive questionnaires, provides another
example (Harding and Garside, 1996). In this case, there was an
attempt at a bottom-up strategy, using the planning for real
approach and other techniques to try to generate consensus
amongst residents over the redevelopment and layout of the area.
This even got into the detail of allowing individuals to choose the
design of housing interiors. The survey showed 'a strong feeling'
that participation had been 'effective and worthwhile'. While there
was a core of non-participants, only 8% felt the views of local
residents had been disregarded, and 58% felt they had enough
opportunity to get involved in deciding how Hulme should change.

Others, however, remain critical about the impact of participation
processes, and are more pessimistic in their analysis. Hoggett wrote
a much-quoted piece in this vein (1995). Similarly, the analyses in
Chapters 11 and 13 of this book (on housing and planning, and on
Urban Development Corporations (UDCs) and ethnic groups)
seem to fit into the top-down strategy, where consultation and
legitimation was really all that the council or the UDC aspired to.
Part of the pessimists' analysis is that councils cannot succeed when

they try to go beyond the top-down approach and have dialogue and genuine discussion via one of the other strategies. This is because the impact of the participation process is structurally constrained. It is circumscribed by the overall lack of resources, so detailed participation can lead to residents getting a childrens' playground, allotments and recycling facilities, but not a multi-purpose community centre, retraining packages and better public transport. The pessimists see the redesign of Hulme as a special case resulting from the exceptional levels of resources available through the City Challenge response to a 20-year-old planning controversy.

It is possible to find examples to confirm both the optimistic and pessimistic interpretations, but more research is needed to work out the balance between them. A longer-term perspective on the experiments of the early 1990s is needed to see whether participation turns out to be about where to put the playground, for example, or whether local people are having an influence on a wide range of issues. From both a sustainable development and a social regeneration perspective, this needs to be measured not just in terms of housing and the built environment, but in terms of broader issues like jobs, crime and poverty. In the LA21 context, the optimistic interpretation would need to show that the more ambitious and innovatory strategies have produced outputs that have changed council strategies, budgets and statutory plans. In the Gloucestershire case, for example, the question that arises is the extent to which the detailed working party reports that went into the Vision 21 exercise to produce the county's LA21 changed the county council's subsequent approach on policies and spending.

Working out the balance between the optimistic and the pessimistic positions has also been made more difficult by changes in the way councils have approached participation in the 1990s. The experiments suggest that councils are using it less in a top-down way for consultation and legitimation of their proposals, and more to promote dialogue and empowerment. In Stoker's terms, this relates to whether councils are trying to endorse their proposals, to negotiate with local people, or 'to act as a referee and provide a framework for a participatory "game" for local residents' (Stoker, 1997b, p. 34).

The extent to which policy-makers' attitudes are changing is unclear. But the variety of innovatory approaches and the scale on which they are being adopted seem more substantial than at any time since the 1969 Skeffington Report (Boaden *et al.*, 1980). The participation strategies being promoted in the 1990s represent British local government's most serious attempt to date to move away from top-down consultation. A significant proportion of councils are developing strategies that involve creative dialogue and attempts to empower local communities, giving these communities greater influence over the built environment, social conditions and economic opportunities around where they live. The extent to which the optimistic scenario can be sustained in reality is closely linked to how widespread and serious this change of attitude amongst policy-makers actually proves to be.

Environmental participation and local governance

The most important part of LA21 has been the way in which the LA21 participation programmes have become a conduit for the unleashing of energy and ideas into the wider arena of the attempts to regenerate local democracy (Young, 1997b). The more imaginative LA21 participation programmes need to be considered in this wider context of innovation in democratic practice (Stewart, 1995). Outside the LA21 context other approaches are being developed (Stoker, 1997b). With citizens juries, for example, the commissioning organisation picks representative citizens as jurors and defines the policy issues to be addressed (Stewart, Kendall and Coote, 1994; Coote and Leneghan, 1995). The jurors receive evidence and cross-examine witnesses. Their conclusions are set out in a non-binding report which is seriously considered by decision-makers. Initially in Britain, this approach was used in the health field, but by 1996 had been applied to local government issues. Hertfordshire County Council, for example, used one to tackle waste disposal.

One of the main problems to emerge on the participation side has been the need for a longer-term approach – for a more linear strategy. The vast majority of participation programmes are one-off exercises relating to a specific development or plan. The linear approach gives people lots of information at the start and maintains links to them for a period of years. If they are involved via citizens juries and similar devices early on, then they can understand the technical details that lie behind proposals for landfill sites or reservoirs. Giving people lots of data can make it possible to reconcile micro-level demands with strategic concerns. Participants can then see if different conclusions can be drawn. With this approach, the process either affects policies and outputs, or helps make proposals more acceptable (Muir and Veenerdall, 1996). Such an approach is being used with regard to water planning in the USA (Walsh, 1995) and work is being done on it in the context of waste management in Britain (Petts, 1995). The same principle of involving people over time appears in some of the monitoring approaches in City Challenge/SRB areas. It is more developed in Hamilton-Wentworth in Canada where stakeholders are involved in monitoring the impact of the LA21 on policies and budgets over time. Business has a specific role (Whittaker, 1995, pp. 48–52). The linear approach strengthens the participatory process, maintains early momentum, addresses the problem of raised expectations and helps rebuild trust in local democratic institutions. Community-based partnerships can also be seen as a linear approach, developing from an analysis of what local people think needs doing at the micro level.

The growth of these community-based partnerships also fits in with the wider changes in local governance, with the continuing moves away from bureaucratic, paternalist, welfare provision towards a different model. Increasingly, smaller, more flexible, enabling councils are working not just through partnerships with industry, but also with a whole variety of voluntary and not-for-profit organisations. By helping to promote empowerment and the expansion of the social economy, LA21 is helping to shift the balance of provision between public, private and voluntary sector bodies. If this shift in local governance is to take place on a significant scale, then central and local government need to develop capacity-building programmes to target skills and re-sources more effectively (Skinner, 1997), following the example of councils like Barnsley. It is at the micro level of the urban neighbourhood, the estate, and the village that bottom-up empowerment programmes can be developed as a means of tackling social exclusion, alienation, and loss of faith in the capacity of local government to deliver (Gibson, 1993; Geddes, 1995; Taylor, 1995; Thomas, 1995; Stoker, 1997b, pp. 31–4; Young, 1996). This will help to build up social capital and strengthen the weakened links between the local state and civil society (Putnam, 1993; Knight and Stokes, 1996).

The role of the elected councillor has been complicated by these developments however. At present, British local government is established on the basis of the representative democracy model. Ultimately, after all the participation programmes have been completed, local governments have to govern. When there are conflicts at the micro level, or between strategic and more local approaches, councillors have to make decisions in the public interest for the whole of their areas. Some councillors, however, feel that the experiments with participation are starting to undermine this role, and to leave too many decisions about local priorities to local people. In addition, some of the bigger community-based partnerships are making decisions about resource allocation at the ward level. These developments are starting to move us towards more of a participatory democracy model, as is the use of information technology (Percy-Smith, 1995; Stoker, 1997b, pp. 42–3; Young, 1996, pp. 73–5). In contrast, the growth of community-based partnerships gives expression to the associational model of democracy (Achterberg, 1996).

The development of empowerment fits into this broader context because of its links to the citizenship debates (Wheeler, 1996). It promotes conceptions of citizenship in the civic republican tradition. These build from a set of rights to emphasise participation, the practice of citizenship, and involvement in debate and decision-making. This runs counter to the Right's more liberal interpretations which were prevalent in the 1980s and early 1990s. They emphasised citizens being able to make more choices as parents, tenants, consumers, and customers of health services.

There is a tremendous opportunity here for the innovative, people-centred approaches to participation of the mid-1990s to become established as best practice. In the past, interest in participation has waxed and waned with periods of intense interest and others of disillusionment (Boaden *et al.*, 1980; Gyford, 1991; Stoker, 1997). Some of the ideas pushed by the New Urban Left councils in the 1980s (Stoker, 1988, Chapter 9), however, were subsequently applied more widely. Their policies towards the disabled and ethnic minorities – derided by some at the time – have been widely adopted as the mainstream, conventional approach a decade later. The watershed on participation that is now coming into view will have a much broader significance for the regeneration of local democracy, however.

About this study

This project was entitled 'Participation, Partnership, and Sustainable Development: Promoting Local Agenda 21s'. The first aim was to draw together data on different approaches to participation in local government, particularly in connection with Local Agenda 21 (LA21). The second aim was to collect material on the range of community-based partnerships of the kinds discussed in the text above; and to analyse their dynamics and the ways they can relate to sustainable development. The project thus linked into the themes of empowerment, local citizenship, and the changing roles of the voluntary sector being explored through the ESRC Local Governance Programme as a whole.

At ten months, this project was one of the smallest in the Programme. It was carried out only by the author, and the methodology was developed accordingly, with three simple stages – data-collection from primary and secondary sources, interviewing, and analysis. Seventy-five semi-structured interviews were conducted with key figures in pioneering authorities and organisations at all levels, from the national down to the neighbourhood. They were held in urban and rural areas, and included some in Denmark and the Netherlands, where some academics were also interviewed. Many interviews developed beyond information-gathering into detailed discussions about different approaches. In such a swiftly developing field, it proved especially useful to talk to people at the cutting edge of these developments.

The main document from the project (Young, 1996) is a 40 000 word report which aims to relate the project's findings to the needs of practitioners. Part 1 focuses on promoting participation. Part 2 analyses how capacity-building techniques can be used to promote community-based partnerships, and Part 3 identifies and discusses 16 issues arising from the project where further research is needed. These can be tackled via comparative case-study approaches in dissertations or through more ambitious programmes. It is available *free* in exchange for reports and information on individual councils' or other organisations' involvement in this sphere; or for academic papers on these issues. Send an A4 size envelope with stamps to cover postage – 64p or 300gms – to S.C. Young, Government Department, Manchester University, Manchester M13 9PL, UK.

11 Technical Expertise and Public Participation in Planning for Housing : 'Playing the Numbers Game'

Jonathan Murdoch, Simone Abram and Terry Marsden

Introduction

The concept of governance illuminates how local political ensembles of interacting agencies have emerged in a more turbulent socio-economic environment and directs our attention to the multitude of public and private institutions now involved in the local delivery of policies, strategies and services. In effect, 'governance is about governmental and non-governmental organisations working together' (Stoker, 1997a, p. 1) in non-hierarchical and flexible partnerships (often characterised as 'networks' (Rhodes, 1995)). The emergence of partnerships as key mechanisms of local governance ensures the inclusion of new partners in the delivery of policies and services. Frequently these partners are established institutional actors who have the 'positional strengths' (Harding, 1997, p. 643) to deliver the required resources. However, as Young has shown in the previous chapter, the partners are often local communities (or their representatives) who are incorporated into new participatory arrangements aimed at promoting creative and innovative solutions to local problems.

The new terminology of governance directs our attention to change. The traditional institutions of local government are deemed to be failing and come to be replaced by more fluid assemblies, ensembles or networks of actors. In essence, it is argued that when government hierarchies fail to find distinctive solutions to local problems they are replaced by more creative, interactive sets of relations which permit the deployment of strategies and policies tailored to the specificities of local requirements. Thus, where 'government' is hierarchical, 'governance' is characterised by flattened and fluid sets of relations; where 'government' is rigid and bureaucratic, 'governance' is flexible and interactive. In our view, however, it is worth counselling caution in tracing such a shift from government to governance. As with many general movements of this nature, there is a danger that the emphasis on change may result in a neglect of stasis. In this case, there is a danger that existing arrangements of hierarchical and bureaucratic relations come to be viewed as residual legacies of an earlier phase of local politics which is now in the process of being replaced. Such a perspective may severely underplay the stability of these 'residual' arrangements.

In this chapter, we illustrate how more traditional forms of local government continue to dominate certain policy areas and we examine a structure of government which has maintained its hierachical and bureaucratic shape. The structure extends from the national down to the local level in a form which positively excludes, rather than includes, new partners. In particular, this structure permits the involvement of local communities on only the most constrained of terms. Thus, the innovative strategies of community participation outlined by Young in the previous chapter are quite lacking in this sector. This exclusionary complexion is seemingly necessitated by the desire on the part of central government to ensure that local government delivers the requisite policy. The policy is planning for housing, and we argue below that a centralised planning-for-housing structure is required to ensure the delivery of housing units at the local level. Thus, the planning-for-housing structure sets its face against new institutional innovations, for it is believed that if local systems of governance assume exclusive responsibility for housing delivery, then there is every chance that in certain anti-growth areas no houses will be built. A strong central to local hierarchy ensures that local aspirations are forcefully constrained by central direction.

Having outlined the planning-for-housing structure, we go on to examine how this structure imposes itself upon one anti-growth locality. In the context of the Buckinghamshire Structure Plan

Review Process we show that the use of particular forms of technical expertise in the planning-for-housing arena necessarily displaces the non-technical views of local (anti-growth) participants. We, thus, outline how local opinion is marginalised by top-down modes of central regulation (akin to those discussed by Young in the previous chapter). In conclusion, we examine whether this top-down structure of government is likely to survive the challenges now being made on its mode of operation.

Planning for housing

Although local authorities can no longer build houses, they are charged with ensuring that sufficient land is made available to meet likely housing requirements in their administrative areas. Thus, within local plans, authorities are required to show how demands for housing will be met. The calculations of levels of demand come, however, from central and regional tiers of government. Essentially, the system is driven by the desire of central government to ensure that 'a decent home is within reach of every family' (quoted in HC, 1996, p. ix). A strong central-to-local structure is evident in the planning-for-housing arena and this structure ensures that local areas make decisions which accord with national goals.

The planning-for-housing structure is held together by forecasts of housing demand. The forecasts are ostensibly utilised to make future trends apparent to all involved in the planning process. The forecasts also serve to hold the structure together, however for, as we shall show below, they align the behaviours of governmental and non-governmental actors in a diverse number of (local) situations as all are called upon to deliver the requisite numbers of new units. The numbers act as 'automatic technical mechanisms for making judgements, prioritising problems and allocating scarce resources' (Rose, 1991, p. 674). They permit a form of 'remote control' to emerge (Cooper, 1992) wherein local decisions are forced to conform with those made at the centre. Moreover, this 'remote control' can be achieved in ways which ensure that responsibility for action becomes distributed away from central government towards the regions and the localities. In short, 'decisions are broken up into pieces' (Star, 1995, p. 114), that is, they occur across a range of differing sites which are linked only by technical forms of calculation.

This distribution of action within the planning-for-housing system is manifested in the various governmental layers which make up the structure (see Figure 11.1). The layers are held together by a formal

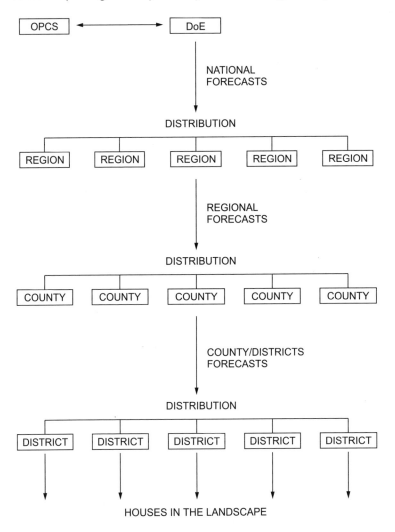

FIGURE 11.1   The planning-for-housing network

technical procedure which runs as follows. The Department of the Environment (DoE) produces detailed household projections or forecasts for England and Wales (these appear every three years or so). The forecasts are based on the most recent population projections prepared by OPCS. The projections are trend based. Historical information on household formation (the propensity of different categories of individuals to form households) is projected forward using an intricate statistical method. The household projections are compiled by applying projected household membership rates to the projections of the private household population disaggregated by age, gender and marital/cohabitational status, and summarising the resulting projections in terms of household formation. Basically, the numbers illustrate what would happen if past trends in household formation were to continue into the future.

In general, the figures are disaggregated from the top down (Holmans, 1996, p. 9) and, once a set of national projections has been calculated and accepted, then these are converted into dwelling requirements at the regional level. This exercise (which is generally carried out by regional planning fora and statisticians from the DoE) aims to arrive at a recommended base set of figures for housing requirements in each region. The national figure provides a 'control' total to which the sum of the regional estimates must agree. In making the regional calculations, a whole range of factors are taken into account – number of households in the area, surveys of housing quantity, scope for conversions, vacancy rate estimates, and so forth – so that a set of workable figures are produced within regional policy guidance. Any regional constraints on meeting regional targets only begin to emerge as the figures move further down the planning hierarchy and it is when the forecasts become included in structure plans that the potential problems associated with actually finding space for new housing come into sharp focus. The counties are expected to distribute their dwelling requirements amongst district authorities. The district councils are obliged to find sites in order to meet the perceived levels of 'demand'. It is this obligation which emerges from the way local authorities are incorporated into the national-to-local structure of housing provision.

In short, the whole structure is held together by numbers. Figure 11.1 shows how the figures flow down the hierarchy from the DoE through the regions, counties and districts as dwelling projections to be incorporated into plans and, finally, emerge as buildings in the landscape. However, while the numbers appear to be the 'glue' which holds the whole ensemble together, the DoE (now DETR) – which sits at the apex of the hierarchy – emphasises that the construction of these statistics is not an 'exact science', but is rather one which seeks a 'balance' between 'demands and needs, provision and environmental considerations' (HC, 1995, p. 43). Nevertheless, the system of regulation is orientated towards statistical objectivity in order to give a firm basis on which to plan. The Head of Housing Policy at the DoE recently explained that although the forecasts are based on a range of assumptions 'they are assumptions really designed to give as neutral a picture as you can of the future' (HC, 1995, p. 43). This assumed neutrality easily translates into a form of objectivity which comes to be seen as somehow 'apolitical'; neutrality and objectivity render invisible the political priorities which lie within the figures (for comparable analyses see Winner, 1985; Star, 1995).

The DoE is also keen to stress that the forecasts should not be regarded as a *determinant* of local housing requirements, for they merely *indicate* the likely levels of demand which may exist in a local area over a given time period. They say the numbers

> provide a starting point for policy decisions. The projections cannot be regarded as precise predictions for future years and the sources of uncertainty have to be borne in mind. Uncertainty increases with the degree of detail, both geographically and by category of household; and with distance into the future (DoE, 1995, p. 13).

As we illustrate below, however, while uncertainty might increase as the figures move down the hierarchy so does their authority.

Linking in the local: a case study

In order to examine the extent to which the numerical calculations are resistable at the local level (where, after all, they are finally turned into houses) we turn to the Buckinghamshire Structure Plan Review process. Buckinghamshire provides a useful case study of the conflict between growth and environmental protection for population growth in the county has been particularly intense in recent years – between 1971 and 1991 it had the fastest population growth in the UK (an increase of approximately 30%). The county also has a long tradition of middle-class in-migration to the rural areas. As the south east – particularly those counties to the west and north of London – has seen a growth in this social strata (see Hamnett, 1986, 1987), so the most attractive environments in Buckinghamshire have witnessed a continued in-migration of wealthy residents, particularly into the preserved southern districts. In previous work (Murdoch and Marsden, 1994) we have shown that villages in this county are becoming increasingly middle class in character. We found, on average, that around two-thirds of village residents had moved into their houses within the last 10 years and that almost half rural residents fell into socio-economic groups 1, 2 and 3, with a further third in the economically inactive (retired) category. Almost all the residents in these villages showed themselves to be strongly opposed to economic development with the vast majority (70–80%) wishing to see no more new homes or development opportunities in the countryside (see Murdoch and Marsden, 1994, especially Chapter 2).

It is also important to note the spatial distributions of development within the county over recent years, for this indicates where the most pressurised and protected enclaves lie. Prior to the recent local government review (which took effect after the events described here) Buckinghamshire was made up of five districts: Milton Keynes and Aylesbury Vale in the north; High Wycombe, South Buckinghamshire and Chiltern in the south. The initial growth centre was High Wycombe where, during the 1960s, the Labour-controlled council sanctioned a policy of substantial public housing investment. By the early 1970s, however, a coalition of conservation groups, spearheaded by the local branch of the Council for the Protection of Rural England (CPRE) and the Chilterns and High Wycombe amenity societies, forced the adoption of a much more restrictive growth policy in the south of the county, an area which comprises mainly of Green Belt and an Area of Outstanding Natural Beauty (AONB) (Healey *et al.*, 1982). Further growth was, therefore, pushed into the north, notably the town of Aylesbury and the new city of Milton Keynes. Throughout the 1980s, growth levels within the county remained high and the planning restrictions in the south ensured that Aylesbury Vale (which grew by 8.2% between 1981 and 1991) and Milton Keynes (which grew by 39.2% during the same period) took the bulk of the new population (in the south population numbers remained almost static (Buckinghamshire County Council, 1996)).

During this period, the Structure Plan's policies of containment in the south and urban expansion in the north came to be bolstered by a local political coalition – made up of amenity societies, action groups, local residents, county and district councillors – which had come into existence as a 'second line' of defence against any incursion into the rural areas of both the south and the north. This coalition would only accept growth in the urban areas of Aylesbury and Milton Keynes, and to a lesser extent High Wycombe, and sought to ensure that development plan policies adhered to these protectionist principles. In the review of the Structure Plan being examined here, the protectionists made their views plain from the beginning when a group of county councillors (mostly drawn from the southern districts) insisted on the rigorous protection of the Green Belt and AONB areas in the south and the rural areas in the north. According to a planning officer who was involved in drawing up the plan, the councillors were concerned to ensure that the Green Belt and the AONB were sacrosanct: 'they've always made clear right from the word go that they wanted the Green Belt protected and they wanted the AONB protected. You've got those two fixed starting points which they were firmly attached to' (interview).

From the beginning of the review process, therefore, members of the anti-growth coalition ensured that earlier Structure Plan policies of Green Belt/AONB protection were maintained. Having re-established this policy, the County Council then attempted to gain the districts' acceptance of this general approach. Not surprisingly, the policy of maintaining Green Belt and AONB boundaries in the south, and thus focussing development activity in the north, was welcomed by the southern districts of Chiltern and South Buckinghamshire. More unexpectedly, however, the northern districts also went along with the strategy. For Milton Keynes, the role allocated to the borough was very much in line with its expected course of development up to 2006 when it was still expected to play a regional growth role; thus, it was happy enough to play its part in soaking up development pressures from the south of the county (even though planners in the city were sceptical that Milton Keynes relieves any pressure from the south of the county). Crucially, Aylesbury Vale District Council were also supportive of the distributional strategy and seemed happy for the town of Aylesbury to continue to act as a regional growth centre. The districts were keen to behave responsibly in accordance with the demands being made of the county at the regional level. Thus, the town of Aylesbury – whose population had grown by 200% between 1960 and 1990 – was to be a focal point for development throughout the plan period. The planners here seemed to view accommodating future development as something of a challenge: as one said during interview 'it's a good fun place to work...where you've got a reasonable amount of development pressure, and you've got certain problems to be overcome as well. It's an art of achieving a balance between these'.

This strategy of spatial distribution of development indicates that the decisions taken during that earlier phase of strategic planning had become entrenched, not just in planning policies, but in the coalition of actors surrounding the review. However, while a local anti-growth coalition, constituted around protection of the rural environment, was firmly in place in Buckinghamshire, the county could not reject development emanating from within the region as a whole. The planners, because they were incorporated into planning-for-housing structure, had the responsibility of providing for levels of housing provision determined by the numerical calculations of national, regional and local housing demand. At the time (1992), it had been calculated that the south-east region would require 222 250 new homes during the Structure Plan period (1991–2011) and Buckinghamshire County Council initially agreed to provide 62 600 of these. In line with the general strategy, supplemented by the generally supportive attitudes of the districts, the housing distribution figures allocated the vast bulk of new housing to Milton Keynes, Aylesbury and High Wycombe (it was expected that the total figure of 62 600 would be distributed in the following way: Milton Keynes would take 37 200; Aylesbury Vale 14 300; Wycombe 6700, Chiltern 1900 and South Bucks 2500).

Almost from the very beginning of the review process, then, the whole complexion and direction of the plan was shaped around the two objectives of rural protection and the need to meet regional housing requirements. Protectionism in the south and regional responsibilities in the north combined in a consensus amongst the planners on the required levels of development and their spatial distribution. Yet this strategy emerged from a very select group of local decision-makers, effectively made up of planners and local councillors. Thus the next stage of the plan review process – the public consultation exercise – provided an opportunity for a much broader range of participants to challenge the assumptions which lay at the heart of the plan. In practice, however, many of these assumptions were strengthened rather than weakened by the consultation process. A key part of the strategy – growth in the north and protection in the south – was supported by the most influential local actors, such as local amenity societies, parish councils and environmental groups.

This perception of local support for the plan was reinforced by the muted response from urban areas within the county. Residents of Aylesbury, for instance, a town which was set to bear the brunt of new development, produced almost nothing in response to the plan policies. It is hard to find any clear reason for this, but it was suggested to us by various respondents that it might be due to the fact that the town is not parished so there is no focal point for any anti-development sentiments. There seemed to be no history or tradition of collective action in response to planning issues in the town. Moreover, the levels and types of development already experienced may have resulted in a fatalism towards future development trends. It was mentioned to us by one planning officer that this fatalistic attitude is linked to the entrenchment of the strategic policy in the county: in his view, the policy has become 'fixed in people's minds; this is how it's been done and always will be done'. Thus, in Aylesbury apathy seemed to prevail largely as result of the entrenched assumptions around development. There was, therefore, effectively no local (urban) counterweight to the protectionist (rural) ensemble (a situation which was reinforced by the political make-up of Aylesbury Vale District Council which was at this time Conservative dominated; there were no Conservative councillors in Aylesbury itself).

While there was undoubtedly a great deal of local support for the distributional strategy there was, however, some disquiet about the overall levels of development expected in the county as a whole. Many members of the anti-growth coalition who lived in the south and in the rural areas of the north, although pleased that the countryside was to be offered protection, worried that levels of development were too high in the county as a whole. They recognised that *all* residents would be affected by significant growth in the population. Thus there was a general feeling of disquiet about the levels of housing proposed in the plan and some attempt was made to question the need for growth on the scale proposed. Raising this question, however, proved much more difficult than arguing for the straightforward protection of environmental designations, even for these resourceful and articulate people.

Although central government's Planning Policy Guidance Note 3 (Housing) makes clear that: 'Structure Plans will need to explain how the housing figures have been derived and the assumptions underlying them' (Department of the Environment, 1992, para.11) it became evident during the review process that only those participants with sufficient resources to engage in the technical arguments necessary to undo the 'facts' coded into the housing policies could hope to challenge the power of the numbers at the local level. The assumptions upon which the figures were based – DoE household formation calculations, census data, vacancy rates and so on – were hard to scrutinise. Moreover, the numbers came from national and regional institutions which seemed to have already rendered them 'factual'. Yet the government claims – in its planning guidance – that these numbers should be 'tested' during the Structure Plan review process. In this case, however, the only actors with the expertise to undertake this task were the house builders and their objective was simply to get the numbers increased.

A full-blown debate about the housing numbers took place over two days at the Enquiry in Public (EiP). Here the house builders – who were assembled *en masse* – took issue with the policies underlying the County's figures. They challenged the figures from a number of different directions, arguing, for instance, that the County Council had over-estimated the strength of the east–west shift (provided for by the development of the so-called 'East Thames Corridor') and had underestimated both in-migration pressures and the potential for job growth. The vacancy rates used by the County in their calculations were also criticised as too modest. The HBF provided a set of comparative figures and projections which gave alternative scenarios to those provided by the County Council and proposed a figure of 79 500 dwellings between 1991 and 2011 (around 17 000 higher than the County Council's figure). Other developers provided their own housing projections (ranging from 64 000 to 74 000 for the plan period) and all concentrated on undermining the County Council's housing projections, using alternative calculations.

Effectively, the professional planning consultants and the other representatives who spoke for the house builders used their expertise and technical resources to open up the housing calculations in order to expose the political assumptions which they believed lay within them (one HBF officer said during interview that 'it's political pressure that is leading them to adopt the figure they have . . . . It's the politics that leads to this'). Nevertheless, the figures could only be disputed in technical not political terms. Thus, alternative numerical calculations were used to argue for increased dwelling figures on the basis that in-migration patterns would be higher or that the vacancy rates were too low. It was also noticeable at the EiP that other participants, who also wished to challenge the housing numbers, were not so well equipped to formalise their arguments. Amenity societies, parish councils, the CPRE and voluntary agencies all actively opposed the figures. Their arguments, however, were neither technical nor numerical; they were simply 'political'. As a consequence, those local participants who expressed deep reservations about the validity of the statistics, the assumptions about the 'need for growth' and so on, but who did not put forward a thorough numerical analysis, using alternative calculations, were not able to make any impact on the projections.

From the final report of the EiP panel came a recommendation that the housing figures should be increased marginally. Having thoroughly checked the County Council's figures, the Panel concluded that net in-migration would be higher than the County had allowed, particularly in the latter half of the plan-period. It was also noted that the County had underestimated vacancy rates. Thus, the total number of houses to be provided during the plan period was raised from 62 600 to 66 500. In their response to the EIP panel report, the County Council argued that its in-migration figures were sound but accepted that the vacancy rate had been too low. It settled on a figure of 64 000 houses throughout the plan-period, an increase of 1400 houses above the original total. This figure was included in the final, adopted version of the Structure Plan (Buckinghamshire County Council, 1996).

To summarise this section, the whole debate around levels of development revolved around the figures. Even though a well-organised and long-standing anti-growth coalition was deeply suspicious of the 'numbers game' that they were forced to play, they could find no way to resist the technical calculations coming down from 'on high'. The only actors with the required technical knowledge to play the game successfully were the house builders. They too were suspicious of the numbers, but *only* those calculated at the local level; they accepted the national and regional projections and used these as a basis from which to launch their assault on the County Council's calculations. They successfully employed the national and regional figures in their debate with the local authorities. Thus, the configuration of local argument by the national-to-local calculations of housing demand enabled the house builders to dominate the debate about the required levels of housing development in Buckinghamshire.

Some concluding comments.

In the case study outlined above, the planning-for-housing structure employed a considerable array of technical resources as it, firstly, brought future trends in household formation and housing demand into the calculations and then ensured that these calculations cascaded down the planning hierarchy, thereby configuring decisions made at the local level. It was evident that the technical resources available to the national-to-local stucture far outweighed those available to local actors, even though the local actors (middle class, committed, articulate, knowledgeable, etc.) showed themselves, in many respects, quite capable of effective participation. They simply could not resist the technical forms of expertise which bound their locality into a long chain of national-to-local regulation. By comparison with these objective technical facts, their own representations seemed emotional, partial and parochial; in short, *political*.

In many ways, this finding simply reiterates the tensions which have frequently been observed between technical forms of planning and the requirement to include members of the public in decision-making processes (Stoker, 1997b). It has long been understood that public participation sits uneasily with 'scientific' planning (Reade, 1987; Short *et al.*, 1986; Thomas, 1996). Yet the claim is frequently made that planning should provide an effective and even-handed arena in which a variety of participants can debate their differences and reconcile their conflicts. The analysis presented above indicates, however, that this process of mediation is formalised in such a way as to ensure that local communities are obliged to accept new houses whether they like it or not (this finding mirrors that presented by Short *et al.*, 1986).

It is, therefore, implicit in the structure which governs the planning-for-housing process that national goals (provision of housing) must be permitted to override local preferences. This aspect of the regulatory system – which in many ways conforms to traditional conceptions of local government – ensures that the structure is hierarchical and technocratic. Such an observation gives rise, however, to the question of stability; given the changes currently sweeping through local government – as outlined in the chapters of this book – can this structure be maintained or will it succumb to the general shift towards governance? In speculating upon this issue we can point to two main sources of pressure on the planning-for-housing structure.

As we have seen, the forecasts hold together a national-to-local structure and effectively constrain the ability of local actors (those situated in the counties and districts) to dislodge the assumptions which lie at the heart of the calculations. However, the hierarchical and coercive dimensions of the structure have not escaped the notice of those groups which oppose new house building in the countryside. The CPRE, for instance, recognises that the technical calculations hold together the institutional framework and they see the projections as the fundamental driver of the planning for housing process. In evidence presented to the House of Commons Environment Committee, the group has argued that the planning-for-housing structure is *dominated* by the household projections because, in practice, local planning bodies simply accept the figures. Worried by possible government intervention (as in Berkshire where the Secretary of State recently forced the Council to adopt higher regional totals after an 'unacceptably' low figure was included in the structure plan) or legal challenges from the house builders (as in Buckinghamshire where planners were concerned that their refusal to take the EiP recommendations fully on board would result in a court action) councils err on the side of caution and work to the figures coming down from above.

The CPRE has, therefore, recently attempted to weaken the power of the housing projections by lobbying for their downgrading in the structure planning process (the group maintains that authorities should be free to adopt lower figures if they so wish; in their view this is a local matter for local planning authorities to decide upon) and strengthen the environmental capacity calculations included in national and regional housing forecasts. It is argued by CPRE that regional policy guidance should give *equal* weight to environmental capacity considerations when deciding on regional housing requirements (HC, p. 131). The interest group, along with other commentators (such as Baker and Wong, 1997), also believes that the process should be rendered more transparent through the encouragement of more active debate at the regional level. Thus, the number of participants in the planning-for-housing process should be expanded to include the whole range of interested parties (perhaps using some of the innovative procedures outlined in the previous chapter by Young), not just those involved in planning and house building. These arguments would now seem to have been largely accepted by the new labour Government (see DETR, 1998)

Pressures for change in the composition of the institutional structure are also emerging as a result of the forecasts themselves. The aim of the housing forecasts is to bring future housing demand to the attention of policy makers and planners in order to ensure that housing provision is forthcoming, But the forecasts also render future trends visible and allow a consideration of the predicted developmental scenarios. Such a consideration seems to be occurring the prediction that in the wake of 4.4 million houses will be needed before the year 2016. The sheer scale of the housing numbers involved has prompted much discussion around the question 'where will the people go?' (see DoE, 1996; Breheny and Hall, 1996) and has unleashed a whole host of other questions – such as how do we reverse two centuries of anti-urban culture in England and how do we change the 'grisly' present-day experience of urban living? (Cordy, 1997, p. 6) – questions which led into the recent deliberations of the Urban Task Force (DETR, 1999). At the present time, these issues are giving rise to demands for a new approach to housing-for-planning policy and for the elaboration of a new relationship between local and national systems of regulation Again, the labour government has been forced to formulate a responsible (DETR 1998).

Both these sets of pressures seem to indicate that the technical framework which governs the planning for housing arena has perhaps reach the limit of its adequacy. It is now argued by many concerned commentators that a much more inclusive regime is required, one which permits an open and free-ranging debate on the whole range of issues which are raised by the high levels of development expected in future years. The concerns which have emerged in response to the housing forecasts derive in part from a perception that certain social groups are being ill-served by the 'numbers game'. As in other areas of governance, technical expertise in the planning for housing structure functions as 'a nodal point' around which perceptions, explanations and arguments are organised. At present, the only actors with the ability to circle this nodal point are policy-makers, developers and, to a lesser extent, those seeking to protect the rural environment. There are many potential participants who are currently excluded from the decision-making process such as those urban dwellers in places like Aylesbury who are faced with continued development into the forseeable future, with all the environmental disruptions and social upheavals that this entails. The technical and hierarchical arrangements which despite the new labour government's amendments, still compose the planning-for-housing sector do little to bring the concerns of these groups to the fore. It is to be hoped that an increasing recognition of this failing prompts a search for a more inclusive and transparent form of governance in the planning-for-housing sphere.

About this study

Under the ESRC's Local Governance Programme this project – entitled *Exclusive space? Networks of participation and forward planning in a rural locality* – followed the Buckinghamshire Structure Plan Review process throughout 1994 and 1995. The main participants, such as planning officers, councillors, amenity groups, developers, local residents and parish councils, were interviewed and many planning meetings, including the Enquiry in Public, were attended. We are grateful to all our respondents for their patience and time. In particular, we would like to thank Chris Kennenford of Buckinghamshire County Council who was especially generous with his time and knowledge. Further findings from the project can be found in: Murdoch, J., Abram, S. and Marsden, T. (1996) 'Modalities of planning: arenas, actors and strategies of persuasion in the development plan review process' *Papers in Environmental Planning Research* No. 5, Dept. of City and Regional Planning, University of

Wales Cardiff; Abram, S., Murdoch, J. and Marsden, T. (1996) 'The social construction of "Middle England": the politics of participation in forward planning' *Journal of Rural Studies* 12(4) pp. 353–364; Abram, S., Murdoch, J. and Marsden, T. (1998) 'Planning by numbers: migration and statistical governance', in Boyle, P. and Halfacre, K. (eds) *Migration into rural areas: theories and issues*, Wiley, London; Murdoch, J. and Alram, S. (1998) 'Defining the limits of community governance', *Journal of Rural Studies* 14 pp. 41–51; Cowell, R, and Murdoch, J. (1999) 'Land use and the limits to (regional) governance' *International Journal of Urban and Regional Research*, forthcoming; Murdoch, J. and Abram, S. (2000) *Governing growth: discourses of development and environment in planning for housing*, Ashgate, forthcoming.

12 User Participation in Community Housing: 'Is Small Really Beautiful'?

David Clapham, Keith Kintrea and Helen Kay

Introduction

This chapter seeks to examine the experience of community-based housing organisations (CBHOs) in Scotland as a form of local governance. Compared with many of the processes and institutions discussed in this book, what is particularly distinctive about CBHOs is their community base and their very small scale; typically CBHOs own and manage between 100 and 500 dwellings, serving a population of around 1500–1800 at the most.

The theoretical (or hoped-for) advantages of small institutions of governance are many and include the prospect of greater effectiveness as service providers, the availability of participative democracy as a means for better decision-making, and greater accountability to residents. At the same time they need not remain isolated, but can participate in partnership with other organisations and therefore have access to wider resources and power.

After an outline of CBHOs, this chapter considers four main issues. First, the effectiveness of the organisations as housing providers is assessed; how successful are CBHOs as housing managers? Second, the accountability and legitimacy of the CBHOs is examined; do residents trust the organisations, what mechanisms of accountability exist, and how effective are they? Third, the wider relationships of the CBHOs within the local governance network are discussed; to what extent are the organisations able to be independent players and shape their own destiny in the name of resident control? Finally, an overall assessment of the significance of CBHOs for the development of systems of governance is made. How can community-based housing associations be best understood; are they a real alternative to traditional forms of governance, offering an insight into the possibilities of a new community-based governance where opportunities for deliberation and local response result in better government?

The origin and characteristics of community-based housing organisations

CBHOs, in this context, refers to small housing organisations run by residents established following the transfer of housing stock from the ownership of local councils. In legal terms they are either cooperatives or housing associations registered with Scottish Homes, the government's housing agency in Scotland, and often described as Community Ownership schemes. They originated in Glasgow in the mid-1980s as a result of pressure by residents in six local areas to improve their housing conditions and their neighbourhoods. The council lacked the funds to pay for improvements and sought a mechanism whereby affordable rented housing could be retained, but improvements carried out. After lengthy negotiations with the Scottish Office, and following a vigorous campaign by the residents, the first schemes were formed in 1986 and 1987. These were soon followed by others in Glasgow and elsewhere and, after 1989, under Scottish Homes, it became policy throughout Scotland to promote Community Ownership as part of estate regeneration schemes.

There are now around 40 Community Ownership organisations in Scotland to which nearly 13 000 houses had been transferred by 1995. This represents 69% of all council stock in Scotland transferred to new owners since the mid-1980s, not including Right-to-Buy sales (Taylor, 1996). Some other Community Ownership schemes have been created by the disposal of Scottish Homes' own housing stock.

Although the CBHOs are highly distinctive, they are part of the changing shape of the governance of public services and have some parallels with institutions in other services, such as grant-maintained schools. In housing, CBHOs are part of the move away from direct provision of housing by local councils and towards the creation of a diversity of providers including housing associations, Housing Action Trusts and, more recently, local housing companies, as well as the decentralised management of existing council housing in tenant management cooperatives and estate management boards. Government housing policy has varied between England and Scotland with CBHOs being a distinctively, if not uniquely, Scottish phenomenon.

CBHOs are highly distinctive organisations within the housing field; four points stand out. First, they are, in principle, community controlled and led. All residents in the area are entitled to become members, members elect the Management Committee, and committee members are almost exclusively local people. Second, they have a full range of responsibilities in relation to their stock; they own it, and are responsible for housing development (improvement and/or new building) and housing management. Third, they are small and highly localised with only a few hundred houses in their control, usually all situated in a few roads or streets. Fourth, they operate in very deprived areas. Most CBHOs were established as a matter of policy in the most deteriorated and deprived areas of council housing, and have been ascribed a key role in Scottish urban policy in helping to transform the most difficult estates (Scottish Office, 1988).

This chapter focuses on four of the original six Community Ownership schemes established in Glasgow in 1986 and 1987. Two of the schemes are in post-war peripheral estates, one is an isolated 'cottage' estate, while the fourth is part of an inter-war slum clearance estate recognised as one of the most deprived areas of Scotland (for more details see Clapham *et al.*, 1989; and Clapham, Kay, and Kintrea, 1996).

Effective housing provision

At the outset the primary motivation of tenants was to achieve better housing conditions and this was also the main objective of the council. The residents had a largely instrumental approach: the fact the CBHOs were resident-controlled was an exciting bonus but not in itself an objective. In fact, the council was probably more interested in resident control than were the residents, as was the Scottish Office which wanted to reduce the role of the council and to promote self-help. The success of resident control was dependent on the Community Ownership model proving itself to be an effective and sustainable means of delivering housing services, otherwise the support from tenants necessary for its survival would not be forthcoming.

The research showed that housing improvement had been undertaken in an effective manner to the satisfaction of most tenants and the other agencies and that housing management services were being delivered successfully. Tenant satisfaction with the service provided by the council in 1986/87 was compared with that provided by the Community Ownership organisations in 1989. In all areas, a majority of tenants said that the service under Community Ownership was better than that under the council, and overall 68% of tenants said the service was better (Clapham, Kintrea and Whitefield 1991).

These findings are mirrored by those of other studies, which show that local resident-controlled housing agencies provide a more effective service as measured by tenant satisfaction (Clapham, 1992; Price Waterhouse, 1995). By 1989, however, the new organisations had not had much time to establish themselves. It could be argued that the success of housing improvements influenced perceptions of the housing management service and that this effect would wear off as other neighbouring properties were brought up to a similar standard and the improvements aged. Further, it could be argued that the success was due to substantial tenant involvement which would be difficult to sustain in the long term. Tenant satisfaction with the service in 1989 was therefore compared with 1994. Levels of satisfaction in all the CBHOs were high in 1994 and in all but one case had increased since 1989: 81% of tenants said they were satisfied with the service provided by the CBHOs in 1994 compared with 72% in 1989.

Tenants in 1994 also held the view that the service was getting better. Across all four schemes, 40% said the service was improving and only 6% said it was getting worse. It was evident from the interviews with staff and committee members that over the years since the previous evaluation, the associations had developed their housing management systems and adopted a more professional approach whilst retaining the commitment to community involvement and accountability which was a key element of their initial success.

In summary, the evidence of the research is that locally-based resident-controlled housing organisations can not only provide an effective service but, crucially, can sustain this over a considerable period of time.

Accountability and legitimacy

Residents' views on accountability

The extent to which CBHOs were accountable to residents, and regarded as legitimate by them, was explored in the household survey. In particular, the focus was on the attitudes of respondents to their local CBHO and to Glasgow City Council, which was the former landlord of many residents, and which remains, by far, the largest provider of social rented housing in Glasgow.

The survey shows that CBHOs were regarded much more highly than the council: 70% or more of respondents believed that ordinary residents have no say in the council, that councillors are out of touch, that officials do not care and that local government affairs are too complex. Over 60% thought that the council wastes a lot of money, although 44% did say the Council 'can be trusted to do what's right', which seems rather surprising in view of the other findings. In contrast, a majority disagreed with the contentions that the CBHO committees are out of touch, that the staff don't care, and that a lot of money is wasted, and three-quarters believed that the CBHOs can be trusted to 'do what's right'. Although there are some problem areas (over a third believe they have no say in the CBHOs and nearly 40% think the CBHOs' affairs are too complex to understand), it is evident that the CBHOs are trusted and respected to a far greater extent than traditional local government, at least in the form of Glasgow City Council.

Further evidence of the perceived legitimacy of CBHOs is shown in comparisons of interviewees' confidence in various UK institutions. CBHOs emerge as the institution in which the greatest proportion of respondents (38%) felt they could place 'complete' or a 'great deal' of confidence, with Parliament, local councils, the civil service, and business and industry all generating positive responses from fewer than 10% of respondents.

Mechanisms of accountability

There are two potential mechanisms for accountability to local residents in the CBHOs. First, residents may participate directly in the decision-making processes of the CBHOs. The second mechanism is the Committee which is elected by local residents. The Nolan Committee on Standards in Public Life (1996a) has encouraged all housing associations to adopt both of these mechanisms.

Active participation in the CBHOs was examined by asking about respondents' attendance at meetings in 1994 and 1989. Over 60% of people in the later survey had ever attended some kind of meeting, most commonly the AGM or another public meeting. Of those attending meetings, over three-quarters reported they had been to a meeting during the previous 12 months, therefore around 46% of all residents had been to some kind of meeting during the last year. The proportion who had ever attended a meeting, and the proportion who had attended one in the past year both fell between the two surveys, however, although the proportion of residents who had attended a committee meeting of some kind (almost certainly as a committee member) rose.

Some of those interviewed, particularly longer-standing committee members, were disappointed with the level of interest shown by residents in the CBHOs in the 1990s. They contrasted the apathy of the present day with the enthusiasm of the mid-1980s. One reported:

> Some of the original tenants have moved out and other types of tenants have come in...[All they want] it is to have a decent house,...they don't care what happens round about them in the area, as long as they get a decent house to live in, the whole place could go to pot really.

A committee member elsewhere also cast doubt on residents' interest:

> ...most of the tenants at the present time are quite happy to get a house, shut their door, and forget what is going on. Whether any of them really know what [the organisation] is doing I don't know.

These kinds of complaints, though, must be seen in the context of organisations which were set up with a cooperative ethos that is still held proudly by some. The survey figures in fact suggest that active participation in the CBHOs has held up very well as the organisations have matured, in spite of the slow-down or even halt of housing development activity which, of all housing activities, usually attracts the most active participation. The survey strongly suggests, at the very least, that the CBHOs have the potential to be held accountable to those residents who take up the frequent opportunities to access the staff and committee members. The high proportion of residents attending AGMs when committee members are elected certainly seems to confound the criticisms made by the Nolan Committee (1996a) that the boards or committees of housing associations in general were often accountable only to themselves. Indeed, an experienced observer offered evidence to the Nolan Committee that 'membership [of housing associations] in terms of shareholding membership, nearly always means absolutely nothing' (Richard Best in Committee on Standards in Public Life, 1996b, p. 150). This certainly does not seem to be the case here.

Committee members

'Who are the governors' in the new local governance is a frequent question which has preoccupied critics, with the implication that decision-makers are out of touch with, and unrepresentative of, service recipients. In the CBHOs, the formal control is held by the committee; evidence about committee members is available from the household survey, where 15% of individuals interviewed were current or former committee members, and from interviews.

The constitutions of the organisations mean that all elected committee members are local residents; who come from tightly circumscribed areas. This means that nearly all committee members are tenants or, failing that, local owner-occupiers.

The survey enables comparison to be made between committee members and other residents. Overall, in terms of age, gender balance, educational qualifications, and employment status, committee members are very similar to the respondents as a whole. Committee members were slightly more likely to have formal educational and occupational qualifications, more likely to have at least one person in the household in work, and fewer were in the very lowest income brackets. This demonstrates a key point: a leading management role in the CBHOs is clearly held by the average – or near average – housing estate resident. CBHO committee membership contrasts strongly with most board members in local public spending bodies, recently said to be 'still drawn from a narrow and homogeneous social stratum with a preponderance of white, middle class, middle aged to retired men' (Greer and Hoggett, 1997, p. 3).

Although committee members were more or less average local people, this does not in itself mean that they actively represent the people who live in the area. In the 1994 survey, nearly half the respondents (47%) said they had not spoken to a committee member in the past year, which suggests that committee members are not constantly in touch with other residents. At the same time, almost three-quarters said it was very easy to talk to a committee member, which suggests that they can be approached.

The qualitative interviews with the committee members showed a wide range of approaches to representation. None saw themselves as representing any particular point of view or political party, and none made any particular effort to canvass the tenants' views, or make themselves available in any kind of 'surgery'. The more experienced members were happy to bring up cases as they came across them, or to represent individual's positions at the committee or, occasionally, directly to the staff. This kind of practice was enthused about by a Scottish Homes Board Member, and a former CBHO chairperson, in oral evidence to the Nolan Committee:

> From the accountability side, it is very important to understand that tenants who are on a committee and live in a street, like I do and I am on the committee, you are more accountable to your local neighbours than you are to private organisations or Scottish Homes because you have accountability, walking down your own street and out your own front gate... (Frances McCall in Committee on Standards in Public Life, 1996b, p. 436)

In contrast, a few committee members avoided all contact with ordinary tenants. Indeed, in some of the CBHOs, there was a rule which forbade committe members from answering any query brought by tenants, instead, they were instructed to direct tenants to the CBHO's office to have the matter handled by the staff. A staff member reported the situation:

> It's a rule of the cooperative that the committee members can't discuss tenants' complaints in the street; your first approach is through the office.

Such practices seem to challenge the role of the committee member as a representative. It could be argued that the CBHOs are an exercise in participatory, rather than representative, democracy, and a breakdown in the representative role is of no consequence. Given that a majority of residents in any one year do not take an active part in the CBHO, however, it seems surprising at first sight that the representative and advocacy role of committee member is limited by policy. Equally, it could be argued that the role of the committee member is that of a trustee, rather than a representative, but there was no evidence that the role of committee members had been thought through in depth in any of the organisations studied, so that committee members remained in an ambivalent position – representatives often without the means to represent.

The staff and committee interviews suggested several reasons for the deliberate limiting of the representative role. Chief among these were the personal pressures on committee members when there were scarce resources to allocate or controversial decisions to take, but there was also evidence that some committee members were too inexperienced or unfamiliar with the policies and practices of the CBHOs. The CBHOs wanted to avoid damaging rumours sweeping the neighbourhood based on errors of fact or judgement. One experienced committee member reported:

> In my opinion there is really only five or six people who are really effective. [others] have been here as long as I have, one of them has been doing it longer than me, but they still don't know what they are doing.

> ... they are basically scared, and they don't know how to sort that. They have had lots of chances to train, but they say it's too far away – and it's just a taxi ride.

Elsewhere, a staff member reported that committee members sometimes took an exceptionally narrow view of their representative roles to the detriment of policy-making and strategy:

> Last year what was happening was that committee members were coming to meetings and bringing up their six repairs and not talking about what's on the agenda.

There are clearly, then, some shortcomings in involving large numbers of residents in committee elections and in other meetings with the CBHOs, and some practical problems in the representative role of the committee. It is clear, however, that the community basis of the housing organisations considered here is solid, that they have managed to sustain quite a substantial degree of active participation over nearly 10 years since they were founded. It is also clear that the kinds of people who govern the CBHOs are the same as those who receive the services and that this is true to a much greater extent than in regional or national housing associations or other local public spending bodies. Perhaps a more important question, however, is what difference this community support and apparent representativeness makes to the decisions which are taken.

Decision-making in the CBHOs

Earlier research (Clapham *et al.*, 1989) showed that the local people who formed the first action groups and campaigned for their houses to be improved were critical to the support which was generated from central and local government. However, having persuaded government and its agencies to back them in the mid-1980s they were then inevitably caught up in a decision-making process which involved powerful agencies. Also, by employing staff, the experience, views and values of staff came into play, together with a less direct role for the committee.

Three of the four CBHOs examined here employ a small staff team headed by a Director. The fourth organisation employs one staff member as a coordinator and buys in most services. Senior staff are all experienced, well-qualified and well-paid, and to a large extent, professionalised; they see the reference points for their jobs as outside the CBHOs. The standards of service they promote largely come from the housing profession, the housing association movement and the best practice guidance of the Scottish Federation of Housing Associations and Scottish Homes.

Committee–staff relations

The interviews with staff and committee members showed that staff tend to take the lead at the operational level, by leading on agenda setting and strategy. Several established committee members believed that staff had too much power, and could not quite accept that the organisations had become professionalised and more distant from them as they matured. A committee member referred to the CBHO as 'a monster which got out of control' and claimed she had to spend as many as 180 hours a month on CBHO business. 'If I didn't, we would have the tail wagging the dog'. Another complained: 'Staff take too much to do with it these days' while another believed that committee members' views were not always recognised:

> I think...when you are suggesting something I always feel as if you are getting put off. [The staff] don't really say 'Well, that isn't right, we will do it our way', but I think it could happen.

Others, though, felt the committee, or at least some of its members, did have sufficient influence, but only after they had gained experience:

> we used to be like noddy dogs and be likely only to say 'if you think so!' Now, if we don't like something...we say 'we don't like that', whereas we have got management [Committee Members] who would just say 'yes', but then I think we all start out like that but we have to progress on to being big mouths like I am now.

Certainly it was evident in the interviews with senior staff that they sometimes saw it as part of their job to persuade their committees to behave in a 'responsible' manner in line with good practice. This was concerned as much with committee behaviour, rather than policy. One director reported:

I think that probably, when I was first here, I was quite inclined to the view that 'it's the committee's decision' and 'the committee are right',

but she went on to say she had quite quickly had to move and intervene into what she saw as breaches of discipline amongst committee members.

It was evident, however, that power was sometimes more evenly balanced. Another senior staff member reported:

Sometimes we have quite long and fought battles... I think they do listen... they might do what they want at the end of the day but they will give you a hearing.... Certainly if I am saying 'Well, look, it's illegal and you really cannot do that' they will listen ....At the end of the day (referring to policy on tenancy conditions) if they decide it's no budgerigars and hang the hamsters we are going to have to run with that.... I think what you have to accept as a member of staff is that you are not always right.

Overall, the evidence from the household survey shows that the majority of committee members were satisfied with their level of influence, but over 40% of current committee members believed that the committee should have more influence. Almost no one believed the committee should have less influence.

Relationships with Scottish Homes

Scottish Homes provides the majority of funds for housing development and has a statutory role to regulate and monitor housing associations. In evidence to the Nolan Committee, the Chief Executive of Scottish Homes explained the agency's approach to influencing housing associations:

We are in a somewhat difficult position because housing associations are independent, voluntary bodies notwithstanding that something like, for mainstream rented accommodation, 83% of the cost of every unit is borne by us, so they clearly need us. We fund them. We cannot, except *in extremis*, order them to do things and we would not be prescriptive. We believe, for example, that in the code of conduct area it is better to suggest to associations, and the Federation of Scottish Housing Associations joins us in this, better ways of doing things and expect them to adopt them. (Peter McKinlay in Committee on Standards in Public Life, 1996b, p. 435)

The evidence to the Nolan Committee did not, however, recognise that Scottish Homes may seek to influence housing associations in two ways. Certainly Scottish Homes approves and monitors associations for compliance with recommended financial and administrative procedures, and for adherence to good practice. Second, and often more importantly, Scottish Homes controls the development funding of CBHOs. Evidence from the study shows that both types of influence led the CBHOs to compromise their policies to suit Scottish Homes' rather than to suit themselves.

A feature of the relationships between the CBHOs and Scottish Homes is the very limited role of the CBHO committees. Committees meet Scottish Homes' staff on the occasion of three-yearly monitoring visits, but otherwise only rarely. Nearly all other relationships with Scottish Homes are handled by staff, including critical meetings, such as the annual programming meeting when the forthcoming year's development programme is discussed, as well as all day-to-day contacts about development projects; therefore, staff are usually the messengers for Scottish Homes' views. Interviews with committee members reveal that they sometimes did get involved directly, however. For example, in one of the CBHOs there had been several meetings with Scottish Homes' staff as part of a process to decide whether to expand the organisation's area of operation. The committee had also visited Scottish Homes 'in force' to protest at the high rent assumptions made by Scottish Homes' staff in order to calculate the available funding for a new development. The rather remote position of the committees in the 1990s, however, provides a stark contrast with the early days of the CBHOs, when the residents' representatives had a hands-on role in campaigning for and running the organisations, including dealing with Scottish Homes.

Two issues serve to illustrate the influence Scottish Homes has over the CBHOs' independence; these concern the selection of tenants and the development of houses for sale. The first of these is a classic problem for all kinds of community-based organisations, which are often recognised as having less ability to promote equity and prevent discrimination than public sector organisations (Osborne and Gaebler, 1993). Scottish Homes' (and the Scottish Federation of Housing Associations') recommendation is that selection and allocation of tenants should be on the basis of need and that local people should not be favoured (Scottish Federation of Housing Associations and Scottish Homes, 1990, 1996). Committee members, however, usually take the view that the CBHOs should select people on the basis that they will be good cooperators and neighbours, and that the committee should have a leading role in making the selections. This seems understandable in the context of housing estates which have difficult problems of anti-social behaviour, crime and drugs. One committee member was not alone when she lamented that her committee now had no control:

> The reason how ours [i.e. the CBHO] worked great at the beginning was because we were really committed . . . but legislation would have to be changed somehow to give the co-op more power [over] who is coming into your houses; I would like to see changes made . . . because those tenants we got at the very beginning were contacted because they said on their transfer form that they would like to get involved in a housing co-op.

All of the CBHOs had changed their selection processes over the years in line with recommended practice. In at least one, this was the subject of a major battle between the committee and staff, with Scottish Homes supporting the staff. A staff member reported:

> They wanted basically for the whole community to pick who got the houses, and didn't see anything wrong with that . . . I said 'You cannot just do that', [it was] a real ding dong.

Scottish Homes, at a visit to the CBHO, then supported the staff view, and the committee relented their position. The staff member reported:

> They just said, 'Oh OK, it's out of our hands'. But that is unfortunate for them because that was one of the things they thought they could keep hold of as a community, not as a personal power thing . . . they thought they could have more control

over allocations and I think if you asked the general people here they would think that too.

The other issue which illustrates Scottish Homes' power over the CBHOs relates to development policy. Scottish Homes commonly proposes particular dwelling and tenure mixes and rents as a condition of development funding, but these often contradict the priorities of the CBHO. One staff member reported:

We go through all this, you know, 'the people are in control' and I think the Committee here accept along with me that they are not in control and, at the end of the day the rents are determined by how much HAG [Housing Association Grant] you get, how much loan you have to take, so very little is actually determined by you.... by the time you finish going through the regulations, you've been to Planning and you've been to Roads and you've been to Scottish Homes, you get beaten down to whatever a solution is. It's not what you started with and it never will be.

A CBHO a staff member was asked:

Researcher: Is it possible for the Committee to say 'We don't want any shared ownership'?
Staff member: They can say whatever they like. Scottish Homes will probably issue you with an offer of loan and say 'This is what we are prepared to give you'. This is what they're going to do at [name of scheme] where we can't reach consensus.
Researcher: So there is no negotiation?
Staff member: It's theoretical negotiation. Practically, there's no negotiation.

The Scottish Homes Development Manager for the area, referring to the same issue, stressed that Scottish Homes would ensure that, if shared ownership failed, the CBHO would be protected financially, but explained:

we've got targets and obligations from the government to introduce home ownership and certainly in an area like [name of estate] we would be quite up-front and say it is one of our objectives to achieve a balance of tenure – there isn't a balance at the moment.

The manager went on to explain:

> If the committee had come back and set their faces against, there might have been a bit of a go slow in terms of the investment that was made available.

> We've never actually said 'Well, if you don't do shared ownership, or whatever, we're not investing'. It's come to that yet.

This research supports the Nolan Committee's rather tentative conclusion about the relationship between Scottish Homes and housing associations in Scotland. Referring to Scottish Homes (and also to Tai Cymru in Wales) the committee reported, 'it appeared to us that the funding bodies are sometimes seen as over directive by the housing associations' (Committee on Standards in Public Life, 1996a, p. 90).

Our evidence suggests strongly that Scottish Homes has not been adhering to the Nolan Committee's second 'fundamental proposition', which concerns the need to limit regulation to effective audit, while allowing independent organisations to be independent.

At the time of writing, Scottish Homes is moving towards allowing at least some housing associations greater freedom at the price of all associations completing extensive documentation. Associations which perform well on paper and are highly-rated by monitoring staff are to be permitted three-year (rather than one-year) development programme agreements, streamlined funding procedures and less frequent monitoring visits (Scottish Homes, 1996).

Relationships with the local authority

The other important domain of relationships for CBHOs is with the local authority, in this case Glasgow City Council. The key set of relationships for actively developing CBHOs covers development strategy, and the role of individual CBHOs in planning and implementing the redevelopment of the wider estates in which they operate, since they have been ascribed a key role in the City Council's strategy for regenerating its run-down housing estates.

In evidence to the Nolan Committee the Director of the Scottish Federation of Housing Associations sought to explain the relationship which Scottish housing associations had with local authorities and Scottish Homes (although not specifically referring to CBHOs):

> The other thing which is particularly important about Scottish housing associations is the extent to which they work in partnership with local authorities and, indeed, with Scottish Homes. The whole culture is one of partnership where associations, local authorities and Scottish Homes believe that there is such a community of interests, and although we do not always agree, we do believe that cooperation is the most appropriate way for meeting our respective agendas and objectives. (David Orr in Committee on Standards in Public Life, 1996b, p. 448)

The research revealed that, in fact, the CBHOs were weak and largely dependent players in these local partnerships. This is best illustrated by the situation of one organisation which operates within an Urban Partnership, one of Scotland's 'flagship' estate regeneration projects (McAllister, 1996). Together with other CBHOs in the estate, the CBHO was important to the Urban Partnership's strategy of achieving housing improvement and tenure diversification. Yet the CBHO has had no direct access to the decision-making machinery of the Partnership. As a result, the CBHO perceived that its development strategy was compromised by decisions made by the City Council and its partners that were outside its control, and the CBHO cited several examples of development decisions which went against its interests.

In principle, most of the CBHOs have links with the council at the political level through the cooption of local councillors to their management committees. In practice, councillors rarely attend meetings, mostly take little interest in the CBHO and are not an effective means of partnership between the CBHOs and the council.

Two of the case studies reacted to their local powerlessness by forming alliances with other CBHOs in their areas. Both alliances were intended to examine strategic questions, such as the use of development sites, and to raise the profile of the CBHOs. A Committee member explained:

> When you get a lot of wee co-ops individually basically they are useless; they have not got any power, but if all these wee co-ops got together and had one big organisation representing them you have a lot of power.

Neither group, however, was having much success, and the more formal of the two groups has now been wound up. One senior staff member related how their local group had tried to assert itself:

> We have tried as far as we could by making a video, having a launch, making a publication to say 'We are here! Listen to us!' but we have not got our feet under the table yet.

Conclusions

The CBHOs are an unusual form of micro-local governance; housing services which were formerly provided by large, traditionally organised local government departments have been handed over for residents in deprived areas ostensibly to run themselves. They stand in sharp contrast not only to most local government housing departments, but also to the large national and regional housing associations that dominate the English housing association sector.

The CBHOs have delivered many of the advantages sought in small-scale institutions of governance, and confounded many of the criticisms levelled at local public spending bodies outwith local government. Most importantly, they deliver accountability 'downwards' to communities, and are open to the influence, in practice not just in principle, to most of the people they serve. Moreover, they seem to be successful in delivering services which satisfy most people – nor is this a flash in the pan; good services have been sustained for 10 years. If the objective of developing new forms of governance is better government, then Community Ownership seems to have met with success.

The evidence, however, shows that not much real power has been handed over to these deprived communities. There is no danger that they will run outside the control of the state as a kind of radical, people-based alternative to the mainstream. Committee members do have important powers over the policies, staff, and housing development projects which enable local needs and wants to be addressed, but they have, in reality, little possibility of making major development or strategic decisions for themselves. Committees are highly reliant on their staff, the CBHOs are far less powerful than the other key players in the hierarchy, and in reality they are highly dependent, rather than independent.

What has happened is that the conditions have been created for successful collaboration between deprived communities and local and central government agencies, and they all get something out of the arrangement. The council is able to get rid of its most deteriorated housing stock and residents get improved houses, a better service and the possibility of being actively involved. In the final analysis, however, the CBHOs can be seen more as vehicles for delivering the government's housing agenda for restructuring social housing, rather than as springboards for local democracy and independence.

About this study

This chapter presents some of the results of the third stage of a programme to monitor the progress of the Community Ownership schemes. The first stage involved interviews with tenant leaders and a survey of residents in all six areas immediately before the introduction of Community Ownership. (Clapham *et al.,* 1987). The second stage, in 1989, involved further interviews with committee members of the new organisations; a follow-up tenant survey, group discussions with tenants, and interviews with representatives of Scottish Homes, the council, and association staff. The main aim of these stages was to evaluate the success of the six original associations in implementing an improvement programme and managing their housing stock (see Clapham et al, 1989; Clapham, Kintrea and whitefield, 1991; Clapham and Kintrea, 1994).

Stage three of the research was undertaken in 1994 and 1995. In this stage, the objective was to examine CBHOs as institutions of governance, in particular to assess the durability of the Community Ownership schemes, the motivations and attitudes of volunteers, the commitment of residents, and the organisations' place in the local governance network. Methods are described in Clapham, Kay and Kintrea (1996) and again involved a combination of surveys and interviews with key actors.

13 Patterns of Inclusion and Exclusion: Ethnic Minorities and Urban Development Corporations

**Sue Brownill, Konnie Razzaque,
Tamsin Stirling and Huw Thomas**

Introduction

The implications for black and ethnic minorities of the changes in local governance, we would argue, have been, as yet, relatively underexplored. This chapter will assess the impact of the emerging system of local governance on black and ethnic minority influence over policy formulation and practice.

By focusing on Urban Development Corporations (UDCs) we show how the changing face and style of operation of local governance is interacting with relations of race and racism at national and local levels to produce new patterns of exclusion. Not only is this leading to changes in power over policy formulation and implementation, but also to shifts in the racialisation of policy – that is the extent to which notions of 'race' enter into policy discourse and decision-making. Contradictions in this process, however, mean new, albeit limited, spaces for influence can be opened-up within the changed governance terrain and variations over time and space are marked.

While there is some debate about whether such changes can be viewed as a deracialisation of local governance, we conclude the chapter by discussing the wider implications for local governance research and practice of the restructuring of the relationship between public policy and its governance, and racism and exclusion.

UDCs and the changing pattern of local governance

We begin by familiarising readers with UDCs and their place within the emerging system of local governance. While no one agency or organisation can be taken to exemplify all the changes in local governance, UDCs exhibit many of the features outlined in this volume and elsewhere (Stoker, 1991). Initiated in 1981, they were intended to be short-life agencies set up to replace local authorities in the narrowly defined task of 'regenerating' specified inner-city areas through maximising private investment. Since that time, 13 UDCs have been designated and by 1998 the majority had been wound down. The research underlying this chapter involved analysis of six UDCs with populations over 1000: Birmingham Heartlands, the Black Country, Bristol, Cardiff, London Docklands, and Tyne and Wear. Whereas there are similarities between these areas in terms of the common experience of a UDC, it is also important to stress the differences. For example, the proportion of the population which is black or ethnic minority varies from 1% in Tyne and Wear to over 25% in London and Cardiff. Further, it would be a mistake to see these communities as homogenous, as each are made up of a variety of black and ethnic minority groups which have different experiences, demands and relationships with political institutions.

UDCs were characterised by a lack of direct local electoral accountability, with decision-making dominated by a board of government appointees, an emphasis on facilitating or levering action and investment by other agencies, a tightly drawn 'mission', an attention to centrally devised performance indicators and the promotion of an organisational culture which replaced the 'red-tape' of bureaucracy with the 'can-do' mentality of the private sector.

In focusing on UDCs, we had two main questions. Firstly, what are the implications for black and ethnic minority influence of the changes in local governance? While no one can pretend that local authorities represent the pinnacle of inclusivity (see critiques of local authorities and anti-racism such as Gilroy, 1987; Ben Tovim *et al.*, 1986; Solomos and Back, 1995), nevertheless, it is widely recognised that some have made significant advances in equal opportunities policies and programmes. Will their demise/restructuring lead to a reversal of these gains or, alternatively, the breaking down of institutions and networks subject to closure and racism? In addressing these questions, we focused on policy processes within UDCs, which we discuss later.

Secondly, a question that developed over the course of the research concerned the interaction between patterns of governance, the racialisation of urban policy and the racialisation of politics at national and particularly local levels. Originally developed by Robert Miles (1982) in relation to labour migration, the concept of racialisation arises out of a critique of essentialist and biologically given notions of 'race'. Miles argues that race should be accepted as an ideology and as a socially constructed concept. Categories such as 'race', he argues, are actually produced through human action and interaction and through relations of domination and subordination. Analysis should focus instead on examining specific process of 'racialisation':

> those instances where social relations between people have been structured by the signification of human biological characteristics in such a way as to define and construct differentiated social collectivities (Miles, 1989, p.75).

The concept of racialisation has been widened by later writers from Miles' original usage, refering to the construction of racial categories, to a wider process by which this socially constructed notion of 'race' enters into social, economic and political relations, and political and policy discourse (which itself has an impact on how racial categories are constructed). Thus, writers such as S. Smith (1989) have examined the dynamics of 'race' and residential segregation and Solomos and Back (1995) have looked at the racialisation of local politics in Birmingham. The strength of such work is that it enables us to see such ideological constructions of race change and develop through time, space and across different policy areas. However, there is a danger that racialisation could become a catch-all concept, losing its specificity in ever-widening applications to a range of situations. This does not, in our opinion, undermine its usefulness for our purposes.

We also agree with Solomos and Back (1995), who indicate it is important to investigate the racialised context within which *local* policy-makers are making decisions. Previous research has shown how agencies and institutions of governance, even those supposedly insulated from local politics, are influenced by the social relations within their operational areas (Duncan and Goodwin, 1988; Imrie and Thomas, 1993). It is important that the racialisation of these relations is taken into consideration, something not prioritised in previous work. We discuss these issues of 'race' and racialisation in more detail elsewhere (Thomas *et al*., 1995, Brownill *et al*., 1996c). UDCs provide fertile ground in which to explore questions about the racialisation of public policy and local politics. The inner-city has long been associated with 'racial problems' (CDP, 1977; Atkinson and Moon, 1994). We have charted elsewhere (Brownill *et al*., 1996c) the evolution of this racialisation of urban policy and discussed recent assertions that we are witnessing the emergence of an 'ethnically blind' approach (Burton, 1994) or even the deracialisation of urban governance.

Such views are given support by the fact that the legislation setting up UDCs (the Local Government Land and Planning Act) made no reference to equalities, nor did the performance indicators through which 'success' in regeneration was measured, concentrating, as they did, on physical outputs such as roads and floorspace built or private money levered in. As a result UDCs, with only one or two exceptions, have failed to monitor either their activities or employment ethnically. Government ideology asserted that the benefits from regeneration would 'trickle down' to an undifferentiated local population reflecting the neo-liberalism of the Conservative governments of the 1980s which saw equal opportunities as not only an example of all that was wrong with local government, but also as an unnecessary interference in the market. Previous work by Munt (1994), however, indicated how this shift from social to physical regeneration operated to the relative disadvantage of black and ethnic minority residents. While, as we shall argue later, the contradictory results of the evolution of inner-city policy make a simple reading of deracialisation inadequate, what is revealed as important is to look at the relationship between changes in the racialisation of policy, patterns of exclusion and inclusion within governance, and the relationship of the changing face of local governance with these processes. This became the framework for our study of UDCs.

The operational style of UDCs and black and minority ethnic influence

In this section, we discuss the ways in which the decision-making processes of UDCs are structured in ways which tend to marginalise black and ethnic minority influence. There are dangers in generalising, because there is some evidence of local distinctiveness in the style of UDCs as they bed themselves down into, and are influenced by, their local political and institutional circumstances (Imrie and Thomas, 1993). Nevertheless, UDCs share sufficient organisational similarities – in particular their insulation from local democracy and the importance of central government patronage in appointing key personnel – to sustain useful conclusions about patterns of inclusion and exclusion in their decision-making processes.

The key factor structuring the ways in which UDCs operate is the lack of influence of local councillors over their day-to-day operation because of their being governed by a board of nominees of the relevant Secretary of State (of the Environment in England, or of Wales). To become a candidate for nomination to boards such as these, people must have a certain social prominence.

Being an important local politician is one method of securing prominence, as all UDC boards have a minority of places for local councillors appointed in a personal capacity. Black and ethnic minority politicians, however, remain under-represented in the higher echelons of local politics in most areas. Advancement in business and the professions is another common ways of gaining the prominence needed to even qualify for nomination. These kinds of societal rewards, however, are themselves distributed unequally between racial or ethnic groups (and, indeed, between other social categories, e.g. by gender). As a result, nominations to boards of UDCs tended to reflect and reinforce patterns and processes of racialised exclusion in society in general.

While recognising that a seat on the board does not equate automatically with influence and that the assumption that black individuals are there to represent solely black interests is fallacious, a key indicator of *potential* influence and power is the presence on the boards of UDCs of black and ethnic minority members. The lack of ethnic monitoring carried out by the vast majority of UDCs has made inquiry difficult, but our research indicates that of the six UDCs examined, each with a shifting board membership of 12 at any one time, there have been only three black or ethnic minority members. Two of these people were on the same UDC at different times (London) and the third (a prominent local businessman) served on both the Birmingham and Black Country boards. Such a picture contrasts with research by Geddes (1993), which indicates that the number of black and ethnic minority councillors in local government is increasing (although the proportion stands at only 2%, as opposed to the 6% of the UK population which is non-white). As far as our information shows, this picture of UDCs is reinforced by the lack of black and ethnic minority senior officers.

The second consequence of having a *nominated* board is that its membership is extremely unlikely to contain fundamental or vociferous critics of government policy. UDC board members were typically drawn from the private sector, particularly the property development world and the institutions which finance it.

Such closure is reinforced by the fact that UDC boards are not open to the public, and minutes and agendas are not made public. The implications for power are clear. As Coulson (1993) noted, it amounts to a patron/client model of central/local relations, at the heart of which is the concentration of power in the hands of the patron. In theory, it enables the key 'mission' of central government to be carried out without any of the annoying 'implementation gaps' associated with local democracy, and it needs to be legitimised only to a distant parliament and not to local interests. Our work shows that this is exclusionary in terms of black and ethnic minority influence.

A final consequence of the importance of the nominated board, and the unimportance of local councillors, is that the decline of the elected councillor not only gives more power to nominees, but also to officers. Above, we indicated the place taken by UDCs within the rise of 'entrepreneurial governance', as some have termed it (Burchell, 1993; Du Gay, 1996). Within this, officers, and often the private consultants brought in to supplement the deliberately small permanent staffs, are no longer bound by bureaucratic procedures (which may include practices to ensure equality), but are there to carry out the organisation's mission in the quickest and most cost-effective manner. In practice, this gives officers a high level of autonomy to carry out their roles and to influence strategy.

Du Gay (1996) has raised questions as to the impact on equity within governance in general of this form of management. Our research indicates that there are definitely grounds for these concerns in relation to black and ethnic minorities, but as we shall show later, this new culture also provides some openings for black and ethnic minority influence.

The impact of exclusion on the racialisation of urban policy

'So what?', we hear readers ask. It is not new for ethnic minorities to be excluded from decision-making, it is also not new to state that UDCs have not been involving or benefiting their local communities. What are the effects of the processes we are discussing on black and ethnic minorities? The lack of ethnic monitoring within UDCs makes answering such questions difficult. From our own perspective we were also concerned with how decisions were made rather than with policy outputs, which does provide a partial picture, it has to be admitted. Where evidence does exist (e.g. Docklands Forum, 1993; DCC/ALA, 1992), it suggests that black and ethnic minorities have been excluded from the benefits of regeneration to a greater degree than their white neighbours. It is not possible to attribute this solely to lack of influence, however, or to draw firm conclusions from the evidence available.

What is clearly different about UDCs is the racialisation of urban policy and strategy that they represent. Again, while it is not possible to directly attribute this to the emergence of a new system of local governance, it is important to discuss the changes and the implications that one may have for the other. Whilst, earlier in this chapter, we set out the legislative and ideological background to UDCs, evidence from the day-to-day operation of UDCs provides a clearer picture of how they approached the question of race and regeneration.

As indicated by the following quotes, race could easily be removed from policy discourse, because of government ideology linked to a narrow remit, the culture and policy processes within UDCs outlined above, and the need for speed:

If you spoke to the Corporation at high level and say 'what does the race question mean to the Corporation' you would get a reasonably blank look, I think, because they do see themselves as single issue, short-life organisations (UDC Community Development Officer (CDO))

in the legislation there is no mention from the government about equality... so there is no signal from anywhere (Local authority officer) we do not have a race committee (UDC CDO)

we've never differentiated in terms of sex or race or any other (UDC Business and Community Liaison Officer)

There is also evidence of these 'ethnically blind' views translated into the actions of the 'entrepreneurial bureaucrat'. One UDC officer recounted how he prefaced an address to a Black Business organisation with the words 'I don't approve of your organisation'. He went on to explain that a business person was simply that – and not a black business person. In our interviews with UDC officers the community often emerged as a homogenous 'other' – something out there, unknown and lacking a realistic form, even a threat. Interestingly, this echoes the way in which many writers on race and ethnicity report white people perceiving black and ethnic minorities (e.g. Solomos and Back, 1996). This 'ethnically blind' view was not unchallenged within UDCs, for example, in one interview we conducted with a (black) community development officer and his (white) superior, the latter was arguing that an approach which did not positively discriminate would still benefit ethnic minorities while his colleague argued that this denied the operation of racism in society restricting access to services and facilities in the first place. Yet it was unusual for these challenges to become official policy.

A focus on mission can have positive effects, however. UDCs have approved places of ethnic worship purely on floorspace grounds – they will fill up undeveloped land – and as they are immune from electoral 'whitelash' could make decisions solely on these grounds. Where poor race relations was seen as threatening property development and profitability, for example the election of a British National Party candidate in the London Dockland Development Corporation (LDDC) area, action may be taken. In this case, the banks in control of the Canary Wharf development at that time donated money to alleviate the social housing shortage, seen as the trigger of tension.

Yet the goal of private-sector-led regeneration which drives UDCs can also be seen as leading to the removal of race and equality from the policy agenda, lending support to the deracialisation thesis. To attract private investment, UDCs have paid particular attention to the image of the areas which they are promoting; the transformation of London Docklands from run down port to yuppie playground is a case in point here (for a fuller discussion see Brownill, 1993; Thomas *et al.*, 1996). The uncoupling of race from the inner city as a way of making areas 'safe' to invest in is a part of this process.

In UDC literature we came across constant references to 'balanced communities'. Such a term is never defined, but the implication, backed up by the visual imagery in the literature, is that the multi-racial nature of areas is to be restructured. Thus, in Cardiff Bay, the area of Tiger Bay, nationally synonymous with a multi-racial area, is referred to as Butetown. The Cardiff Bay Development Corporation (CBDC) Regeneration Strategy carries proposals for a 'Butetown Bazaar', where an African woman walks through a 'festival shopping' development with goods balanced on her head. Black residents are thus transformed from the stereo-typical inner city rioters to participants in the mission of property-led regeneration. We explore the role that the transformation of local governance has in the restructuring of space, and the 'imagineering' of areas of cities in more detail elsewhere (Thomas *et al.*, 1996).

The impact of this can be exclusionary, for example a Community Development Officer within one UDC commented that work done on equality was 'perpetually challenged at officer level, because people don't regard it as being part of what urban regeneration is all about'. Yet the example of Cardiff shows that these images, and the regeneration strategies behind them, can be challenged. Not only does the Cardiff Bay Regeneration Strategy make mention of the fact that UDC policies 'pay proper regard to the multi-racial dimension in every significant development' (CBDC, 1988, p.94), but the local community has actively organised around challenging the reconstructed image of their area. For example, a local community newspaper, *Making Waves* (itself partially funded by the UDC), has celebrated the multi-cultural nature of the area and has constantly sought to place the black and ethnic minority population within the redevelopment process. Thus, a struggle over the racial-isation of regeneration in Cardiff Bay has been on-going, both in terms of the image of the area being promoted and the question of who should benefit. This indicates the influence which the local politics of race can have on the racialisation of urban policy within particular localities.

Consultation, legitimation and new patterns of inclusion

The argument that changing patterns of local governance are part of a restructuring of the racialisation of urban policy, rather than its deracialisation, are lent further weight when we examine patterns of consultation and community development within UDCs. Whilst some of the patterns of exclusion noted above are mirrored, we can also see new spaces opening up within the changing governance picture.

Despite, or perhaps because of, the lack of local accountability, UDCs have retained the need for legitimation. Thus, all UDCs have engaged in some form of public consultation, from publishing newsletters to holding public meetings. Where the black and ethnic minority population is seen as being important in achieving this legitimation, organisations and individuals may well find themselves involved, as examples from Cardiff and London have already indicated. Whether we are witnessing genuine consultation or the incorporation of potential protest and exercises in public relations is a matter of debate (Brownill, 1993), and it is interesting to note that little concrete action has followed from the CBDC strategy statement referred to above.

As UDCs are not required by legislation or the need to ensure accountability (and re-election of councillors) to consult, they need not be inclusive. Consultation is also influenced by the need for short-life agencies to act quickly and not to interfere with the 'entrepreneurial' image of corporations (one Chief Executive of the LDDC called consultation a relic of the local authority days). These restructured processes can exclude ethnic minorities, for example by relying on pre-existing networks that are themselves racist or by ignoring black and ethnic minority populations due to the perceived time-consuming nature of consultation with them (we have anecdotal evidence of this leading to the total exclusion of the area of Saltley, with its large Asian population, from the Birmingham Heartlands UDC). The fragmentation of governance means that communities need to know both of the existence of agencies and areas of responsibility they have. Surveys carried out in some UDC areas showed that black and ethnic minority communities had less knowledge of UDCs than the population as a whole. The focus on planning and redevelopment within UDCs is also not one that black and ethnic minority organisations have traditionally organised around.

This being said, our research also revealed how consultation could include black and ethnic minorities, particularly within the area of community development, showing the variation in practice across policy areas. In part, this is the result of the autonomy of individual officers within the UDC culture discussed above. This autonomy meant that, where relevant officers chose to develop networks which included black and ethnic minorities and to adopt strategies which benefited them, they could have a major impact on the flow of benefits (in the form of grants) and on the views included in consultation. As one CDO said, 'I'm afraid that's the way things work. It's key individuals saying "I'm quite interested in that"'.

It is also significant that a number of UDCs employed ethnic minority community development officers. In areas such as London and Cardiff this fortuitous situation led to increased attention to the black and ethnic minority population. In other areas, where the CDO did not make it a priority, exclusion was the norm. Direction from the top by key senior officers was also reported. For example, a sympathetic (but unfortunately not long-lasting) Chief Executive was instrumental in one of the black board members being appointed to the LDDC.

We are mindful here of two issues. First, it would be wrong to divorce this idea of 'networking' from the context, structures and the social relations which create the space for it and constrain it. In this context, this includes the need for legitimacy, the reflection or challenging of racism, the regeneration brief and the focus on regeneration. Secondly, we would not want to overplay the significance of this 'buffer' of professionals, be they black or white, between the community and government or suggest that it is unproblematic (Cain and Yuval Davis, 1990). It is also interesting to speculate, however, on how such networks can present opportunities of 'backchannels' for political expression for those excluded from the mainstream, particularly if that exclusion is related to institutional racism (Herbst, 1994). These points are discussed more fully in H. Thomas *et al.* 1996.

The marginalisation of any influence gained through these processes must also be noted. Only one UDC, London, had a corporate structure which placed community development within the higher levels of decision-making. Marginalisation can also be noted in the areas of activity into which black and ethnic minorities are drawn.

We have already noted that UDCs operate within a narrow regeneration brief. Within this, the area of training seems to have been earmarked as one of special relevance for black and ethnic minorities – as a way of tying them into the enterprise economy – despite the fact that other issues may be of greater significance for the black and ethnic minority population. Finally, these advances are vulnerable to changes in the conditions which support them. The situation in London referred to above where a combination of sympathetic officers, community cohesion and resources produced a Community Services Division operating under an explicit recognition of the need to ensure black and ethnic minorities benefitted from regeneration, was eroded in the 1990s by the departure of key officers, racial tension in the locality and fewer resources.

Our work on UDCs shows that the changing face of local governance is producing new patterns of exclusion, but also of inclusion for black and ethnic minorities. Such patterns are leading to changes in influence and power over policy, which, in the context of urban policy, are contributing to a lessening of the links between race and regeneration. The contradictory nature of such developments, however, mean that talk of deracialisation is premature – rather, the racialisation of urban policy must be seen as a contested area, the outcomes of which will vary through time and space.

Conclusions: implications for local governance

While UDCs may be seen as extreme examples of entrepreneurial governance and are now being wound down in favour of so-called 'partnerships', there are a number of implications for local governance in general which we feel are transferable from our research. Firstly, the patterns of exclusion from power and influence found within UDCs may be repeated within other unelected agencies, especially where nominees are key decision-makers. The need for such organisations to achieve legitimation and to promote a positive public image ensures a continued role for public consultation and raises the potential for influence, but the constraints on such openings need to be recognised.

The rise of the 'partnership' should not be seen to be immune from such processes. Whereas partnerships are presented as being more democratic than agencies such as UDCs – representing, in ideal form, local authorities, the private sector, the voluntary sector and the local population – the relative balance of power within such partnerships, and the inclusion or exclusion of potential 'partners', need to be carefully assessed. Further the modes of operation and decision-making associated with such institutional forms, their permeability to black and minority ethnic influence and their inter-relations with the local politics of race need to be identified and analysed. Research indicating the importance of 'networks' in partnership formation and operation needs to be highlighted here, as does the lack of attention to black and ethnic minorities in this work (see, for example, Skelcher *et al.*, 1995).

Secondly, a number of trends which serve to marginalise black and ethnic minorities are also to be found outside UDCs. One is a focus on speed, often associated with the fixed life of such agencies (MacFarlane, 1993). This can also have the effect of leading to manipulation and instrumentalism and the desire to get potential trouble makers 'on board' (Mawson *et al.*, 1995). This would suggest that the targets and timetables set for agencies should allow scope for meaningful consultation with all sections of the community.

Government is increasingly seeking to assert its ideology not through boards of appointees, but through mechanisms such as challenge funding, where resources go to those bids which best represent government priorities rather than to the areas of greatest need. Burton (1994) has commented that within urban policy this is resulting in fewer resources going to areas of concentration of black and ethnic minority populations. In competition, the narrow focus of policy becomes accentuated as agencies try to second-guess governmental priorities. Thus, despite the fact that the successor policy to the UDCs, the Single Regeneration Budget, includes meeting the needs of ethnic minorities as a policy aim, in the first three rounds only two bids, out of over 500 that have gained funding, make this their overall priority (Loftman, 1997). We could speculate about the continuation of the trend we noted in UDCs that, in the (re-) presentation of a place as one where success is likely, the downplaying of race is seen as a desirable strategy.

The promotion of an over-riding, and more often than not narrowly-defined, mission for governance agencies can impact upon black and ethnic minorities. The regular review of performance against a limited number of indicators can add to these processes of marginalisation, particularly where the focus is on outputs and not processes. Where there is no legislative or other requirement that agencies consider equality in their activities, such arrangements can be particularly exclusionary. We would argue that, not only should government policy and performance indicators make explicit reference to equal opportunities, but that the lead agencies in partnerships require all other partners to show a commitment to race equality as a pre-requisite of funding or partnership.

Access to knowledge and information about the structure, *modus operandi* and access points within the plethora of governance agencies that now exist is also an issue that needs to be addressed. Evidence suggests that black and ethnic minority organisations and individuals are likely to be disadvantaged in this respect and there is a definite need for a spread of information and capacity building.

Thirdly, our research raises interesting conclusions in relation to the discussion on equity and public management. Entrepreneurial governance may well exclude equality from its agenda, however we would not wish to suggest that local government was immune to institutional racism and that, therefore, such findings are solely a result of changes in governance. As as we have also seen, the implications are not totally negative – there is nothing which states that the entrepreneurial bureaucrat cannot have a concern with equity and cannot use this to secure results, although we would be the first to admit the limited nature and extent of the spaces thus opened up. We have suggested elsewhere (Brownill *et al.* 1996a) that the remits and missions of officers need to make specific reference to the needs of black and ethnic minorities.

Finally, it is important to be aware of the influence of local social relations and the racialisation of local politics on the ways in which agencies work and how influence is wielded within them. Our research has indicated some quite dramatic differences between agencies with ostensibly the same structure and remit as a result of a combination of pressures exerted from outside and the influence of key individuals within those organisations. It is likely that these patterns will be repeated elsewhere.

Our research indicates that changing patterns of governance are reflecting and reinforcing relations of racism, exclusion and marginalisation in society in new and dynamic ways. This process is not monolithic, however, and new, albeit limited, spaces have opened up, particularly within certain areas with a high degree of racialisation

of politics. Rather than labelling this the deracialisation of governance, we would prefer to see these trends as the ongoing restructuring of the relationship between the forms and processes of
governance and the racialisation of policy and practice at local
and national levels. Further research and action is needed to intervene in these processes to ensure that race equality does not slip
even further down the governance agenda.

About this study

The research was carried out between October 1994 and October
1995. It was based on nearly 100 semi-structured interviews with
'key informants' within and outside the six UDCs mentioned above,
supplemented by a variety of official publications and secondary
sources. Analysis concentrated on three main policy areas: development strategy, housing, and community development. In addition, case studies of particular events, policies or proposals within
these policy areas were conducted. Two methodological issues arose
within the research. The first related to the secrecy of organisations
like the UDCs and the problems this presented in terms of access to
information, compounded by the lack of ethnic monitoring in most
UDCs. The second related to the political sensitivity of the topic
under consideration and the multi-racial nature of the research
team. This may have resulted in respondents giving responses they
thought appropriate, rather than truly reflecting the facts. In addition to the references already quoted further discussion can be
found in Thomas, H. *et al.* (1998) *Ethnic Minority Influence in
Urban Policy: Policy Processes in UDCs*, Project Working Paper No 4
(Cardiff: Dept of City and Regional Planning, University of Wales)
and Brownill, S. and Thomas, H. (forthcoming) 'Urban Policy and
Britain's Racialised Minorities', in O. Yiftachel *et al.* (eds) *The
Power of Planning* (Kluwer).

14 Feminist Intervention and Local Domestic Violence Policy

Stefania Abrar

'Domestic violence', in this chapter, means mental, physical, sexual, emotional or economic abuse of one partner by another. It is largely perpetrated by men over women. Here, we examine the ways in which feminists have operated to influence the uptake of policy on domestic violence by the local state. Policy promotion at this level has been crucial since it is here that women experiencing domestic violence have been in direct contact with public officials. Three localities are compared to investigate the factors leading to the adoption of policies. The process surrounding their institutionalisation illustrates the nature of local feminist intervention.

Commentators in the USA and Canada have noted the importance of local feminist advocacy groups in setting local agendas on domestic violence, however there is a recognition that these groups need allies to achieve success. Andrew's detailed account of the establishment of the Centre Against Violence (Ottawa-Carleton, Canada) stresses the interrelationships between community mobilisation and the local state. The establishment of this centre was the result of a coalition forged by a female local councillor with an interest in domestic violence. Institutional structures and local political agendas played an important part in legitimising the coalition (Andrew, 1995). Brownill and Halford's (1990) critique of the distinction often made between women's 'formal' and 'informal' political organising is reflected in Andrew's analysis. They argue that there are significant similarities and interconnections between feminist action both inside and outside the state. Indeed, on a practical level 'people are constantly meeting, consulting or working jointly and resources may change hands'. For them, unravelling this process is central. 'We need to challenge and transform such categories as the informal and the formal to tease out the political processes which underlie them. These processes included gender, differing access to executive power and differing agendas for change' (Brownill and Halford, 1990). Therefore, to understand how local policy on domestic violence is made it is necessary to consider the nature of local institutions, women's mobilisation and the dynamics of the relationship between them. We must also consider how the political agendas of the various camps coincide to produce policy which works in the interests of women.

Other useful public policy perspectives focus more explicitly on interest group analysis. Some point to the significance of particular configurations of policy networks (Marsh and Rhodes, 1993) and coalitions (Sabatier, 1993), others, most notably Dowding (1995), focus on the bargaining capacity of interest groups and their differential access to power resources. Dowding, informed by a rational choice perspective, identifies a number of resources used by groups to further their interests: legitimate authority, information and expertise, reputation, and conditional/unconditional incentives (such as money). The distribution of these resources among actors in a policy network can be assessed to predict the policy influence of any group. Change is the result of a change in the resources available to groups, often brought about by an exogenous event.

These approaches may complement each other. Dowding suggests that systematic inequalities in power depend upon resources which themselves may depend upon social location. Thus, the institutionalisation of male interests in society, together with what Schattschneider has called 'the mobilisation of bias' against new interest groups, may explain the consistent exclusion of women's interests from the policy process (Gelb, 1982) In addition, ingrained cultural hostility towards both female presence and feminist intervention has made change even more complex, leading to feminist political action occurring at the margins and incrementally. Thus, the policy networks approach, though useful in mapping resources, must be complemented by the consideration of contextual factors which shape the distribution and use of these resources.

Accordingly, we detail the policy history of domestic violence in three local authorities to examine the exogenous factors shifting the distribution of resources and then describe the ways in which these opportunities have been managed by feminists to achieve woman-centred policies. First, a brief summary of the wider national context which forms the backdrop to local policy-making on domestic violence.

Domestic violence: the rise of a woman's issue in public policy

Woman's issues have traditionally been classified as private issues outside the public policy domain. Where public policy has focused on women, it has been to reinforce their domestic and familial roles. A functionalist and professionalised ethos in public service agencies, together with male-dominated hierarchies, have tended to obscure and exclude women's interests. The 1977 Homeless Persons Act, which imposes a statutory duty upon local authorities to rehouse woman with children and women subject to domestic violence, is the only piece of legislation securing the rights of women to service delivery. To this day, there is no other statutory duty preventing local authorities from discriminating against women in terms of service provision. (The 1975 Sex Discrimination Act placed obligations on local authorities as employers rather than as service providers and, with the exception of education departments, local government services were exempt from the effects of the Act.)

Despite the 1977 Act, domestic violence is a relatively new issue on the public policy agenda. Its location in the private sphere has meant that historically it has been regarded as a legitimate feature of interpersonal relations. As late as 1975, the Association of Chief Police Officers maintained that, in a domestic violence case, 'every effort should be made to reunite the family' (Hamner, 1989). Moreover, research on the incidence of the crime suggests that it is severely under-reported to statutory agencies and in national crime surveys. The North London Domestic Violence Survey, for example, found that in 78% of cases violence was not reported to any agency (Mooney, 1993).

The rise of domestic violence to the national public agenda has had a profound impact on its uptake at a local level. Its origins lie in the feminist movement, in particular the women's refuge movement which emerged in 1974 as the Women's Aid Federation. By 1987, the English branch of the federation included 200 refuges. Although primarily engaged in providing shelter to women fleeing violence, it was committed from the beginning to educating the public. One of its five aims is to: 'educate and inform the public, the police, the courts, the social services and other authorities with respect to the battering of women, mindful of the fact that this is the result of the general position of women in our society'. It had significant input into legislation in the 1970s.

Despite the passing of the Domestic Violence and Matrimonial Proceedings Act (1976), the Magistrates Courts Act (1978) and the Housing (Homeless Persons) Act in 1977, both the police and local authorities remained unwilling to use the law to protect domestic violence victims until well into the 1980s. Change came about principally as the result of the legitimation crisis faced by the police in the early 1980s. This created the opportunity for a combination of women's agitation, increased service provision for women, critical feminist research and media attention to sexual violence to bring the issue to the attention of the national criminal justice community. During the 1980s, a number of agencies produced reports on domestic violence. In 1986, a Home Office circular prompted the Metropolitan Police to set up a working party which led to Force Order in 1987. By the late 1980s and early 1990s, domestic violence units started to appear in police forces across the country. Interest extended to other agencies in recognition that domestic violence crossed institutional boundaries. In 1989/90, a senior Home Office researcher produced a report incorporating a feminist critique of statutory agencies and recommended a coordinated multi-agency response to the problem. This was followed by moves, sponsored by the Home Office via the Safer Cities Programme to encourage local crime prevention projects to take up initiatives around domestic violence. Finally, in the 1990s, various national level agencies began to take the issue seriously (Lovenduski and Randall, 1993)

Even so, there was a notable lack of coordination at central government level. Progressive moves at the national level through-out the 1980s and early 1990s masked what is still a piecemeal, fragmented response to domestic violence. This is complicated by the fact that responsibility for domestic violence is shared by a wide range of agencies such as the police, the courts, and the probation, social, health, housing and education services. Until recently, each operated in a discrete policy community. In 1989, Smith stated, 'it almost seems as if each agency defines the problem in such a way that it is someone else's responsibility... the end result is that the victim can be left virtually helpless' (Smith, 1989). The most sig-nificant incentive provided by central government to encourage the adoption of domestic violence policy at the local level has been funding through the Safer Cities projects. This development results from the coincidence of the new 'crime prevention' orthodoxy in the Home Office (Tiley, 1993) and the rise of domestic violence on the national agenda. Since its launch in 1988, 52 cities have been chosen, on the basis of indicators of inner-city deprivation and high crime rates, to receive funding for crime prevention initiatives. By the end of 1993, there had been 111 small-scale initiatives on domestic violence funded by Safer Cities at the local level. Safer Cities initiatives are short-term injections of funds designed merely to stimulate the uptake of crime prevention projects by local agencies. No permanent funding is available.

At the local level, where the agencies dealing with women experiencing violence are situated, response is patchy and underfunded. A survey by the London Housing Unit found that local authorities vary in their definitions of domestic violence as well as in how they interpret the notoriously unclear statutory duty to rehouse women experiencing violence (London Housing Unit, 1995). Some housing departments have adopted the feminist approach of taking a woman's word as proof of violence and follow the Department of Environment's Code of Guidance (a progressive interpretation of the 1985 Housing Act), whereas others require legal action as evidence of abuse. The practice of social services departments also varies widely. Some local authorities lead a coherent, multi-agency response, others deny that domestic violence is a problem in their communities. A few have developed good practice guidelines at the corporate level, together with information/education campaigns and training of their front-line service deliverers. Most will at least have produced a leaflet on accessing help. A commitment to employing paid officers is key: as one domestic violence expert put it:

> a lot depends on the particular officers in post. Where there are officers in post, they do all this outreach work, they have lots of conferences. Other local authorities are either not spending the money or are not putting the same energy in. You don't expect Tory authorities to do this stuff.

Our research indicates that the most 'feminist' and most developed policies are multi–agency initiatives with a number of officers in dedicated posts. Although such initiatives occurred almost exclusively in Labour controlled areas, many Labour authorities had only minimal policies, suggesting that partisan explanations could offer relatively little illumination of the reasons for varying practices.

The uptake of domestic violence projects by local authorities has had a distinctive dynamic. A key role has been played by women's committees and/or established posts with special responsibility for women's issues in local authorities. These are mainly to be found in progressive Labour local authorities which, responding to changes in party membership and feminist involvement after 1979, altered local policies on women and women's issues. This has not been a uniform development across the country and is largely dependent on particular local social relations and the locality's overall economic and political profile (Halford, 1988). In 1991, less than 12% of local authorities in mainland Britain had set up women's committees (Edwards, 1995).

The development of domestic violence policy in three local authorities

The three case study authorities are a provincial city, Radicalton, and two inner-London boroughs, Progressiveham and Toryville. These are very different in their structure, culture, political complexion, feminist presence and the way in which they have implemented local government reform. Radicalton is a provincial metropolitan local authority under Labour control throughout the recent period of local government reorganisation. Although some streamlining took place there, comparatively little structural change had taken place in its institutions by the time our fieldwork was completed. This is an active, politicised local community with a strong and continuing feminist presence. Radicalton set up a council women's committee following local feminist activism that had been strong since the 1970s. Progressiveham is a modern, recently decentralised, Labour-led council with a national reputation for initiatives to promote changes in gender relations. A women's committee was set up there in 1981 but, unlike Radicalton, this council has not been directly influenced by a local feminist movement. Toryville is a modern, fully reformed, Conservative-led council with little interest in feminist projects, but with a commitment to efficient delivery of national policy. Feminist activism in Toryville stayed firmly outside the local state. Progressiveham and Toryville should be assessed in the light of the nature of feminist politics in London which has a number of distinctive features. London is a national and international centre for feminism in which most strands of feminist thought and types of feminist activity are present. It is characterised by intense and lasting divisions among feminists over issues of violence, difference, race and sexuality that affect the patterns of activity and cooperation more than in other parts of the country, where such divisions exist but have been less likely to prevent collective action in support of particular policies.

Radicalton

Radicalton in the late 1970s and early 1980s was characterised by active feminist mobilisation around issues of male sexual violence which was strengthened by the psychological landmark created by a series of widely publicised and brutal murders of women in the area. The significant role played by women's groups in lobbying for the establishment of the women's committee in 1982 led to their strong input into committee decisions through a system of community representatives. The interest in sexual violence in the community was thus reflected in the work of the committee and the single local government women's officer from an early stage. Radicalton City Council became the first council in the country to sponsor conferences on sexual violence and succeeded in raising the profile of male sexual violence against women as a matter for public policy. In addition, access to the police through the county council police committee, enabled the women's committee to pursue legitimately a critical part of the domestic violence problem – its 'no crime' status with the police. Senior police officers' attitudes to this involvement were initially hostile. 'The man in the street', the women's committee representatives were told at their meeting with the police, 'is simply not interested in prosecutions for domestic violence'. Determined to change this attitude, the women's committee continued to meet with the police throughout the early 1980s to discuss women's policing needs. Meanwhile, a wider legitimacy crisis was occurring in the district police: race issues, the miners' strike and media exposés of police treatment of rape victims undermined the force's credibility.

In 1985, media coverage of the case of a local victim of a domestic killing once more brought police practice under intense scrutiny. Bowing to public pressure, the police allowed feminist activist researchers, funded by the county council, to investigate the force's response to domestic violence. The recommendations of the subsequent report were strongly endorsed by the Chief Constable, thereby symbolising a new commitment by the police to multi-agency cooperation and a formal recognition of the crime status of domestic violence. The women's committee, led by its chair, a former community representative, was able to capitalise on the publicity generated by the Chief Constable's statement by organising an inter-agency working party on domestic violence, which she chaired. This included a core of representatives from local authority departments and the voluntary sector.

As a networking device it proved useful. Initially comprising committed individuals rather than influential policy makers, members of the inter-agency working group were able to lobby inside their own agencies. In the housing department, for example, this resulted in the employment of a women's officer with special responsibility for domestic violence. The need for a full-time worker to develop the multi-agency work became apparent, however, and the chair was able to secure funding from the three council committees most directly implicated in domestic violence work: Housing, Social Services and Equal Opportunities. A coordinator with extensive experience of sexual violence work at Rape Crisis was appointed. Her background, and the close working relationship that the women's committee had built up with women's organisations over a number of years, ensured close links with the voluntary sector.

The Radicalton Inter-Agency Project, as it became known, is one of the most comprehensive and successful projects of its kind in the country. Its unusual structure – part-voluntary sector, part-local authority – enabled it to secure funding from a variety of sources and allowed it autonomy with political backing from the local authority. Funding was secured for 11 workers, with the Home Office providing the leading contribution of 25% of the project's total funding. Some of the posts are funded by the local authority, others through central government Section 11 money (available specifically for the employment of black workers) and other posts receive funding as short-term 'action research projects'. Its resources and expertise have meant that, according to its coordinator:

> [Radicalton]... Inter-Agency Project is extremely well-respected and we are seen as a very professional organisation, we deliver very good quality training, we go in and negotiate... we are seen as being quite powerful locally... we do have political support, we have the support of a huge number of agencies.

There are three elements to its work: its inter-agency forum, a comprehensive domestic violence training scheme; the development of good practice guidelines and policies with agencies; and, most notably, the Good Practice Pilot project which has been launched in one area of the city. This has entailed the training of all relevant workers in the locality and the establishment of special education-, health-and court-based projects in the area.

Policy change has occurred in a range of agencies both inside and outside the local authority: housing, social services, health, Crown Prosecution Service (CPS), police, probation, and education. Local authority policy is a model of women-centred practice on the issue, but more dramatic changes are starting to occur in other local agencies. The project coordinator is beginning to see the results of five years' work:

> Just the other day there was a criminal prosecution that was taken forward and the CPS prosecutor was absolutely brilliant. Apparently, the magistrate who was there gave this man 80 hours of community service, which is, I think, unheard of... the magistrate has been brought through our training programme. The different agencies are actually starting to support each other. It's wonderful.

Although the main avenue for policy change has been the Inter-Agency Forum, where high-level decision-makers from agencies meet once every three months, policy change has been most apparent when there are institutionalised gateways into organisations such as women's officer posts, where sympathetic individuals are in positions of authority, and where the project coordinator has been able to build upon external events such as national level inter-agency agreements.

Progressiveham

Women's safety issues had been a concern of the Progressiveham women's committee since its inception in 1981. Unlike in Radicalton, there was no active women's movement forcing the council to take the lead on domestic violence policy and coordination. Rather, progress in the borough was the by-product of increasing pressure on the Metropolitan Police by feminists (both in the Greater London Council and in London-wide pressure groups) and the media to offer more effective policing of domestic violence. This led most notably to the Metropolitan Police's Force Order in 1987 and a commitment to the establishment of domestic violence units across the city. By the 1990s, multi-agency working was also coming into vogue having been pioneered by cities such as Radicalton. Thus, in 1990, a local female police officer encouraged the women's unit to revive a domestic violence working party that had existed in the early 1980s.

In the light of growing awareness of domestic violence in the borough and at a national level, the women's committee produced a report detailing inconsistency in council provision for domestic violence victims. However, the Director of Housing and Social Services, whose department was targeted by the report, was unsympathetic and was able to ignore the report's recommendations that staff with responsibility for the issue be appointed. Fortunately, the establishment of one of the Home Office Safer Cities projects in Progressiveham in 1991 provided a second forum for the report and the head of the women's unit was successful in securing temporary funding for a domestic violence coordinator post based inside the women's unit.

Full funding of the post was taken over by the council two years later. This came about because of a number of factors. The rising profile of domestic violence nationally, and the presence of a high prestige Home Office action research project for policing domestic violence and offering crisis intervention work in one of Progressiveham's policing divisions (itself the result of collaboration by London-based feminist academics with ties to the Home Office, Progressiveham Police and the Safer Cities Coordinator for the borough), gave the issue a particularly strong legitimacy with decision-makers. The results of a domestic violence survey commissioned by the council shocked councillors. Its findings that a high percentage of women in the area had experienced domestic violence made a strong case for the importance of the issue in the locality. These factors, combined with the ability of the coordinator to produce guidelines and develop networks over the preceding two years, convinced leading members of the council to support the application for permanent funding for the post. As was the case in Radicalton, the decision, by the head of the women's unit and the women's committee, to employ a worker with a background in Women's Aid tapped directly into voluntary sector expertise.

Located inside the council's women's unit, the coordinator develops good practice and policy, training, and facilitates the borough-wide domestic violence working party established by the council in 1990. The location of the women's unit at a corporate level has given the domestic violence coordinator direct access to powerful and supportive senior officials. The downside of her location inside the bureaucracy is that the coordinator has had to work hard to neutralise the negative reputation that being a member of the women's unit entails. A number of strategies help her to do this. Within the authority, she seeks to foster personal relationships in order to establish informal avenues for her work. In her dealings with external agencies, she seeks to influence policy through training and through guidelines to front-line service deliverers at the forum. The women's unit did secure representation on what is known as the Safer Progressiveham Strategy Group, a multi-agency group of senior decision-makers, but policy change has not occurred here. In any case, links with the criminal justice community have been considerably less important than in the case of Radicalton. This is a direct result of the presence of a unique Home Office crisis intervention project in the borough which concentrates on fostering these links. That project is also staffed by feminists and although policy networks rarely overlap, relationships between the two foci for domestic violence policy are cooperative.

Toryville

Despite the rise of domestic violence on the national and London-wide agenda, Toryville council has done little about domestic violence policy beyond disbursing funding to the local refuge and fixing a limited number of alarms in women's homes. In 1983–84, a Toryville 'Women speak out' survey, sponsored by the Toryville Policing

Campaign and funded by the Greater London Council's police and women's support committees, had little impact on the locality in terms of public policy (though the council may have dismissed the GLC report for political reasons). In the 1990s, initiatives at a borough-wide level did occur due to the establishment of a Safer Cities initiative in the area which, unusually, had an all female staff. In 1991, the feminist assistant coordinator, inspired by Home Office conferences and her period of study with a prominent domestic violence activist and academic, set up the multi-agency Toryville Domestic Violence Forum. Drawing on her extensive links with the voluntary sector and initial support from the police (due to her previous crime prevention work in the borough), links were made relatively easily. However, she was unable to secure high-level political or officer support from Toryville council. Persistent hostility from the council, which perceived the autonomy of the Safer Cities project as a threat in itself, scuppered both its chances of policy influence and the sustainability of its initiatives: 'they saw us as being radical and, as far as they were concerned, Safer Cities was there to give them money to supplement the poll tax, they were flooding us with applications to mend roads and fences. They felt they owned Safer Cities'. Resistance to council domination led to 'the most terrible antagonism that continued from start to finish'. This meant that a crucial part of the domestic violence policy network was closed off: 'Trying to get domestic violence policy incorporated as general council policy was impossible, so we had to settle for what we could do as individuals who were committed to working together setting up projects that we could do'. Relations with the council were so antagonistic, in contrast to Radicalton and Progressiveham, that no funding bid was submitted to the council for a coordinator to continue with the Safer Cities work. Instead, the domestic violence forum became reliant on the intermittent patronage of the police and the probation service for support.

By mid-1995, the forum was without influence and funds, and had no coordinator. It relied on the goodwill of the front-line service-delivery agencies to sustain it. With the end of Safer Cities funding, outstanding work was 'sneaked through typing pools'. Its continued existence was viewed by participants primarily as an 'elaborate statement of our good will'. By comparison to Radicalton and Progressiveham, its achievements were minor, limited to small-scale promotion of awareness of domestic violence in the community and the facilitation of rudimentary and intermittent networking by policy advocates.

Feminist intervention at the local level

The three policy histories reveal a two-stage process. The first stage consists of a series of events which enable feminists to establish the need for specific posts to coordinate local approaches to domestic violence. These events are exploited by a variety of feminists located both inside and outside the state, confirming Brownill and Halford's (1990) hypothesis that formal and informal distinctions collapse in the arena of feminist political action. The second stage is the development of resources by feminist lobbyists to push for domestic violence policy. This occurs in a series of bargaining situations with sections of the local bureaucracy or other agencies.

All three localities experienced varying types of feminist intervention. In Radicalton, feminist activists, academics and politicians coordinated their efforts to create structures that were feminist-led but partially autonomous from the council. In Progressiveham, the intervention was largely bureaucratic, with the head of the women's unit securing funds, initially from external sources, to create a feminist post within the council. In Toryville, such activity that there was, was driven temporarily by a feminist located in the Safer Cities project. The initiatives in these arenas built upon the activities of a wider feminist movement active in a variety of ways since the 1970s. Radicalton was the only area to experience direct impact from the local feminist movement. In London, a more direct effect was apparent as feminist ideas trickled down to the local level after surfacing first at the metropolitan and national levels (many London activists in fact doubled as national activists). In all three localities, those in London in particular, the legitimacy of local authority-sponsored posts to promote domestic violence policy was partly dependent on wider cultural and political changes occurring in other professions and agencies (Dobash and Dobash, 1992), particularly the police. Indeed, police participation in local government domestic violence networks accorded feminists with prestige which enhanced their reputation in the local authority setting.

The case studies suggest that the issue of domestic violence receives the most adequate local attention when feminists are established in the relevant local institutions and when the support of local politicians is available. It can be seen that even though the Radicalton and Progressiveham women's committees benefited from what Dowding (1995) would term 'legitimate authority' or what Brownhill and Halford (1990) would call 'high levels of executive access', both committees sought to develop their legitimacy in the issue area and to take on new personnel to work on domestic violence. Women's committees seeking to establish their legitimacy and to increase their staffing faced two obstacles, however: their marginalised status in male-dominated local authorities and funding constraints operating on local authorities in the 1980s, which made local councils resistant to the growth of innovative posts. Local government women's committees are marginal and largely deprived of the most powerful resources for influencing outcomes: statutorily defined responsibility, money and, in many cases, 'reputation' among other bureaucrats. Instead, their bureaucrats and politicians have had to take advantage of externally created opportunities to launch their initiatives. As a result, policy influence has been incremental but patchy, characterised by a long preparation of the ground, followed by a ruthless seizing of opportunities presented by external events:

> It is a process of talking to people, seizing opportunities. It is an intensely personal process which uses political machinery as a way of developing that into actual action. You talk to them within the confines of the Labour group, you talk to them at the Labour Party, you raise issues where you think they are pertinent and you might be able to draw connections between one issue and another. Occasionally you jump up and down and have a real go at them, but largely you don't do that, or you will get side-lined into a corner somewhere. Politics is a male arena and you are likely to be told 'well, this is political reality; you either play by the rules or you do not play at all'.

The wider institutional context is important in establishing legitimacy. Most crucially in Radicalton, the women's committee had access to police governing structures which enabled them to force a relationship with the police. This made them the natural custodians of the inter-agency domestic violence initiative recommended in the feminist academics' report. The women's committee in

Progressiveham had the support of politicians but lacked guaranteed access to the Metropolitan Police, and were thus without the same opportunities to benefit from the reputation gained by such a liaison. They had to wait until the establishment of the Safer Cities project before they were able claim a legitimate role.

In Toryville, feminists had neither political support nor institutional resources. The absence of a women's committee or any other suitable conduit into the local authority, combined with a political ideology hostile to feminism (one prominent female councillor remarked: 'I do not feel as a local authority it is [our] job to change society and the role of women') meant that the Safer Cities coordinator never found high-level support for a policy intervention. In the minds of council officials, domestic violence, women's committees and Labour Party politics all merged into one political demon. One consequence was that Toryville alone out of the 32 London boroughs did not participate in the 1993 London Zero Tolerance (of violence to women) campaign. The Assistant Coordinator of Safer Cities was discredited by her advocacy of domestic violence initiatives: 'I was seen as this radical feminist, leftie, every label that could get attached, and therefore not to be touched with a large barge pole'.

Women-centred policy change rests on the ability of feminists to control and construct an influential policy network. Initially, all the local authorities lacked coordination, and a coherent policy on domestic violence. Agencies failed to cooperate with each other and essentially operated in a series of closed policy communities. In Radicalton and Progressiveham, well-placed feminists were able to change this. By securing funding for initiatives and placing feminist officers at the centre of inter-agency networks, feminists within the local state created a base from which to push for the acceptance of women-centred policies. There are substantial differences in the policy changes achieved by the two feminist networks, however. This can be ascribed principally to the differing levels of resources, primarily money, that the initiatives have been able to secure.

The greater success of the Radicalton project in attracting resources is the result of at least six factors. These included, first, the high level of political support from its inception; second, the successful mobilisation of support by the founder members of the inter-agency group from within their own agencies; third, the existence of women's officers in agencies who provided a channel for joint working; fourth, the part-voluntary sector, part-local authority status of the project, enabling it to bid for a variety of funding; fifth, the strong emphasis on race inequality, enabling the project to bid for Section 11 funding; sixth, and most importantly, the 'pilot' orientation of the project (one of the coordinator's original ideas), enabling the project to become eligible for one-off action-research funding popular with the Programme Development Unit of the Home Office in the early 1990s. This amalgam of resources and expertise enabled the inter-agency project to extend its network. Such resources meant it was able to employ specialised workers attached to particular sections of a wide-ranging network, such as the health sector, which had proved impenetrable in the past.

By contrast, in Progressiveham, the incorporation of the officer into the bureaucracy meant that her role was centred on influencing the local authority staff. The inter-agency working group and her training initiatives did give her access to a wide range of front-line service deliverers, however securing significant policy change in other agencies was less feasible since she had less scope as a single worker than the 11 workers in Radicalton. Nevertheless, she was able to promote good practice policy and used the authority of her position in the council, as well as her considerable personal reputation for expertise, to do so. The absence of women's officers in other agencies and departments of the authority made informal networking important: 'I take the time to remember what is happening in people's lives and meet up with them every so often'. Unlike in Radicalton, the coordinator could not benefit from important resources available from the criminal justice community as the separate network created by the Home Office action-research project. Progressiveham police station won the funding available for such work. The combined policy outreach of the two initiatives was significant, even though it did not enhance the resource base of the officer in the local authority.

Toryville illustrates the consequences of failure to create a feminist-led policy network. The council's refusal to participate constructively imposed a block on policy activity. The other potential ally, the police, proved unreliable and unwilling to provide financial support beyond funding its own domestic violence units.

Reconciling different agendas for change has been a significant problem for feminists in all three localities. In Radicalton, the principles of the Radicalton Inter-Agency Project, which promotes a challenging analysis of domestic violence through its training and projects, comes under intermittent criticism for privileging women's perspectives. Project workers endeavour to overcome hostility by establishing relationships that benefit those dealing with domestic violence victims. Problems of this kind occurred most often when reorganisation has occurred in partnership institutions, necessitating a long process of renegotiating relationships with new decision makers. In Progressiveham, the postholder also sought to promote a feminist interpretation of domestic violence. In the format of training sessions and paper guidelines, this proved relatively unthreatening to the institution. Where the contradictions in political agendas become apparent is in situations of resource conflict. For example, where radical definitions of domestic violence extend expenditure to marginal groups, these definitions have been challenged. In the case of housing allocation policy, the coordinator and the women's committee had to accept a wording change to the proposed policy in order to win the bulk of their demands. In Toryville, the lack of strong feminist leadership of the forum, together with political conflicts, meant that agendas differed to the degree that the local Women's Aid was a rare participant at the forum. It would be wrong to imply, however, that institutional political agendas are monolithic and uniform. Within a given institution a range of sympathies exist. Where feminists were able to access most corners of the network, blockages were offset by the discovery of other influential actors. This did not happen in Toryville due to the absence of a legitimate base from which to cultivate such networks.

Lastly, not all policy change is dependent on the network itself. Political will and resource scarcity proved to be important variables. Success in changing policy beyond the employment of a domestic violence officer has been easiest in situations where resources are plentiful. Housing is a case in point. Levels of conflict faced by feminists trying to shift housing policy to prioritise women who had experienced domestic violence were directly related to resource scarcity. In Radicalton, where council housing resources were under less pressure than in Progressiveham and Toryville, proposals to change housing policy encountered little significant resistance. Inner London authorities, by contrast, have traditionally faced greater housing demands and have thus felt the effects of central government legislation prohibiting the construction of public sector housing more acutely. Indeed, financial constraints in the early

1990s led some London authorities to reverse provisions for women experiencing domestic violence. In Progressiveham, the women's committee had to wage a three-and-a-half year battle to change housing policy. The situation was particularly acute in Toryville, where an aggressive 'right-to-buy' policy was promoted. This led to sections of housing stock being ring-fenced for sale, forcing the housing department to be increasingly ruthless in its allocation of properties. It was said to be operating a 'how desperate are you?' policy, designed to put people off applying for accommodation, rather than encouraging it. Women's groups felt that lobbing for policy change was useless in such an environment.

Conclusion

In the three case studies, feminist bureaucratic and political structures provided crucial avenues for the introduction of domestic violence policy at the local level. In Toryville, where there was no women's committee, the local authority was resistant to policy change on the issue, content instead to define it as the responsibility of the voluntary sector. The mere presence of feminist political and bureaucratic structures, however, has not been the cause of change. The events leading to domestic violence initiatives are the culmination of years of feminist pressure groups' activities in a number of national and local sites. What local women's committees provided was a vehicle for change generated outside the local authority by local-level feminist political action, the rising influence of feminist activism and expertise at a national level, changing professional orientations and the opening up of policy communities in previously closed professions such as the police and social work.

The skill with which feminists have manipulated the resources at their disposal is testimony to the expertise of feminists situated both inside and outside the state. Almost 15 years of experience of women's committees has equipped feminists with a range of strategies to manipulate state resources. Nonetheless, domestic violence coordinators have certainly been an island of growth in an era which has otherwise been characterised by the disestablishment of women's officer posts.

Finally, employing feminists directly from voluntary-sector sexual violence projects has meant that state feminists have reinforced links with feminist activities. With backgrounds in the feminist sexual violence networks, many of those appointed identify with radical feminist perspectives and maintain close ties with radical feminist activities and workers in the voluntary sector. Thus, on a day-to-day basis, women's political organising on domestic violence issues is a joint effort and continues to operate across formal and informal boundaries.

About this study

This chapter is based on the Gender and New Urban Governance Project (ESRC award no L1311250304901) conducted by the author, Joni Lovenduski, Helen Margetts and Patrick Dunleavy. An earlier version was published in *Parliamentary Affairs* in January 1996.

Bibliography

Achterberg, W. (1996) 'Sustainability and Associative Democracy', in W. M. Lafferty and J. Meadowcroft (eds) *Democracy and the Environment* (Cheltenham: Elgar), pp. 157–74.

Aglietta, M. (1979) *A Theory of Capitalist Regulation* (London: Verso).

Alexander, E.R. (1995) *How Organizations Act Together: Interorganizational Coordination in Theory and Practice* (Amsterdam: Overseas Publishers Association).

Andrew, C. (1995) 'Getting Women's Issues on the Municipal Agenda: Violence against Women', *Urban Affairs (Special Issue)*.

Arrowsmith, S. (1990) 'Judicial Review and the Contractual Powers of Public Authorities', *Law Quarterly Review*, vol. 106, pp. 277–92.

Ascher, K. (1989) *The Politics of Privatisation* (Basingstoke: Macmillan).

Ashford, D. (1982) *British Dogmatism and French Pragmatism: Central–local Policymaking in the Welfare State* (London: George Allen and Unwin).

Atkins, Robert (1992) 'Making Use of Complaints: Braintree District Council', *Local Government Studies*, vol. 18, no. 3, pp. 164–71.

Atkinson, R. and Moon, G. (1994) *Urban Policy in the UK* (London: Macmillan)

Axford, N. and Pinch, S. (1994) 'Growth Coalitions and Local Economic Development Strategy in Southern England: A Case Study of the Hampshire Development Association', *Political Geography*, vol. 13, no. 4, pp. 344–60.

Bailey, N., Barker, A. and McDonald, K. (1995) *Partnership Agencies in British Urban Policy* (London: University College Press).

Bakan, J. and Smith, M. (1995) 'According to Rights: The Charlottetown Accord and Rights Politics', *Social and Legal Studies*, vol. 4, no. 3, pp. 367–90.

Baker, M. and Wong, C. (1997) 'Planning for Housing Land in the English Regions: a Critique of Household Projections and Regional Planning Guidance Mechanisms', *Environment and Planning C: Government and Policy*, vol. 15, pp.73–87.

Baker, S., Kousis, M., Richardson, R. and Young, S. C. (1997) *The Politics of Sustainable Development* (London: Routledge).

Bakshi, P., Goodwin, M., Painter, J. and Southern, A. (1995) 'Gender, Race, and Class in the Local Welfare State: Moving Beyond Regulation Theory in Analysing the Transition from Fordism', *Environment and Planning A*, vol. 27, pp. 1539–54.

Barnes, M. Harrison, S., Mort, M., Shardlow, P. and Wiston, E., (1999) 'The New Management of Community Care: User Groups, Citizenship and

Co-production', in G. Stoker (ed.) *The New Management of British Local Governance* (London: Macmillan).

Barry, B. (1991) 'Is it Better to be Powerful or Lucky?' in B. Barry, *Power and Democracy* (Oxford: Clarendon Press).

Bassett, K. and Harloe, M. (1990) 'Swindon: The Rise and Decline of a Growth Coalition', in M. Harloe, C. Pickvance and J. Urry (eds) *Place, Policy and Politics: Do Localities Matter?* (London: Unwin Hyman), pp. 42–61.

Bell, D., Newby, L., and Sheth, R. (1994) *Approaches to Community Participation* (Leicester: Environ).

Ben Tovim, G. *et al*. (1986) *The Local Politics of Race* (London: Macmillan).

Bendor, J. and Dilip, M. (1987) 'Institutional Structure and the Logic of Ongoing Collective Action', *American Political Science Review*, vol. 81, pp. 129–54.

Biggs, S. and Dunleavy, P. (1995a) 'Changing Organizational Patterns in Local Government: A Bureau-Shaping Analysis', paper to the *1995 Annual Conference of the Political Studies Association*, University of York, April 18–20.

Boaden, N., Goldsmith, M., Hampton, W. and Stringer, P. (1980) *Public Participation in Local Services* (London: Longman).

Borgatti, S. P., Everett, M.G. and Freeman, L.C. (1992), *UCINET IV* (Columbia: Analytic Technologies).

Bovaird, T. (1994) 'Managing Urban Economic Development: Learning to Change or the Marketing of Failure?', *Urban Studies*, vol. 31, no. 4/5, pp. 573–604.

Boyle, R. (1990) 'Regeneration in Glasgow: Stability, Collaboration, and Inequity', in D. Judd, and M. Parkinson (eds) *Leadership and Urban Regeneration: Cities in North America and Europe* (Newbury Park, CA: Sage), pp. 109–32.

Breheny, M. and Hall, P. (1996) 'National Questions, Regional Answers' in Breheny M. and P. Hall, *The People – Where Will They Go? National Report of the TCPA Regional Enquiry into Housing Need and Provision in England* (London, TCPA) pp. 31–61.

Bridges, L. *et al*. (1987) *Legality and Local Politics* (Aldershot: Gower).

Brindley, T., Rydin, R. and Stokes, G. (1996) *Remaking Planning. The Politics of Urban Change* (London: Routledge).

Brownill, S. (1993) *Developing London's Docklands* (London: Paul Chapman).

Brownill, S. *et al*. (1996a) 'Race Equality and Local Governance', *Final Report to the ESRC, Available as Project Paper No. 3* (Cardiff: Department of City and Regional Planning; Cardiff: University of Wales).

Brownill, S. *et al*. (1996b) 'Local Governance and the Racialisation of Urban Policy in the UK: The Case of Urban Development Corporations', *Urban Studies*, vol. 33, no. 8, pp. 1337–56.

Brownill, S. *et al*. (1996c) 'Urban Policy Deracialised?' *Paper Presented to the Joint European and American Schools of Planning Conference*, Toronto, Canada, July 1996.

Brownill, S. and Halford, S. (1990) 'Understanding Women's Involvement in Local Politics: How Useful is the Formal/Informal Dichotomy?' *Political Geography Quarterly*, October.

Buchanan, J. M. (1965) 'An Economic Theory of Clubs', *Economica*, vol. 32, pp. 1–14.

Buckinghamshire County Council (1994) *Buckinghamshire County Structure Plan Consultation Draft* (Aylesbury: Buckinghamshire County Council).

Buckinghamshire County Council (1995) *Enquiry-in-Public: Report of Panel* (Aylesbury: Buckinghamshire County Council).

Buckinghamshire County Council (1996) *Buckinghamshire County Structure Plan Adopted* (Aylesbury: Buckinghamshire County Council).

Bulpitt, J.G. (1967) *Party Politics in English Local Government* (London: Longman).

Bulpitt, J.G. (1982) 'Conservatism, Unionism and the Problem of Territorial Management' in Peter Madgwick and Richard Rose (eds) *The Territorial Dimension in United Kingdom Politics* (London: Macmillan), pp. 139–76.

Burchell, G. (1993) 'Liberal Government and Techniques of the Self', *Economy and Society*, vol. 22, no. 3, pp. 266–82.

Burns, D., Hambleton, R. and Hoggett, P. (1994) *The Politics of Decentralisation: Revitalising Local Democracy* (Basingstoke: Macmillan).

Burton, P. (1994) 'Ethnic Justice and Urban Policy' *Paper Presented to ESRC Urban Policy Evaluation Seminar*, University of Wales, Cardiff, Sept.

Butcher, H. *et al.* (1990) *Local Government and Thatcherism* (London: Routledge).

Byrne, Liam (1996) *Local Government Transformed* (Manchester: Baseline).

Cain, H. and Yuval-Davis, N. (1990) 'The Equal Opportunities Community and the Anti-Racist Struggle', *Critical Social Policy*, vol. 10, no. 2, pp.5–26.

Cardiff Bay Development Corporation (1988) *Regeneration Strategy* (Cardiff: CBDC).

Cattell, C. (1994) *A Guide to Co-operative and Community Business Legal Structures* (Leeds: Industrial Common Ownership Movement).

Caulfield, A. (1991) 'Community Power, Public Policy Initiatives and the Management of Growth in Brisbane', *Urban Policy and Research*, vol. 9, no. 4, pp. 209–19.

Caulfield, A. and Wanna, J. (eds) (1995) *Power and Politics in the City: Brisbane in Transition* (Melbourne: Macmillan Australia Educational).

Cawson, A. (1986) *Corporatism and Political Theory* (Oxford: Basil Blackwell).

CDP (1977) *Gilding the Ghetto* (London: CDPPEC).

Church, C. (1995) *Towards Local Sustainability: A Review of Current Activity on Local Agenda 21 in the UK* (London: United Nations Association).

City of Edinburgh (1995) *An Economic Strategy for Edinburgh* (City of Edinburgh).

City of Sunderland (1995) *Unitary Development Plan (Deposit Version)* (Sunderland: City of Sunderland).

Clapham, D. (1992) 'The Effectiveness of Housing Management', *Social Policy and Administration*, vol. 26, no. 3, pp. 209–25.

Clapham, D., Kemp, P. and Kintrea, K. (1987) 'Co-operative Ownership of Former Council Housing' *Policy and Politics*, vol. 15, no. 4, pp. 207–20.

Clapham, D., Kintrea, K., Malcolm, J. and Whitefield, L. (1989) *The Origins and Development of Community Ownership in Glasgow* (Edinburgh: Scottish Office).

Clapham, D., Kintrea, K. and Whitefield, L. (1991) *Community Ownership in Glasgow: An Evaluation* (Edinburgh: Scottish Office).

Clapham, D. and Kintrea, K. (1994) 'Community Ownership and the Break Up of Council Housing in Britain', *Journal of Social Policy*, vol. 23, no. 2, pp. 210–45.

Clapham, D., Kintrea, K. and Kay H. (1996) 'Direct Democracy in Practice: The Case of Community Ownership and Housing Associations' *Policy and Politics*, vol. 24, no. 4, pp. 359–74.

Clarke, M. and Stewart, J. (1994) 'The Local Authority and the New Community Governance', *Local Government Studies*, vol. 20, no. 2, pp. 163–76.

Cochrane, A. (1994) 'Mapping Change in Local Government', in J. Clarke *et al.* (eds) *Managing Social Policy* (London: Sage).

Cochrane, A., Peck, J., and Tickell, A. (1996) 'Manchester Plays Games: Exploring the Local Politics of Globalisation', *Urban Studies*, vol. 33, no. 11, pp. 1319–36.

Cole, A. and John, P. (1995), 'Local Policy Networks in Britain and France: Policy Coordination in Fragmented Political Sub-Systems', *West European Politics,* October, vol. 18, no. 4, pp. 89–109.

Collins, K. and Earnshaw, D. (1993) 'The Implementation and Enforcement of European Community Environment Legislation', in D. Judge (ed.) *A Green Dimension for the European Community* (London: Cass).

Commission for Local Democracy (1995) *Taking Charge: The Rebirth of Local Democracy* (London: Municipal Journal Books).

Commission of the European Communities (1992) *Towards Sustainability: Fifth Action Programme on the Environment* (Brussels: CEC).

Committee on Standards for Public Life (The Nolan Committee) (1996a) *Standards in Public Life: Local Public Spending Bodies, Volume 1, Report.* CM3270–I (London: HMSO).

Committee on Standards for Public Life (The Nolan Committee) (1996b) *Standards in Public Life: Local Public Spending Bodies, Volume 2, Transcripts of Oral Evidence. Cross Section,* CM3270–II (London: HMSO).

Community Development Project (CDP) (1977) *Gilding the Ghetto* (London: CDPPLC).

Cooke, P. (1988) 'Municipal Enterprise, Growth Coalitions and Social Justice', *Local Economy*, vol. 3, no. 3, pp. 191–9.

Coombs, Anthony (1983) 'Privatisation: The Birmingham Experience', *Local Government Studies*, vol. 9, no. 2, pp. 1–5.

Cooper, B. (1993) 'Technology of Representation' in P. Ahonen (ed.) *Tracing the Semiotic Boundaries* (Berlin: Mouton de Gruyter).

Cooper, D. (1994) *Sexing the City: Lesbian and Gay Politics within the Activist State* (London: Rivers Oram).

Cooper, D. (1995a) *Power in Struggle: Feminism, Sexuality and the State* (Buckingham: Open University).

Cooper, D. (1995b) 'Defiance and Non-Compliance: Religious Education and the Implementation Problem', *Current Legal Problems*, vol. 48, pp. 253–80.

Cooper, D. (1996a) 'Institutional Illegality and Disobedience: Local Government Narratives', *Oxford Journal of Legal Studies*, vol. 16, no. 2, pp. 255–74.

Cooper, D. (1996b) 'Talmudic Territory: Space, Law and Modernist Discourse', *Journal of Law and Society*, vol. 23, pp. 529–48.

Cooper, D. (1997a) 'For the Sake of the Deer: Land, Local Government and the Hunt', *Sociological Review* vol. 45, pp. 668–89.

Cooper, D. (1997b) 'Governing Troubles: Authority, Sexuality and Space', *British Journal of Sociology of Education*, vol. 18, pp. 501–17.

Cooper, D. (1998) *Governing Out of Order: Space, Law and the Politics of Belonging* (London: Rivers Oram).

Coote, A. and Lenaghan, J. (1995) *Citizens Juries: Towards Best Practice* (London: Institute for Public Policy Research).

Cordy, T. (1997) 'Questions of Quality Control', *Guardian*, 22 Jan, pp. 6–7.

Cornes, R. and Todd, S. (1996) *Externalities, Public Goods, and Club Goods*, 2nd edn (Cambridge: Cambridge University Press).

Coulson, A. (1993) 'Urban Development Corporations, Local Authorities and Patronage in Urban Policy' in R. Imrie and H. Thomas (eds) *British Urban Policy and the UDCs* (London: Paul Chapman)

Coulson, A. (1997) 'Transaction Cost Economics and its Implications for Local Governance', *Local Government Studies*, vol. 23, no. 1, pp. 107–13.

County Planning Officers' Society LA21 Task Group (1995) *Report on Methods Adopted by Task Group Members in Involving the Public in LA21* (Stafford: Staffordshire County Council).

Crozier, M. and Thoenig, J.-C. (1975) 'La régulation des systèmes organisées complèxes', *Revue française de Sociologie*, vol. 16, no. 1, pp. 3–32.

Department of the Environment (1990) *This Common Inheritance*, Cm 1200 (London: HMSO).

Department of the Environment (1992) *Planning Policy Guidance Note 3: Housing* (London: DoE).

Department of the Environment (1995a) 'Memorandum' in House of Commons Environment Committee Session 1995-6, 2nd Report, *Housing Need*, vol. 2 Minutes of Evidence and Appendices 22–II (London: HMSO).

Department of the Environment (1995b) *Community Involvement in Planning and Development Processes* (London: HMSO).

Department of the Environment (1995c) *Involving Communities in Urban and Rural Regeneration: A Guide for Practitioners* (London: HMSO).

DETR (1998a) *Planning for the Communities of the Future* (London: DETR).
DETR (1998b) *Modern Local Government: In Touch with the People* (London: HMSO).
DETR (1999) *Towards an Urban Renaissance* (London: DETR).
DiGaetono, A. and Klemanshi, J.S. (1993) 'Urban Regime Capacity: A Comparison of Birmingham, England and Detroit, Michigan', *Journal of Urban Affairs*, vol. 15, no. 4, pp. 367–84.
Dobash, R. and Dobash, R. (1992) *Women, Violence and Social Change* (London: Routledge).
Docklands Consultative Committee and the Association of London Authorities (DCC/ALA) (1992) *How the Cake was Cut: Ten Years of the LDDC* (London: DCC/ALA).
Docklands Forum (1993) *Race and Housing in Docklands* (London: Docklands Forum).
Dowding, K. (1991) *Rational Choice and Political Power* (Aldershot: Edward Elgar).
Dowding, K. (1995a) 'Model or Metaphor? A Critical Review of the Policy Network Approach', *Political Studies*, vol. 43, pp. 136–58.
Dowding, K. (1995b) *The Civil Service* (London: Routledge).
Dowding, K. (1996a) 'Public Choice and Local Governance' in D. King and G. Stoker (eds) *Rethinking Local Democracy* (London, Macmillan).
Dowding, K. (1996b) *Power* (Buckingham: Open University Press).
Dowding, K. and Dunleavy, P. (1996) 'Production, Disbursement and Consumption: The Modes and Modalities of Goods and Services' in S. Edgell, K. Hetherington and A. Warde (eds) *Consumption Matters,* (Oxford: Blackwell).
Dowding, K. and King, D. (1995) 'Introduction' in K. Dowding and D. King (eds) *Preferences, Institutions and Rational Choice* (Oxford: Clarendon Press).
Dowding, K., Dunleavy, P., King, D. and Margetts, H. (1995) 'Rational Choice and Community Power Structures', *Political Studies*, vol. 43, pp. 265–77.
Dowding, K., Dunleavy, P., King, D., and Margetts, H. (1999) 'Regime Politics in London Local Government' *Urban Affairs Review*, vol. 34, pp. 515–45.
Dowding, K., Dunleavy, P., King, D., Margetts, H. and Rydin, Y. (forthcoming) *Power in the Metropolis* (Cambridge: Cambridge University Press).
Du Gay, P. (1996) 'Organising Identity: Entrepreneurial Governance and Public Management' in S. Hall and P. Du Gay (eds) *Questions of Cultural Identity* (London: Sage)
Duncan, S. and Goodwin, M. (1985) 'The Local State and Local Economic Development: Why the Fuss', *Policy and Politics*, vol. 13, no. 3, pp. 227–53.
Duncan, S. and Goodwin, M. (1988) *The Local State and Uneven Development* (Cambridge: Polity).
Dunleavy, P. (1985) 'Bureaucrats, Budgets and the Growth of the State: Reconstructing an Instrumental Model', *British Journal of Political Science*, vol. 15, pp. 299–328.

Dunleavy, P. (1989a) 'The Architecture of the British Central State: Part I, Framework for Analysis', *Public Administration*, vol. 67, pp. 249–75.

Dunleavy, P. (1989b) 'The Architecture of the British Central State: Part II, Empirical Findings', *Public Administration*, vol. 67, pp. 391–417.

Dunleavy, P. (1991) *Democracy, Bureaucracy and Public Choice: Economic Explanations in Political Science* (London: Harvester Wheatsheaf).

Dunleavy, P. (1994) 'The Globalization of Public Services Production: Can Government be "Best in World"?', *Public Policy and Administration*, vol. 9, pp. 36–65.

Dunleavy, P., Dowding, K., King, D. and Margetts, H. (1995) 'Regime Politics in London Local Government', *Paper to the ESRC Local Governance Programme Conference*, Exeter, September. 1995.

Dunleavy, P. and Hood, C. (1994) 'From Old Public Administration to New Public Management', *Public Money and Management*, vol. 14, pp. 9–16.

Edwards, S. (1995) *Local Government Women's Committees* (Avebury Press).

Eisenschitz, A. and Gough, J. (1994) *The Politics of Local Economic Policy: The Problems and Possibilities of Local Initiative* (London: Macmillan 1994).

Elkin, S. L. (1987) *City and Regime in the American Republic* (Chicago, IL: University of Chicago Press).

England, Jude (1986) 'The Characteristics and Attitudes of Councillors', in Secretary of State for the Environment, Secretary of State for Scotland, Secretary of State for Wales, *The Conduct of Local Authority Business: Report of the Committee of Inquiry into the Conduct of Local Authority Business*, Research Volume II, *The Local Government Councillor*, Cmnd 9799 (London: HMSO).

Evans, Colin (1985) 'Privatization of Local Services', *Local Government Studies*, vol. 11, no. 6, pp. 97–110.

Ewick, P. and Silbey, S. (1992) 'Conformity, Contestation, and Resistance: An Account of Legal Consciousness', *New England Law Review*, vol. 26, no. 3, pp. 731–49.

Fainstein, N. I. and Fainstein, S. S. (1987) 'Regime Strategies, Communal Resistance and Economic Forces', in N. I. Fainstein, S. S. Fainstein, R. C. Hill, D. Judd and M. P. Smith (eds), *Restructuring the City: The Political Economy of Urban Redevelopment* (New York: Longman), 245–81.

Febbrajo, A. (1986) 'The Rules of the Game in the Welfare State', in G. Teubner (ed.) *Dilemmas of Law in the Welfare State* (Berlin: de Gruyter).

Fudge, J. and Glasbeek, H. (1992) 'The Politics of Rights: A Politics with Little Class', *Social and Legal Studies*, vol. 1, no. 1, pp. 45–70.

Game, C. and Leach, S. (1995) *The Role of Political Parties in Local Democracy* (Commission for Local Democracy).

Game, C. and Leach, S. (1996) 'Political Parties and Local Democracy' in L. Pratchett and D. Wilson (eds) *Local Democracy and Local Government* (London: Macmillan).

Geddes, A. (1993) 'Asian and Afro-Caribbean Representation in Elected Local Government in England and Wales', *New Communities*, vol. 20, no. 1, pp. 43–7.

Geddes, M. (1995) *Poverty, Excluded Communities and Local Democracy* (London: Commission for Local Democracy).

Gelb, J. and Paley, M. L. (1982) *Women and Public Policy* (Princeton: Princeton University Press).

Gibson, T. (1993) *Estate Regeneration at Meadowell* (York: Rowntree Foundation).

Gilroy, P. (1987) *There Ain't No Black in the Union Jack* (London: Hutchinson).

Glagow, M. and Willke, H. (1987) *Dezentrale Gesellschaftssteuerrung: Probleme der Integration polyzentristischer Gesellschaft* (Pfaffenweiler: Centaurus Verlagsgesellschaft).

Gluckman, M. (1940) 'Analysis of a Social Situation in Modern Zululand', *Bantu Studies*, vol. 14.

Goodwin, M. and Painter, J. (1996) 'Local Governance, the Crises of Fordism and the Changing Geographies of Regulation', *Transactions of the Institute of British Geographers*, vol. 21, pp. 635–48.

Goodwin, M. and Painter, J. (1997) 'Concrete Research, Urban Regimes and Regulation Theory' in M. Lauria (ed.) *Reconstructing Urban Regime Theory: Regulating Urban Politics in a Global Economy* (Thousand Oaks: Sage) pp. 13–29.

Grabher, G. (1994) *Lob der Verschwendung* (Berlin: Edition Sigma).

Grafstein, R. (1983) 'The Social Scientific Interpretation of Game Theory' *Erkenntnis*, vol. 20: pp. 27–47.

Grafstein, R. (1992) *Institutional Realism* (New Haven: Yale University Press).

Grant, Wyn (1977) *Independent Local Politics in England and Wales* (Farnborough: Saxon House).

Gray, C. (1994) *Government Beyond the Centre* (London: Macmillan).

Green, D.P. and Shapiro, I. (1994) *Pathologies of Rational Choice Theory* (New Haven: Yale University Press).

Greer, A. and Hoggett, P. (1997) *Patterns of Accountability within Local Non-Elected Bodies: Steering Between Government and the Market* (York: Joseph Rowntree Foundation).

Grubb, M. (1993) *The Earth Summit Agreements* (London: Royal Institute for International Affairs).

Gurr, T. and King, D. S. (1987) *The State and the City* (Chicago: University of Chicago Press).

Gyford, J. (1991) *Citizens, Consumers and Councils* (London: Macmillan).

Gyford, J. *et al.* (1989) *The Changing Politics of Local Government* (London: Unwin Hyman).

Habermas, J. (1986) 'Law as Medium and Law as Institution', in G. Teubner (ed.) *Dilemmas of Law in the Welfare State* (Berlin: de Gruyter).

Halford, S. (1988) 'Women's Initiatives in Local Government: Where Do They Come From and Where Are They Going?', *Policy and Politics*, vol. 4.

Hall, D. (1996) 'The National Labour Party and Local Government: Walsall and its Implications', *Local Government Studies*, vol. 22, no. 4.

Hall, Stephen (1995) 'The Rise and Fall of Local Economic Development: A Case Study of Dudley MBC', *Local Government Studies*, vol. 21, no. 1, pp. 1–10.

Hamner, J. (1989) *Women, Policing and Male Violence* (London: Routledge).

Hamnett, C. (1986) 'The Changing Socio-Economic Structure of London and the South East 1961–81', *Regional Studies*, vol. 20, pp. 391–406.

Hamnett, C. (1987) 'A Tale of Two Cities: Socio-Teneurial Polarisation in London and the South East 1966–81', *Environment and Planning A*, vol. 19, pp. 537–56.

Hancox, Andy, Worrall, Les and Pay, John (1989) 'Developing a Customer Orientated Approach to Service Delivery: The Wrekin Approach', *Local Government Studies*, vol. 15, no. 1, pp. 16–25.

Harding, A. (1991) 'The Rise of Urban Growth Coalitions, UK-Style?' *Government and Policy*, vol. 9, pp. 295–317.

Harding, A. (1992) 'Urban Economic Development Programmes under the Thatcher Governments, 1979–87: An Analysis of Public Policy Making', D Phil. thesis, Nuffield College, Oxford.

Harding, A. (1994) 'Urban Regimes and Growth Machines: Towards a Cross-National Research Agenda', *Urban Affairs Quarterly*, vol. 29, pp. 356–82.

Harding, A. (1995) 'Elite Theory and Machines', in D. Judge, G. Stoker and H. Wolman (eds) *Theories of Urban Politics* (London: Sage).

Harding, A. (1997a) 'Is There a "New Community Power" and Why Should We Need One?', *International Journal of Urban and Regional Research*, vol. 21, pp. 638–55.

Harding, A. (1997b) 'Urban Regimes in a Europe of the Cities?', *European Urban and Regional Studies*, vol. 4.

Harding, A. (1997c) 'Public–Private Partnerships in the UK', in J. Pierre (ed.) *Partnership in Urban Governance: An International Perspective* (London: Macmillan), pp. 72–96.

Harding, A. and Garside, P. (1996) *Hulme City Challenge: First Residents Survey* (Liverpool: European Institute for Urban Affairs, Liverpool John Moores University).

Haughton, G. and Hunter, C. (1994) *Sustainable Cities* (London: Jessica Kingsley Publishers).

Hayward, J. (1986) 'The Political Science of Muddling Through: The *de facto* Paradigm?' in J. Hayward and P. Norton (eds) *The Political Science of British Politics* (Brighton: Wheatsheaf Books).

Healey, P., Davis, J., Wood, M. and Elson, M. (1982) *The Implementation of Development Plans: Report of an Exploratory Study for the DoE* (Oxford: Dept. of Town Planning, Oxford Brookes University).

Herbst, S. (1994) *Politics at the Margin* (Cambridge: Cambridge University Press).

Herman, D. (1994) *Rights of Passage: Struggles for Lesbian and Gay Legal Equality* (Toronto: University of Toronto Press).

Hodge, M., Leach, S., and Stoker, G. (1997) 'More than the Flower Show – Elected Mayors and Democracy', *Fabian Paper No. 32* (London: Fabian Society).

Hoggett, P. (1995) 'Does Local Government Want Local Democracy?', *Town and Country Planning*, vol. 64, no. 4, April, pp. 107–9.

Holgate, G. (1990) 'Local Authorities, Vindictiveness and Bad Faith', *Local Government Review*, vol. 154, no. 38, p. 749.

Holliday, Ian (1991) 'The New Suburban Right in British Local Government: Conservative Views of the Local', *Local Government Studies*, vol. 17, no. 6, pp. 45–62.

Holmans, A. (1996) 'Housing Demand and Need in England to 2011: The National Picture', in M. Breheny and P. Hall (eds) *The People – Where Will They Go? National Report of the TCPA Regional Enquiry into Housing Need and Provision in England* (London: TCPA).

Hood, C. (1983) *The Tools of Government* (London: Macmillan).

House of Commons Environment Committee Session 1995–6 2nd Report *Housing Need*, Vol. 2 *Minutes of Evidence and Appendices 22–II* (London: HMSO).

Hudson, R. (1989) 'Labour-Market Changes and New Forms of Work in Old Industrial Regions: Maybe Flexibility for Some but not Flexible Accumulation', *Environment and Planning D: Society and Space*, vol. 7, pp. 15–30.

Imrie, R. and Thomas, H. (1993) *British Urban Policy and the Urban Development Corporations* (London: Paul Chapman).

Jessop, B. (1992) 'Fordism and Post-Fordism: a Critical Reformulation' in M. Storper and A. Scott (eds) *Pathways to Industrialisation and Uneven Development* (London: Routledge) pp. 46–69.

Jessop, B. (1994) 'Post-Fordism and the State' in A. Amin (ed.) *Post-Fordism: a Reader* (Oxford: Blackwell) pp. 251–79.

Jessop, B. (1995) 'The Regulation Approach and Governance Theory: Alternative Perspectives on Economic and Political Change?', *Economy and Society*, 24 (3), 307–33.

Jessop, B. (1997a) 'A Neo-Gramscian Approach to the Regulation of Urban Regimes', in M. Lauria (ed.) *Reconstructing Urban Regime Theory* (London: Sage) pp. 51–73.

Jessop, B. (1997b) 'The Governance of Complexity and the Complexity of Governance: Preliminary Remarks on Some Problems and Limits of Economic Guidance', in A. Amin and J. Hausner (eds) *Beyond Markets and Hierarchy: Third Way Approaches to Transformation* (Aldershot: Edward Elgar) pp. 111–47.

Jessop, B. (1997c) 'The Entrepreneurial City: Re-Imaging Localities, Redesigning Economic Governance, or Restructuring Capital?', in N. Jewson and S. MacGregor (eds) *Realising Cities: New Spatial Divisions and Social Transformation* (London: Routledge) pp. 28–41.

Jessop, B. (1998a) 'The Rise of Governance and the Risks of Failure: the Case of Economic Development', *International Social Science Journal*, issue 155 pp. 29–46.

Jessop, B. (1998b) 'The Enterprise of Narrative and the Narrative of Enterprise: Place Marketing and the Entrepreneurial City', in T. Hall and P. Hubbard (eds) *The Entrepreneurial City* (Chichester: Wiley) pp. 77–99.

Jessop, B., Peck, J. and Tickell, A. (1999) 'Retooling the Machine: Economic Crisis, State Restructuring and Urban Politics', in A.E.G. Jonas and D. Wilson (eds) *The Urban Growth Machine: Critical Perspectives Twenty Years Later* (New York: State University of New York Press).

John, P. (1994) 'Central–Local Relations in the 1980s and 1990s: Toward a Policy Learning Approach', *Local Government Studies*, vol. 20, no. 3, pp. 412–36.

John, P. (1997), 'Local Governance', in I. Holliday *et al*. (eds) *Developments in British Politics 5* (London: Macmillan).

John, P. (1998), 'Urban Economic Policy Networks in Britain and France: a Sociometric Approach', *Government and Policy*, forthcoming.

John, P. and Cole, A . (1996) 'Urban Regimes and Local Governance in Britain and France' *Urban Affairs Review*, vol. 33, pp. 382–404.

Jones, G.W. (1975) 'Varieties of Local Politics', *Local Government Studies*, vol. 1, no. 2, pp. 17–32.

Judge, D. Stoker, G. and Wolmand, H. (1995) *Theories of Urban Politics* (London: SAGE).

Kantor, P., Savitch, H.V. and Vicari Haddock, S. (1997) 'The Political Economy of Urban Regimes: A Comparative Perspective', *Urban Affairs Review*, forthcoming

Keating, M. (1984) 'Scotland's Capital Change that is Shaping to Become a Head-on Confrontation', *Municipal Journal*, 9 November, pp. 1740–1.

Keating, M. (1988) *The City that Refused to Die* (Aberdeen: Aberdeen University Press).

Keating, M. (1991) *Comparative Urban Politics* (London: Edward Elgar).

King, D. and Stoker, G. (1996) *Rethinking Local Democracy* (London: Macmillan).

Kirklees Metropolitan Borough Council (1995) *LA21 and Transport: Processes and Mechanisms for Change* (Huddersfield: Kirklees Council).

Knight, B. and Stokes, P. (1996) *The Deficit in Civil Society* (Birmingham: Foundation for Civil Society).

Kooiman, W. (1993) 'Governance and Governability: Using Complexity, Dynamics and Diversity', in W. Kooiman (ed.) *Modern Governance: New Government–Society Interactions* (London: Sage) pp. 35–48.

Lafferty, W. M. and Meadowcroft, J. (eds) (1996) *Democracy and the Environment* (Cheltenham: Elgar).

Lafferty, W. M. and Eckerberg, K. (eds) (1997) *From Earth Summit to Local Forum: Studies of Local Agenda 21 in Europe* (Oslo: ProSus).

Lagroye, J. and Wright, V. (1979) *Local Government in Britain and France* (London: Allen and Unwin).

Lansley, S. *et al*. (1989) *Councils in Conflict* (London: Macmillan).

Lauria, M. (ed.) (1996) *Reconstructing Urban Regime Theory* (London: Sage).

Le Galès, P. (1995) 'Urban Regimes and Comparative Urban Politics', *Paper to ECPR Joint Sessions Workshop on 'The Changing Local Governance of Europe'*, Bordeaux, March.

Le Galès, P. and John, P. (1997) 'Is the Grass Greener on the Other Side? What Went Wrong with French Regions, and the Implications for England', *Policy and Politics*, vol. 25, no. 1, pp. 51–60.

Lee, J.M. (1963) *Social Leaders and Public Persons: A Study of County Government in Cheshire since 1888* (Oxford: Clarendon).

Leo (1997) 'City Politics in an Era of Globalization' in M. Lauria (ed.) *Rconstructing Urban Regime Theory* (Thousand Oaks, CA: SAGE)

Levine, M. A. (1994) 'The Transformation of Urban Politics in France: The Roots of Growth Politics and Urban Regimes', *Urban Affairs Quarterly*, vol. 29, no. 3, pp. 383–410.

Lindblom, C.E. (1977) *Politics and Markets* (New York: Basic Books).

Lipietz, A. (1987) *Mirages and Miracles* (London: Verso).

Lloyd, M. G. and Newlands, D. A. (1988) 'The "Growth Coalition" and Urban Economic Development', *Local Economy*, vol. 3, no. 1, pp. 31–9.

Local Government Management Board (1994) *Local Agenda 21 Principles and Process: A Step by Step Guide* (Luton: LGMB).

Local Government Management Board (1995) *Community Participation in LA21* (Luton: LGMB).

Local Government Management Board (1997) *Local Agenda 21 UK Review, 1992–7* (London: LGMB).

Loftman, P. (1997) 'Can the SRB Meet the Needs of Black Communities?', Paper Presented to Black Training and Enterprise Group Conference, Birmingham, March 1997.

Logan, J. and Molotch, H. (1987) *Urban Fortunes* (Berkeley, CA: University of California Press).

Lorrain, D. (1987), 'Le Grand Fossé? Le Débat Public Privé et les Services Urbains', *Politiques et Management Public*, 3–5, Paris.

Lorrain, D. (1993) 'Après la Décentralisation. L'Action Publique Flexible', *Sociologie du Travail*, vol. 3, pp. 285–307.

Loughlin, M. (1989) 'Law, Ideologies, and the Political-Administrative System', *Journal of Law and Society*, vol. 16, no. 1, pp. 21–41.

Loughlin, M. (1994) 'The Restructuring of Central–Local Government Relations', in J. Jowell and D. Oliver (eds), *The Changing Constitution*, 3rd edn (Oxford: Clarendon).

Loughlin, M. (1996) *Legality and Locality: The Role of Law in Central–Local Government Relations* (Oxford: Clarendon).

Lovenduski, J. and Randall, V. (1993) *Contemporary Feminist Politics* (Oxford: Oxford University Press).

Low, N. P. (1994) 'Growth Machines and Regulation Theory: The Institutional Dimension of the Regulation of Space in Australia', *International Journal of Urban and Regional Research*, vol. 18, no. 3, pp. 451–69.

Lowndes, V. (1996) 'Varieties of the New Institutionalism', *Public Administration*, vol. 74, pp. 181–97.

Mabileau, A. (1991) *Le Système Local en France* (Paris: Montchrestien).

MacFarlane, L. (1993) *Community Involvement in City Challenge* (London: National Council of Voluntary Organisations).

Mackinstosh, M. and Wainwright, H. (eds) (1984) *A Taste of Power: The Politics of Local Economics* (London: Verso).

Macnaughten, P., Grove-White, R., Jacobs, M. and Wynne, B. (1995) *Public Perceptions and Sustainability in Lancashire: Indicators, Institutions, and Participation* (Preston: Lancashire County Council for the Centre for the Study of Environmental Change).

Malpas, J. and Wickham, G. (1995) 'Governance and Failure: on the Limits of Sociology', *Australian and New Zealand Journal of Sociology*, vol. 31, no. 3, pp. 37–50.

Manchester City Council, Salford City Council, Trafford Borough Council, Central Manchester Development Corporation and Trafford Park Development Corporation (1994) *City Pride: A Focus for the Future* (MCC/SCC/TDC/CMDC/TPDC).

Marsh, D. and Rhodes, R. (1992) *Policy Networks in British Local Government* (Oxford: Oxford University Press).

Mawson, J. *et al.* (1995) *SRB: The Stocktake* (Birmingham: Centre for Urban and Regional Studies)

Mayntz, R. (1993) 'Governing Failures and the Problem of Governability: Some Comments on a Theoretical Paradigm' in J. Kooiman (ed.) *Modern Governance: New Government–Society Interactions* (London: Sage) pp. 9–20.

McAllister, D. (ed.) (1996) *Partnership in the Regeneration of Urban Scotland* (Edinburgh: HMSO).

McCormick, J. (1991) *British Politics and the Environment* (London: Earthscan).

McEldowney, J. (1994) *Public Law* (London: Street and Maxwell).

Merry, S. (1986) 'Everyday Understandings of the Law in Working-Class America', *American Ethnologist*, vol. 13.

Merry, S. (1990) *Getting Justice and Getting Even: Legal Consciousness Among Working-Class Americans* (Chicago: University of Chicago Press).

Miles, R. (1982) *Racism and Migrant Labour* (London: George Allen and Unwin)

Miles, R. (1989) *Racism* (London: Routledge).

Miller, G. (1981) *Cities by Contract* (Cambridge, MA: MIT Press).

Minogue, Martin and O'Grady, Jeremy (1985) 'Contracting Out Local Authority Services in Britain', *Local Government Studies*, vol. 11, no. 8, pp. 35–50.

Molotch, H. (1990) 'Urban Deals in Comparative Perspective' in J. Logan and T. Swanstrom (eds) *Beyond the City Limits* (Philadelphia, PA: Temple University Press).

Molotch, H. and Vicari, S. (1988) 'Three Ways to Build: The Development Process in the US, Japan and Italy', *Urban Affairs Quarterly*, vol 24, no. 2, pp. 188–214.

Mooney, J. (1993) *Researching Domestic Violence: The North London Domestic Violence Survey*.

Muir, J. and Veenerdall, M. (1996) *Earthtalk* (New York: Praeger).

Munt, I. (1994) 'Race Urban Policy and Urban Problems: A Critique of Current UK Practice' in H. Thomas and V. Krishnarayan (eds) *Race Equality and Planning: Policies and Procedures* (Aldershot: Avebury) pp. 152–186

Murdoch, J. and Marsden, T. (1994) *Reconstituting Rurality: Class, Community and Power in the Development Process* (London: UCL Press).

Norton, Philip (1990) 'The Lady's Not for Turning, But What About the Rest? Margaret Thatcher and the Conservative Party 1979–89', *Parliamentary Affairs*, vol. 43, pp. 41–59.

O'Riordan, T. (1995) 'The Radical Agenda of Localism and Democracy', *Town and Country Planning*, July, pp. 162–3.

Oates, W. E. (1972) *Fiscal Federalism* (New York: Harcourt Brace Jovanovich).

Offe, C. (1975) 'The Theory of the Capitalist State and the Problem of Policy Formation.' in L.N. Lindberg *et al.* (eds) *Stress and Contradiction in Modern Capitalism* (Lexington: D.C. Heath) pp. 125–44.

Offe, C. (1984) *The Contradictions of the Welfare State* (London: Hutchinson).

Olson, M. (1969) 'The Principle of "Fiscal Equivalence": The Division of Responsibilities among Different Levels of Government', *American Economic Review Papers and Proceedings*, vol. 59, pp. 479–87.

Olson, M. (1971) *The Logic of Collective Action* (Cambridge, MA: Harvard University Press).

Orr, M. and Stocker, G. (1994) 'Urban Regimes and Leadership in Detroit', *Urban Affairs Quarterly* vol. 30, no. 1, pp. 48–73.

Osborne, D. and Gaebler, T. (1993) *Reinventing Government: How the Entrepreneurial Spirit is Transforming the Public Sector* (New York: Plume).

Ost, F. (1988) 'Between Order and Disorder: The Game of Law', in G. Teubner (ed.) *Autopoietic Law: A New Approach to Law and Society* (Berlin: de Gruyter).

Painter, J. 1997 'Regulation, Regime and Practice in Urban Politics' in M. Lauria (ed.) *Reconstructing Urban Regime Theory: Regulating Urban Politics in a Global Economy* (Thousand Oaks: Sage) pp. 122–43.

Painter, J. and Goodwin, M. (1995) 'Local Governance and Concrete Research: Investigating the Uneven Development of Regulation,' *Economy and Society*, vol. 24, pp. 334–56.

Peck, J. (1995) 'Moving and Shaking: Business Elites, State Localism and Urban Privatism', *Progress in Human Geography* no. 19, pp. 16–46..

Peck, J. and Tickell, A. (1994) 'Jungle Law Breaks Out: Neoliberalism and Global Local Didorder', *Area*, vol. 26, no. 4, pp. 317–26.

Peck, J. and Tickell, A. (1995) 'Business Goes Local: Dissecting the "Business Agenda" in Manchester', *International Journal of Urban and Regional Research*, vol. 19, no. 1, pp. 55–78.

Percy-Smith, J. (1995) *Digital Democracy: Information and Communication Technologies in Local Politics* (London: Commission for Local Democracy).

Peterson, P. (1981) *City Limits* (Chicago, IL: University of Chicago Press).

Petts, J. (1995) 'Waste Strategy Development: A Case-Study of Community Involvement and Consewsus Building in Hampshire', *Journal of Environmental Planning and Management*, vol. 38, pp. 519–36.

Pickvance, J. (1995) 'Marxist Theories of Urban Politics' in D. Judge, G. Stoker and H. Wolman (eds) *Theories of Urban Politics* (London: SAGE).

Pollitt, C. (1993) *Managerialism and the Public Services*, 2nd edn (Oxford: Blackwell).

Pratchett, L. and Wilson, D. (1996) *Local Democracy and Local Government* (Basingstoke: Macmillan).

Price Waterhouse (1995) *Tenants in Control: An Evaluation of Tenant-Led Housing Management Organisations* (London: HMSO).

Putnam, R. D. (1993) *Making Democracy Work* (Princeton: Princeton University Press).

Quilley, S. (1995) 'Economic Transformation and Local Strategy in Manchester', Ph. D. thesis, Department of Sociology, University of Manchester.

Radford, M. (1991) 'Auditing for Change: Local Government and the Audit Commission', *Modern Law Review*, vol. 54, no. 6.

Reade, E. (1987) *British Town and County Planning* (Milton Keynes: Open University Press).

Renn, O., Webler, T. and Viedemann, P. (1995) *Fairness and Competence in Evaluating Citizen Participation* (Boston: Kluwer).

Rhodes, R.A.W. (1995) *The New Governance: Governing without Government*, The State of Britain Seminars 11 (Swindon: ESRC).

Rhodes, R.A.W. (1997) *Understanding Governance: Policy Networks, Governance, Reflexivity and Accountability* (Buckingham: Open University Press).

Rhodes, R.A.W. (1999). Foreword: Governance and Networks, in G. Stoker (ed.) *The New Management of British Local Governance* (London: Macmillan), pp. xii–xxvi.

Robinson, M. (1992) *The Greening of British Party Politics* (Manchester: Manchester University Press).

Rose, N. (1991) 'Governing by Numbers: Figuring Out Democracy', *Accounting, Organisations and Society*, vol. 16, pp. 673–692.

Royal Commission on Environmental Pollution (1994) *18th Report: Transport and the Environment,* Cm 2674 (London: HMSO).

Rydin, Y. (1997) 'Managing Urban Air Quality: Language and Rational Choice in Metropolitan Governance', *Environment and Planning A*, vol. 30, pp. 1429–43.

Rydin, Y. (1998) 'The Enabling Local State and Urban Development: Rhetoric, Resources and Planning in East London', *Urban Studies,* vol. 35, pp. 175–91.

Sabatier, P. (1993) 'Policy Change Over a Decade or More', in P. Sabatier and H.C.Jenkins-Smith (eds) *Policy Change and Learning: An Advocacy Coalition Approach* (Boulder, Colorado: Westview Press).

Sarat, A. (1990) ' "The Law is All Over": Power, Resistance and the Legal Consciousness of the Welfare Poor', *Yale Journal of Law and the Humanities*, vol. 2, no. 2, pp. 343–79.

Sarat, A. and Kearns, T. (1993) 'Beyond the Great Divide: Forms of Legal Scholarship and Everyday Life', in A. Sarat and T. Kearns (eds) *Law in Everyday Life* (Ann Arbor: University of Michigan Press).

Saunders, P. (1984) 'Rethinking Local Politics', in M. Boddy and C. Fudge (eds) *Local Socialism? Labour Councils and New Left Alternatives* (London: Macmillan).

Saunders, P. (1985) 'Corporatism and Urban Service Provision', in W. Grant (ed.) *The Political Economy of Corporatism* (London: Macmillan).

Saunders, P. (1986) 'Reflections on the Dual Politics Thesis: The Argument, its Origins and its Critics', in M. Goldsmith and S. Villadsen (eds) *Urban Political Theory and the Management of Fiscal Stress* (Aldershot: Gower).

Savas, E. S. (1987) *Privatisation: the Key to Better Government* (Chatham, NJ: Chatham House).

Savitch, H. (1988), *Post-Industrial Cities* (Princeton: Princeton University Press).

Scharpf, F.W. (1994) 'Games Real Actors Could Play: Positive and Negative Coordination in Embedded Negotiations', *Journal of Theoretical Politics*, vol. 6, no. 1, pp. 27–53.

Schneider, M., Teske, P. and Minton, M. (1995) *Public Entrepreneurs* (Princeton: Princeton University Press).

Scottish Federation of Housing Associations and Scottish Homes (1990; 1996) *Performance Standards for Housing Associations* (Edinburgh: SFHA and Scottish Homes).

Scottish Homes (1996) 'Performance Rating of Housing Associations: Rewards and Sanctions' *Guidance Note* SHGN 96/22 (Edinburgh: Scottish Homes).

Scottish office (1998) *New Life for Urban Scotland* (Edinburgh: The Scottish office).

Secretary of State for the Environment, Secretary of State for Scotland, Secretary of State for Wales, *The Conduct of Local Authority Business: Report of the Committee of Inquiry into the Conduct of Local Authority Business*, Chairman Mr David Widdicombe QC, Cmnd 9797 (London: HMSO).

Selman, P. (1996) *Local Sustainability* (London: Paul Chapman Publishing).

Seyd, P. and Whiteley, P. (1992) *Labour's Grass Roots: The Politics of Party Membership* (Oxford: Clarendon Press).

Short, J., Fleming, S. and Witt, S. (1986) *Housebuilding, Planning and Community Action* (London: Routledge and Kegan Paul).

Skelcher, C. *et al.* (1996) *Community Networks in Urban Regeneration: It All Depends on Who You Know* (Bristol: Policy Press).

Skinner, S. (1997) *Building Community Strengths* (London: Community Development Foundation).

Smith, S. (1989) *The Politics of 'Race' and Residence* (Cambridge: Polity Press).

Smith, L. (1989) 'Domestic Violence: A Review of the Literature', *Home Office Research Study No 107.*

Solomos, J. and Back, L. (1995) *Race, Politics and Social Change* (London: Routledge).

Solomos, J. and Back, L. (1996) *Racism and Society* (London: Macmillan).

Stallworthy, M. (1992) 'Local Government Lawyers: The 1980s and Beyond', *Journal of Law and Society*, vol. 19, no. 1, pp. 69–84.

Star, S.L. (1995) 'The Politics of Formal Representations: Wizards, Gurus, and Organisational Complexity' in S.L. Star, *Ecologies of Knowledge: Work and Politics in Science and Technology* (New York: State University of New York Press) pp. 89–118.

Stewart, J. (1995) *Innovation in Democratic Practice* (Birmingham: INLO-GOV).

Stewart, J., Kendall, E. and Coote, A. (1994) *Citizens Juries* (London: Institute for Public Policy Research).

Stewart, J. and Stoker, G. (eds) (1994) *Local Government in the 1990s* (London: Macmillan)

Stoker, G. (1988) *The Politics of Local Government* (London: Macmillan).

Stoker, G. (1991) *The Politics of Local Government* (London: Macmillan).

Stoker, G. (1995) 'Regime Theory and Urban Politics', in D. Judge, G. Stoker and H. Wolman (eds) *Theories of Urban Politics* (London: Sage), pp. 54–71.

Stoker, G. (1996) *Local Political Participation: A Review Paper* (York: Rowntree Foundation).

Stoker, G. (1997) 'Local Political Participation' in *New Perspectives in Local Governance* (York: Joseph Rowntree Foundation).

Stoker, G. and Brindley, T. (1985) 'Asian Politics and Urban Renewal', *Policy and Politics*, vol. 13, no. 3.

Stoker, G. (1998a) 'Theory and Urban Politics', *International Political Science Review*, vol. 19, no. 2, April, pp. 119–29.

Stoker, G. (1998b) 'Governance as Theory Five Propositions', *International Social Science Journal*, vol. 155 (March), pp. 17–28.

Stoker, G. (1998c) 'Public–Private Partnerships in Urban Governance in J. Pierre (ed.) *Partnerships in Urban Governance* (London: Macmillan).

Stoker, G. (1999) 'Introduction: the Unintended Costs and Benefits of New Management Reform for British Local Government', in G. Stoker (ed.) *The New Management of British Local Governance* (London: Macmillan).

Stoker, G. and Mossberger, K. (1994) 'Urban Regime Theory in Comparative Perspective', *Environment and Planning C: Government and Policy*, vol. 12, no. 2, pp. 195–212.

Stoker, G. and Young, S.C. (1993) *Cities in the 1990s* (Harlow: Longman).

Stone, C. (1989) *Regime Politics, Governing Atlanta, 1946–1988* (Lawrence: University Press of Kansas).

Stone, C. (1993) 'Urban Regimes and the Capacity to Govern: A Political Economy Approach *Journal of Urban Affairs*, vol. 15, no. 1, pp. 1–23.

Stone, C. L. (1997) 'Urban Regime Analysis: Theory, Service Provision, and Cross-National Considerations', Paper to the *ECPR Workshop on Local Elites in a Comparative Perspective*, Bern, February–March.

Stone, C. L. and Sanders, H. T. (eds) (1987) *The Politics of Urban Development*, (Lawrence: University Press of Kansas).

Strom, E. (1996) 'In Search of the Growth Coalition: American Urban Theories and the Redevelopment of Berlin', *Urban Affairs Review*, vol. 31, no. 4, pp. 455–81.

Taylor, M. (1995) *Unleashing the Potential: Bringing Residents to the Centre of Regeneration* (York: Rowntree Foundation).

Taylor, M. (1996) 'Transferring Housing Stock in Scotland', *Occasional Paper,* Housing Policy and Practice Unit, University of Stirling.

Tesbelis, G. (1990) *Nested Games: Rational Choice in Comparative Politics* (Berkeley: University of California Press).

Teubner, G. (1986a) 'After Legal Instrumentalism?', in G. Teubner (ed.) *Dilemmas of Law in the Welfare State* (Berlin: de Gruyter).

Teubner, G. (1986b) 'The Transformation of Law in the Welfare State', in G. Teubner (ed.) *Dilemmas of Law in the Welfare State* (Berlin: de Gruyter).

Teubner, G. (1987) 'Juridification – Concepts, Aspects, Limits, Solutions', in G. Teubner (ed.) *Juridification of Social Spheres* (Berlin: de Gruyter).

Thake, S. (1995) *Staying the Course: The Role and Structure of Community Regeneration Organisations* (York: Rowntree Trust).

Thomas, D. (1995) *A Review of Community Development Social Policy* (York: Rowntree Foundation).

Thomas, H. *et al.* (1995) 'Theory, Race Equality and Urban Policy Evaluation', *Project Paper No. 1* (Cardiff: Dept of City and Regional Planning; Cardiff, University of Wales).

Thomas, H. *et al.* (1996) 'Locality, Urban Governance and Contested Meanings of Space', *Area*, vol. 28, no. 2, pp. 186–98.

Thomas, H. (1996) 'Public Participation in Planning', in M. Tewdew-Jones (ed.) *British Planning Policy in Transition* (London: UCL Press).

Tiebout, C.M. (1956) 'A Pure Theory of Local Expenditures', *Journal of Political Economy*, vol. 64: pp. 416–24.

Tiley, L. (1993) 'Crime Prevention and the Safer Cities Story', *The Howard Journal*, February.

Travers, T. (1989), 'The Threat to the Autonomy of Local Government', in C. Crouch and D. Marquand (eds) *The New Centralism* (Oxford: Basil Blackwell).

Trounstine, P. J. and Christenson, T. (1982) *Movers and Shakers: The Study of Community Power* (New York: St Martin's Press 1982).

Tuxworth, B. and Thomas, E. (1996) *Local Agenda 21 Survey* (Luton: LGMB).

Tuxworth, B. (1997) *Local Agenda 21 Case-Studies* (London: LGMB).

Udehn, L. (1996) *The Limits of Public Choice* (London: Routledge).

Vicari, S. and Molotch, H. (1990) 'Building Milan: Alternative Machines of Growth', *International Journal of Urban and Regional Research*, vol. 14, no. 4, pp. 602–24.

Vincent Jones, P. (1994) 'The Limits of Near-Contractual Governance: Local Authority Internal Trading under CCT', *Journal of Law and Society*, vol. 21, no. 2, pp. 214–37.

Walesh, S.G. (1995), 'Interaction with the Public and Government Officials in Urban Water Planning', in H. van Engen, D. Kampe and S. Tjallingii (eds) *Hydropolis: The Role of Water in Urban Planning* (Leiden, The Netherlands: Backhuys).

Walsh, K. (1989) 'Competition and Service in Local Government', in J. Stewart and G. Stoker (eds) *The Future of Local Government* (London: Macmillan).

Ward, K. (1996) 'Rereading Urban Regime Theory: A Sympathetic Critique', *Geoforum*, vol. 27, no. 4, pp. 427–38.

Ward, S. (1993) 'Thinking Global, Acting Local? British Local Authorities and Their Environment Plans', *Environmental Politics*, vol. 2, no. 3, pp. 453–78.

Welsh, P. and Coles, M. (1994) *Towards a Social Economy: Trading for a Social Purpose*, Fabian Pamphlet 564 (London: Fabian Society).

Wheeler, R. (ed.) (1996) *Local Government Policy-Making*, special issue on 'Empowerment and Citizenship', March.

White, L. (1987–8) 'Mobilization on the Margins of the Law Suit: Making Space for Clients to Speak', *New York Review of Law and Social Change*, vol. 16, no. 4, pp. 535–64.

Whiteley, Paul, Seyd, Patrick and Richardson, Jeremy (1994) *True Blues: The Politics of Conservative Party Membership* (Oxford: Clarendon).

Whittaker, S. (ed.) (1995) *First Steps: Local Agenda 21 in Practice* (London: HMSO).

Wilcox, D. (1994) *The Guide to Effective Participation* (Brighton: Partnership Books).

Wild, A. (1996) *Community Participation in Local Agenda 21*, Masters dissertation, University of Sheffield.

Williams, D. and Game, C. with Leach, S. and Stoker, G. (1994) *Local Government in the United Kingdom* (London: Macmillan).

Willke, H. (1992) *Ironie des Staates: Grundlinien einer Staatstheorie Polyzentrischer Gesellschaft* (Frankfurt: Suhrkamp).

Winner, L. (1985) 'Do Artifacts have Politics?', in D. MacKenzie and J. Wacjcman (eds) *The Social Shaping of Technology* (Milton Keynes: Open University Press).

Wolf, C. (1978) 'A Theory of Nonmarket Failure: Framework for Implementation Analysis', *Journal of Law and Economics*, vol. 21, no. 1, pp. 107–39.

Wood, C. (1995) *Stepping Stones II* (Lincoln: Wildlife Trusts).

World Commission on Environment and Development (1987) *Our Common Future* (Oxford: Oxford University Press).

Young, S.C. (1993) *The Politics of the Environment* (Chorlton, Manchester: Baseline Books).

Young, S.C. (1996) *Promoting Participation and Community-Based Partnerships in the Context of Local Agenda 21: A Report for Practitioners* (Manchester: EPRU Paper, Government Department, Manchester University).

Young, S. C. (1997a) 'The United Kingdom: A Mirage Beyond the Participation Hurdle?', in W. M. Lafferty and K. Eckerberg (eds) *From Earth Summit to Local Forum* (Oslo: ProSus), pp. 201–28.

Young, S. C. (1997b) 'Local Agenda 21: The Renewal of Local Democracy?' in M. Jacobs (ed.) *Greening the Millennium: The New Politics of the Environment* (Oxford: Blackwell).

Young, S.C. (1997c) 'Community-Based Partnerships and Sustainable Development: A Third Force in the Social Economy', in S. Baker, M. Kousis, R. Richardson and S.C. Young (eds) *The Politics of Sustainable Development* (London: Routledge) pp. 217–36.

Zacher, H. (1987) 'Juridification in the Field of Social Law', in G. Teubner (ed.) *Juridification of Social Spheres* (Berlin: de Gruyter).

Index

access to knowledge   208–10, 213, 247

accountability
   and decision-making   87–9, 219–24, 232
   and monitoring quangos   130, 144–5, 148–9, 235, 243
   of public–private partnerships   22–3

Agenda   *see* Local Agenda 21

air quality management   105

Andrew, C.   249

appointed boards, assessments of   130–49 *passim*

Arun District Council   174, 177, 179

Ashford, D.   72–3, 74, 75, 89

Associated British Ports (ABP)   87–8

Audit Commission   174

Aylesbury   205, 206, 207
   Aylesbury Vale District Council   176, 204, 205–6, 207

Back, L.   236

Barking and Dagenham, London Borough of   95

Barnsley   195

Berkshire   53, 211

Birmingham   176, 235, 238, 243

Black Country Development Corporation   235, 238

black and ethnic minorities   234–48

Braintree District Council   170–1, 177, 178–9

Bristol   235

Brownill, S.   249–50, 261, 262

Brundtland Report   181, 182

Buckinghamshire   176, 203–10

Bulpitt, J.   161

bureau-shaping thesis   109–11

Burton, P.   246

Business Links   85

Canada   195, 249

Canary Wharf   241

Cardiff Bay Development Corporation (CBDC)   235, 242, 244

Cattell, C.   191

central state
   central–local state relations   63, 72–5, 76, 123, 128, 166–79, 199
   key actor in local development   94–7, 113

Channel Tunnel Rail Link   28, 29, 95

Chesterfield   157–60, 162

Chiltern District Council   204, 205

Church, Dave   152, 161

citizens juries   194

citizenship   196

City Challenge programmes   65, 97, 183, 184

Cleveland   161

club theory   93

Coles, M.   191

collective action, problems of   92–7

collective consumption   106–11

community power   92–7, 182–96

competitive tendering   121

Computer Assisted Telephone Interviewing (CATI)   131–2, 149

Conservative Party
   councillors' views of law   117–28 *passim*

in local government 61, 62,
166–79, 254–5, 259–61
market-led policies 11, 57, 97,
237
Cornwall County Council 169
Coulson, A. 239
Council for the Protection of Rural
England (CPRE) 204,
211–12
councillors, local elected
Labour party groups 150–65
and public participation
strategies 196
and Urban Development
Corporations 238–9
views of local governance
130–49 *passim*
Coventry District Labour
Party 161
Croydon, London Borough of 96,
188
Crozier, M. 74

Dartford 27–9
decentralisation policy, Labour
Party and 152–7
decision-making 87–9
democracy
concepts of 151–2
and elected local
government 141–6
and local politics 162–5, 184
and public participation 194–6,
223–4
Department of the Environment,
Transport and the Regions
(DETR) (formerly
Department of the
Environment (DoE)
and environmental issues 105,
181
guidance on public
participation 8
and housing 202–3, 208, 253
rule-setting 29
support for urban economic
development 63, 67, 95, 96

Derbyshire, local government
reorganisation in 157–60
devolution of local
government 179
see also regions
District Health Authorities
(DHAs) 131, 132–49 *passim*
domestic violence policy 249–67
Dowding, K. 250, 262
Du Gay, P. 239
Dudley Metropolitan Borough
Council 175

East Lindsey District Council 171,
178
Economic and Social Research
Council (ESRC) xi, xv
Edinburgh 59–71, 67–8
education
juridification and 118, 122, 124,
126, 129 n2
partnerships involving 28
reform attempt in Solihull
175–6
research projects in 89
Egan, Lord 98
elected local councillors *see*
councillors
elites
elected councillors and appointed
boards 130–49 *passim*
key decision-makers 59, 70–1,
206–7
Elkin, X. 56, 68
employment *see* labour market
environmental protection
and planning for housing
203–13
LA21 strategies 182–96
public concern 181–2
ESRC (Economic and Social
Research Council) xi, xii
Essex, Braintree District
Council 170–1
ethnic minorities 234–48
Euralille redevelopment
scheme 76, 80–1, 88

European Commission   181
European Union   191
    funding   51

feminist groups   261–6
Fordism and local governance
    34–6
    transition to post-Fordism
        36–43
France
    community-based partnerships
        in   191
    local policy networks in   72–90

Geddes, A.   238
Gender and the New Urban
    Governance project   115
Glasgow City Council   217–18,
    219, 230–1
globalisation   2
Gloucestershire County
    Council   193
governance
    dependent on locality   81–3
    failure   17–23
    mechanisms and rationality   xii,
        xv, 3, 15–17, 198
    and stability of traditional
        hierarchies   198–9
governments
    and appointed boards   239, 246
    policy cycles   15, 31
    role in metagovernance   23–4
Granada TV   64
Gurr, T.   96

Hague, William   179
Halford, S.   249–50, 261, 262
Harris, Toby   99
Hayek, F. von   12
health authorities   28, 131–49
    passim
Hervé (mayor of Rennes)   76, 88
Heseltine, Michael   25
heterarchy   15, 18
High Wycombe   204, 206
Hoggett, P.   192

Home Office   252, 253, 256, 258,
    259, 264
housing provision
    and domestic violence policy
        265–6
    failure of top–down strategies
        183
    in Fordist mode of regulation
        48
    public marginalised in planning
        process   198–213
    success of community ownership
        schemes   215–33
Howard, Michael   98–9
Hudson, R.   47

Independents in local
    government   168–9, 169, 171,
        173, 175
industrial restructuring   46–7, 60–1
INLOGOV   174
inner cities   *see* urban areas,
    regeneration of
institutionalism   1, 3
interest groups and policy-
    making   249–50

Jessop, B.   34, 37–9, 47
juridification of local
    government   117–29

Kennenford, Chris   213
key players in local
    governance   49–50, 59, 65,
        70–1, 87–8
    local politicians   73–4, 74–5,
        80–1, 86, 88–9, 157–60, 162
King, D.S.   96
Kirklees Metropolitan Borough
    Council   77

labour market and economic
    change   37, 40–1, 42, 45–7, 50
Labour Party
    intra-party relationships   150–65
    local councillors' views of
        law   117–28 *passim*

in local government 61–2, 69, 97, 171, 254, 255–9
National Executive Committee (NEC) 153–4, 154
'New Labour' 11
Lambeth, London Borough of 97
Lancashire County Council 188
law in local governance, perceptions of 117–29
leaders *see* key players
Leeds 75
  conflicts in local governance 85–6
  policy networks in 79–80, 83
  power of elected local government 77–8
legitimacy
  of appointed boards 137–8, 243–5, 243
  of community-based organisations 219–24
  in party politics 162–3, 163–5
  of women's committees 262–3
Liberal Democratic (formerly Social Democratic/Liberal) Party 169, 170
Lille
  central–local state politics 74, 76, 79
  conflict between communes 83
  economic development coalition in 80–1, 86
  key role of mayor 88, 89
Lincolnshire 170, 171, 174
Local Agenda 21 participation strategies 182–92, 193
local authorities
  central–local state relations 63, 72–5, 76, 200–3
  and community-based housing organisations 230–2
  domestic violence policy 249–67
  in economic development projects 94–7, 113
  as enabling authorities 57, 76
  Labour Party politics within 150–65

officers of 62
public opinion of 134–44
public participation strategies 182–97
and Urban Development Corporations 238
Local Enterprise Companies (LECs) 131, 132–49 *passim*
Local Governance Research Programme xi–xv
Local Government Management Board 182
local government reorganisation 157–60, 160
local regulatory capacity 43, 52
London
  air quality management 105
  domestic violence policies 251, 253, 254–5, 261
  governance without GLC 97, 98–9, 102–3, 111, 113
  London Docklands Development Corporation (LDDC) 235, 238, 241, 242, 243, 244
  Metropolitan Governance and Community Study 91–2
  Metropolitan Police 252, 258, 263
  support for elected authority 146
  tourism in 102–5
  transport infrastructure projects 95–6, 98–9, 113
  urban regeneration project 94–5
London Science Park 27–9
Lorrain, D. 74
Loughlin, M. 127–8
luck, systematic 93–4

Major governments 11, 26, 166–79
Manchester
  Hulme City Challenge 192, 193
  inner city regeneration programmes 183
  Olympic bid 29–30, 66–7
  urban politics of production in 59–71

market failures   11–13
Marxism   1, 13
Mauroy, Pierre   76, 79, 80–1, 88, 89
Members of Parliament (MPs)   75,
    153–4
metagovernance   23–6
methodology of research
    projects   32, 53, 71, 90,
    115–16, 129, 131–2, 149, 197,
    213, 233, 248
Miles, Robert   236
Milton Keynes   204–5, 206
Mudie, George   75
Munt, I.   237

networks
    interpersonal   29–30, 58, 64–5,
    256, 264
    in local party politics   xiv, 157–60
    see also under policy-making
'New Labour'   11
new public management and service
    provision   xiii–xiv, xv, 106–11
Nolan Committee on Standards in
    Public Life   220, 221, 222, 226,
    227, 230
non-elected bodies   130–49
North Kesteven District
    Council   170, 178
Norton, X.   167

O'Brien, Stephen   99
Offe, C.   35

partnerships   *see* public–private
    partnerships
party politics *see* Conservative
    Party; Labour Party; Liberal
    Democrats
police role in domestic violence
    policy   251, 252, 255–6, 258,
    261, 262–3
policy-making
    networks   79–89, 98–105, 263
    public participation in   182–96
post-Fordist mode of
    regulation   36–43

privatisation of local government
    services   176
public opinion of local
    governance   130–49, 184
public participation
    strategies   182–96
    marginalisation of some social
    groups , 200, 207–13
public–private partnerships   198
    as alternative to market
    failures   11
    balance of power in   245–6
    conflict and cooperation in
    85–6, 87, 98–105
    in economic development   20–3,
    27–9, 49, 51, 63–8, 83–4
    and LA 21 strategies   190–2
    and markets/state   18
    in service delivery   51
    transnational   21

quangos (quasi non-governmental
    organisations)   130–49

racialisation of public
    policy   234–48
racism   126
rational choice theory   91–116,
    250
refuse collection   176
regions
    economic development
    partnerships in   26–32
    organisations   49
    and planning for housing   202–3,
    211–12
    regional assemblies   145–6,
    148–9
regulation theory   33–4
Rennes   76, 79, 83, 86, 88
research methodologies   32, 53, 71,
    90, 115–16, 129, 131–2, 149,
    197, 213, 233, 248
Rio Earth Summit   182
Rochdale, Labour Party in   155–7,
    160, 162
Royal Armouries project   80

Safer Cities Programme 252, 253, 258, 260
Savas, E.S. 107
Schumpeterian 'workfare state' 39, 51
Scotland
  community-based housing organisations 215–33
  Health Board members' opinions 131, 132–49 *passim*
  support for elected assembly 146
  urban development in Edinburgh 60–71
Scott, Sir Bob 30
Scottish Development Agency (SDA) (later Scottish Enterprise) 61, 63
Scottish Enterprise *see* Scottish Development Agency
Scottish Homes 216, 222, 226–30
Scottish National Party 69
service provision
  collective goods approach 106–11
  compulsory competitive tendering 121
  and customer focus of local councils 170, 172, 175, 176–7
  importance of central government 69
  not covered by sex discrimination legislation 251
  opinions on 134–5, 142–4, 147, 148
Sheppard, Lord 98–9
Single Regeneration Budget 51, 85, 183, 184
Skinner, S. 192
Smith, L. 252
Smith, S. 236
'social economy', the 191
Solihull Borough Council 175–6, 179
Solomos, J. 236
Southampton 75, 77–8, 81, 83, 86, 87–8

Southend Borough Council 175, 176
Standing Advisory Council on Religious Education 129 n2
state
  and governance 19, 23–5, 52–3
  neoliberal 11, 14, 26
  and remedying market failure 12–15
  under post-Fordist mode of regulation 39–43
  see also central–local state relations
Stoker, G. xiii–xiv, 68, 193
Stone, C. 56,58, 68
Sunderland, Metropolitan Borough of 43–52
sustainable development 181–2

Tebbit, Peter 175
Thames Gateway initiative 27–9, 95
Thatcher governments
  erosion of elected local government 76–7
  and local Conservative councils 166–79
  slimming-down of state 11, 26,
Thoenig, J.C. 74
Thomas, H. *et al.* 244
Tiebout model 93, 111
tourism 67, 98–9, 102–5
trade unions 158–9
Training and Enterprise Councils (TECs) 65, 131, 132–49 *passim*
transport and infrastructure 95–6, 113, 189, 190
Tyne and Wear 44, 235

UK (United Kingdom) government
  Department of the Environment *see* Department of the Environment, Transport and the Regions
  Home Office 252, 253, 256, 258, 259, 264

uneven development, management
    of   43, 52–3
urban areas
    regeneration of   26, 27–9, 94–5,
    183
    Urban Development
        Corporations (UDCs)
        234–45
    urban regimes   54–70, 83–4, 93
USA (United States of America)
    local domestic violence
        agendas   249
    public participation programmes
        in   195
    urban regime theory in   54–6,
        58, 68, 69

voluntary sector
    in inter-agency project   256–7,
        263–4, 264–5
    networking with   260, 266–7

Wales   53, 146

Cardiff Bay Development
    Corporation (CBDC)   235,
    242, 244
Walsall, Labour Party in   152–5,
    160, 161–2, 163
Walsh, Kieron   xi
Wandsworth Borough
    Council   175, 176, 177
waste disposal   190, 195
Welch, P.   191
Westminster Borough
    Council   175, 177
Whitehead, Alan   75
Widdicombe proposals on local
    government   169, 170
Wilcox, D.   192
Women's Aid Federation   251–2,
    259, 265
women's committees on local
    authorities   254, 255, 256, 258,
    262
Wrekin District Council   177